Annual Report Of The Board Of Trustees Of The Public Museum Of The City Of Milwaukee, Volumes 11-15

Milwaukee Public Museum

ELEVENTH ANNUAL REPORT

—— OF THE ——

BOARD OF TRUSTEES

—— OF THE ——

PUBLIC MUSEUM

—— OF THE ——

CITY OF MILWAUKEE.

SEPTEMBER 1st, 1892, TO AUGUST 31st, 1893.

OCTOBER 1st, 1893.

MILWAUKEE:
ED. KEOGH, PRINTER, 386 AND 388 BROADWAY.
1893.

ELEVENTH ANNUAL REPORT

———OF THE———

BOARD OF TRUSTEES

———OF THE———

PUBLIC MUSEUM

———OF THE———

CITY OF MILWAUKEE.

SEPTEMBER 1st, 1892, TO AUGUST 31st, 1893.

OCTOBER 1st, 1893.

MILWAUKEE:
ED. KEOGH, PRINTER, 386 AND 388 BROADWAY.
1893.

To the Honorable, the Common Council of the City of Milwaukee:

GENTLEMEN:—The Board of Trustees of the Public Museum, in accordance with Section 8, Chapter 328, of the laws of 1882, presents herewith its annual report as required by law. It respectfully refers to the annual report of Mr. Nehrling, the custodian of the Museum, for such details and information as are not contained in this report.

There are at present in the Museum:

113,959 Zoological specimens, valued at....................	$25,856 50
15,739 Botanical specimens, valued at....................	944 90
8,586 Anthropological specimens, valued at.............	6,525 20
11,026 Paleontological specimens, valued at.............	5,167 00
4,035 Mineralogical and lithological specimens, valued at.	3,767 14
5,036 Books, pamphlets, etc., valued at.................	5,074 19
3,035 Birds' eggs and nests, valued at..................	10,000 00
Total valuation.....................................	$57,334 93

The number of visitors during the year was 84,311.

I regret that we have but $50,000.00 insurance, against $60,000.00 of last year. The decrease is due to the great precaution of the insurance companies, and will be increased to the original amount as soon as possible.

The financial statement of the Board is as follows:

Balance in Museum fund September 1, 1892...............	$7,201 12
Appropriation to Museum fund, January 1, 1893...........	11,367 51
From other sources....................................	146 90
	$18,715 53
Total expenditures since last report....................	10,745 33
Unexpended balance in Museum fund, Sept. 1, 1893....	$7,970 20

I desire to express my thanks to the members of the Board, to Mr. Nehrling and to his assistants for their kind co-operation in furthering the best interests of the Museum.

Respectfully submitted,

GEO. W. PECKHAM,

President.

REPORT OF THE CUSTODIAN.

Milwaukee, Wis., September 19th, 1893.

To the Board of Trustees of the Public Museum of the City of Milwaukee:

Gentlemen :—In compliance with Article 6 of your rules and regulations I have the honor of submitting to you my third annual report, being the eleventh in the series of reports since the foundation of the Museum.

In the history of the Museum there has been scarcely a year so successful and important than the present one. We have not only succeeded in obtaining large collections of archæological, palæontological and mineralogical material, but I have also obtained the promise of several foreign commissioners of the World's Columbian Exposition of Chicago to make selections from their zoological and ethnological exhibits. A large number of specimens of almost all branches of natural history have been donated to the Museum by ardent friends of the institution. In addition to the 6,500 square feet already occupied by the collections, the Museum has had the good fortune of securing from the Exposition Association 3000 square feet more. This new annex which is well lighted—in fact, better lighted than the old parts of the institution—offers the possibility of displaying many valuable specimens hitherto kept from public view by lack of room. Twenty-two new cases have been furnished for this new part.

I. ZOOLOGY.

A.—MAMMALS.

Mr. Chr. Preusser, who takes a special interest in the fauna of this country, and especially of the Northwest, donated during the past year quite a number of specimens. I shall only mention the following: Two Western Fox Squirrels (Sciurus niger var. ludovicianus), one Red Squirrel or Chickaree (Sciurus hudsonicus), two Northern Hares or White Rabbits (Lepus americanus), and one Woodchuck or "Ground Hog," (Arctomys monax).

Mr. James Garbarde presented an albino Fox Squirrel, taken by himself at West Bend, Wis.

The celebrated animal dealer, Mr. Carl Hagenbeck, of Hamburg, Germany, visited our Museum several times and was so much pleased with the arrangement and condition of the collections, that he donated a number of very valuable and rare horns of African Antelopes. These horns were collected by the well-known zoologist, Mr. J. Menges, in the land of the Somalis, East Africa. The following species are represented in the collection. Soemmering's Antelope (Gazella Soemmeringi), Waller's Antelope (Lithocranius Walleri), Kudu (Strepsicerus Kudu), Swayne's Antelope (Alcelaphus Swaynei), Imberbis Antelope (Tragelaphus imberbis). Mr. Hagenbeck also donated a dwarf elephant (Elephas indicus sumatranus), which was known to the visitors of the World's Fair as the "Dwarf Elephant Lilly." This very valuable animal died in Hagenbeck's Zoological Arena and Animal Show, Midway Plaisance, World's Fair grounds, Chicago, and was sent immediately after its death to the Museum, where it arrived in good condition.

By purchase the following mammals were acquired: One Ocelot (Felis pardalis), and one Jaguar (Felis onza), both from Honduras, C. A., one Zebu (Bos zebu), one Buffalo (Bos americanus), one Red Fox (Vulpes vulpes), and one Beaver (Castor fiber).

B.—BIRDS.

Mr. Clarence J. Allen, of this city, a warm friend of the Museum, donated a number of birds. mainly belonging to the order Raptores or Birds of Prey. These specimens which were collected at Fox Point, Milwaukee County, were all in fine plumage. They represent the following species: One Pigeon Hawk, (Falco columbarius), one Cooper's Hawk (Accipiter cooperi), one American Hawk Owl (Surnia ulula caperoch), one Barred Owl (Syrnium nebulosum), one Short-eared Owl (Asio accipitrinus).

From Mr. Chr. Preusser the following donations were received: One Canada Jay (Perisoreus canadensis), two Hooded Mergansers (Lophodytes cucullatus), one American Merganser (Merganser americanus), two Bonaparte's Gulls (Larus philadelphia), and one Green Heron (Ardea viresceps).

Mr. H. Hirsch, of this city, donated the following birds: One Red-tailed Hawk (Buteo borealis), one Saw-whet Owl (Nyctale acadica), and one Screech Owl (Megascops asio).

As in former years, Mr. August Stirn donated during the past year a number of rare exotic birds. The following are especially interesting: Six Hummingbirds of a species which I have not yet determined; four white and variegated Bengalese or Japanese Manakins (Urolancha acuticauda var.), and four White Rice-birds (Munia oryzivora var.). The last two species are very interesting, as in Japan they are largely raised in confinement, having lost their original color entirely during their domestication. The Japanese, who have raised these birds through centuries, are just as fond of them, as the bird-fanciers of Europe and America are of their Canaries.

Mr. Oscar Widule donated a Night Hawk (Chordeiles virginianus). These very useful and interesting birds breed abundantly on the flat roofs of the business part of the city.

Miss Fanny Rauterberg presented a Yellow-bellied Sapsucker (Sphyrapicus varius)

A small number of rare North American birds were purchased from Mr. Chas. K. Worthen, of Warsaw, Ill., and about twenty specimens from Central America were bought from Mr. Erich Wittkugel, of San Pedro Sula, Honduras.

C.—REPTILES.

Mr. Adolph Meinecke, Sen., collected near his winter home at Gotha, Orange County, Fla., a number of interesting snakes which he donated to the Museum. Prof. E. D. Cope, who recently visited the Museum, had the kindness to determine most of them.

D.—INSECTS.

A collection of fifty-nine tropical beetles was presented to the Museum by Mr. Adolph Meinecke.

II. MINERALOGY AND LITHOLOGY.

On his way home from Florida, last spring, Mr. Meinecke learned at Cullmann, Ala., that a gentleman there had in his possession an extensive collection of minerals and fossils and that the collection was for sale. On looking over the objects, Mr. Meinecke saw at once that this collection was the life-long work of a specialist, as all the specimens were nicely labeled, well selected and of the very best quality. He purchased the entire collection and donated it to the Museum. The collection of minerals, consisting of about 350 pieces, contains specimens from many parts of the world.

III. PALÆONTOLOGY.

The collection of fossils, which Mr. Meinecke bought at Cullmann, Ala., is very large, consisting of more than 4,500 specimens, almost all from Europe, especially Germany.

Mr. Fred. Krempel, of Santa Ana, Cal., donated a part of a petrified tree.

Mr. Frank W. Suelflow presented nine palæontological specimens found at Cementville, Milwaukee County.

Through the kindness of Mr. Thomas A. Greene the Museum has succeeded in securing by purchase 634 fossils, all from the Palæozoic time, of Illinois and Wisconsin.

IV.   ARCHÆOLOGY.

A peculiar Baptizing Font was added to our collection by Mrs. W. Frankfurth. The specimen was secured by the late Mr. W. Frankfurth at Hettenheim, Germany, and is evidently very old, fonts like this having perhaps been in use during mediaeval times. The same lady donated an old Roman water urn, also from Hettenheim, Germany.

A very valuable donation to our archæological collection was made by Mr. C. A. Read, of this city. He sent through Mr. Chr. Preusser seven fine copper implements "which were found while grading a street near the Kinnic-

kinnic on the old farm of the late Chr. Wahl, Sr., about
where the old glue factory stood."

By purchase the institution acquired the well-known
collection of archæological specimens from Mr. Henry
Haskell, of Aztalan, Jefferson Co., Wis. The collection
consists of 4,000 flint arrow heads of all shapes and sizes,
200 tomahawks, polished stone hatchets, stone axes, hoes,
digging tools, agricultural implements, 200 leaf-shaped
spear heads and spades, 20 copper implements, 6 pipes of
peace, and 12 discoidal stones with balls. As all the
specimens were collected in Jefferson County and the larger
part at Aztalan, and in the Crawfish and Rock River Valley,
the collection is especially valuable and interesting. The
ancient works at and in the vicinity of Aztalan are only a
few miles from Mr. Haskell's residence.

The line of perfectly round mounds—I counted nine or
ten—is still present, but the wall of the "sacred enclosure,"
as shown on plate 34 and 35 of Mr. J. A. Lapham's excellent work, "The Antiquities of Wisconsin," is almost
entirely destroyed. Corn and wheat were growing where
once a great people assembled. A number of the mounds
have been opened at different times, and their contents, having been carried away to all parts of the world, cannot be
recovered.

V. ETHNOLOGY.

Mr. Martin Berliner added to the ethnological department of our Museum a "warrant for £20 to David Hillhouse, for furnishing supplies at the treaty with the Creek
Indians, June 25, 1789."

Ex-Alderman Henry Fischer donated two very interesting copies of newspapers from the last century. One is
"The Boston Evening Post" of April 3, 1765, and the

other "The New Hampshire Gazette" of October 11, 1865. The same gentleman presented two specimens of Confederate States money.

A sword and an iron hatchet, found near Gotha, Fla., and doubtless of Spanish origin, were donated by Mr. A. Meinecke.

We received quite a number of minor donations to this department, all of which are enumerated in the appendix of this report.

The following interesting objects were added by purchase: Five hand-made iron locks from churches and castles in Germany and evidently very old; one pewter lamp, one shade lamp, one candle stick and two pairs of snuffers, all collected in Germany. A necklace of beads, eagle claws and elk teeth and another one of beads, once in possession of the Arapahoe Indians, were also purchased.

DEPARTMENT OF WORKS OF ARTISTIC SKILL.

In a regular meeting of the Board of Trustees of the Public Museum, held January 28, 1893, a new department was added to the Museum. This department is designated to comprise specimens of artistic skill only, and artisans are requested to assist by donations or otherwise in order to make this new department a success. The board was induced to create such a department by a donation of Mr. Nicholas Lorenz, of this city, who presented to the Museum an exquisite silver goblet, thoroughly gilded and ornamented in a most beautiful manner with imitations of precious stones.

OTHER DONATIONS.

Mr. Gustav Preusser donated a portrait of the late Dr. August Luening, one of the founders and first president—from 1857 to 1861—of the once famous society, "Der

Naturhistorische Verein von Wisconsin,'' which in 1888 became the ''Natural History Society of Wisconsin.'' The society, at that time exclusively German, formed large collections of natural history objects, which were generally known under the name of Engelmann Museum. Dr. Luening, as well as Mr. Gustav Preusser and others, donated largely to these collections. In 1883 this Museum was presented to the city, forming the beginning of the fine collections of the Public Museum of the City of Milwaukee of to-day.

LIBRARY.

From the various scientific societies and institutions of this country and abroad a large number of scientific papers, pamphlets and books were received in exchange. The Smithsonian Institution, the National Museum, the Department of Agriculture and the War Department of Washington have donated largely to our library.

Among the books purchased, the following are of special value: Sir William Yardine Bart, ''Humming Birds'' (2 vols.); A. F. W. Schimper, ''Die Epiphytische Vegetation der Erde''; Dr. H. G. L. Reichenbach, ''Trochilinæ,'' ''Conores Exotica''; Dr. Otto Finsch, 'Die Papageien (2 vols.); Bowdler R. Sharpe ''Catalogue of the Passeriformes of the British Museum'' (13 vols.); F. A. Brockhaus, ''Conversations-Lexicon'' (7 vols.); Dr. G. Brown Goode, ''American Fishes.''

Not only strictly scientific books should find a place in our Museum library, popular scientific works should also be added to some extent. Many visitors who look over our collections are desirous of reading about certain objects which have interested them most. They frequently inquire about such books at the Museum office. This is the right

class of visitors, progressive and desirous of getting all the
information they can. In the American Museum of Natural
History, of New York, in the Philadelphia Academy of
Science and in other institutions excellent libraries are con-
nected with the collections free to all visitors. On this
point I have expressed my opinion more elaborately in the
last annual report (p. 14–17) and in my report on Eastern
Museums, to which I refer.

WORK DONE.

Last fall, from Nov. 9th to Dec. 1st, I visited the East
and spent all my time in studying the museum buildings
and the collections exhibited therein. While at Washington, D. C., I visited the Smithsonian Institution, the
National Museum, the Army Medical Museum and the collections of the Agricultural Department. On my way to
New York I spent several days in the Academy of Sciences,
Philadelphia, and in the museum of Princeton College,
Princeton, N. J. The American Museum of Natural History, Central Park, N. Y., made a deep and lasting impression on my mind. The building as well as the beautiful
collections, displayed in the best possible manner, the
scientific laboratories where original research is carried on
by an excellent staff of scientists, celebrated over all the
world, combine to make this institution one of the foremost
in this country. In the Peabody Museum, New Haven,
Conn., the Museum of Comparative Zoology, and Peabody
Archæological Museum, Cambridge, Mass., in the Essex
Institute, Salem, Mass., I also spent many hours. A more
detailed account on these scientific centres was given in my
"Report on Eastern Museums," which was printed in the
course of the year.

The more our collections increase the more work is necessary to keep them in good condition and to display each specimen advantageously in our crowded cases.

The work done in the museum by its custodian is always of a very variable character. It is not readily seen by the casual visitor, but nevertheless, it is very tedious and tiresome and takes much time. Almost every day scientific periodicals and proceedings from American and foreign societies are received. These publications have to be looked over and in many cases carefully read, as they often contain valuable scientific material. Each article of special merit and on special subjects has to be marked for cataloguing.

The mammal and bird collections as well as the collections of Indian relics have to be closely examined each month, which is a very unhealthy and sometimes dangerous work, as the specimens and cases are suffused with arsenic and corrosive sublimate. The odor of camphor and naphthaline, when opening a case, is almost overpowering. It is necessary to be thus on a constant lookout for museum pests, which would soon spoil our collections if allowed to get a foothold.

Much of my time is occupied by writing temporary labels or in looking up those already on the specimens. The thousands of labels of the ornithological collections had to be changed according to the American Ornithologists' Union "Code and Check List." The labels were all printed in the Museum under my supervision, and each one had to be examined again before attaching it to the specimen. All the labels of Mr. Meinecke's very large collection of minerals and fossils which he donated to the Museum, had to be looked up and compared with the standard works on these subjects before entering them into our records.

The correspondence in the interest of the Museum takes a very considerable portion of my time. Rarely a day passed that not several, in many instances long, letters had to be written by me. The business correspondence is mostly done by the assistant secretary, Mr. Carl Thal. Another part of my time is taken up by donors and friends of the Museum who frequently call at the office. This class of visitors, who are usually cultivating a special field of natural history, ethnology, etc., are especially welcome, as they are desirous to study. During a large part of the year quite a number of architects called repeatedly on me in order to get some information regarding the interior arrangements of the new Museum building.

This year of the World's Columbian Exposition has brought a large number of distinguished men to Milwaukee, who almost all visited the Museum. All admired our collections of beautifully mounted and tastefully arranged specimens of birds and mammals, and most of them were struck by the immense material having been brought together with our exceedingly low appropriation. Mr. Carl Hagenbeck, of Hamburg, and Mr. Umlauff, of the same city, both well acquainted with the museums of Europe, pronounced our Museum one of the best of its line. Dr. Carl Peters, the celebrated African explorer, Dr. Hans Virchow, of the University of Berlin, Dr. Feiherr von Schmidt, of the Technical High School of Munich, Mr. Chr. Benkard and a number of foreign commissioners of the World's Fair visited the Museum and were entertained to the best of my ability.

I have spent about thirty-six days at the World's Fair, Chicago, in looking up specimens for the Museum. A large number of specimens were donated, and I was very successful in buying, for a very low price, a large number of fine natural history objects. A good selection of mounted mammals and birds from Ward's Natural History Exhibit in the Anthropological Building was made. This collection, consisting of about 75 excellent specimens, will prove to be a grand addition to our institution.

In the state building of the United States of Colombia I found, early in June, a large collection of bird skins, which had been collected in the Andes Mountains for the World's Fair. Mr. Lemley, one of the commissioners for Colombia, gave me the permission to make a selection for the Museum. I picked out 132 specimens, the cream of the entire collection. From the British Guiana exhibit in the Agricultural Building I obtained most of the bird skins for a very reasonable price. Dr. J. J. Quelch, the commissioner, presented to me a large number of other objects, skins of mammals, a mounted Manatee, specimens of woods, palm logs, etc., all of which will be enumerated in my next annual report.

I carefully studied the large and tastefully arranged collections of natural history specimens in the Government Building, the cases in which they were displayed, etc. Thus the year has been an exceedingly busy one for me. I could scarcely find time to read the most important scientific papers, and to do some extra scientific work was an impossibility.

The business letters have been written by Mr. Carl Thal on the typewriter. He also did the routine work, kept the records and the account books in the best possible manner, and did such other work as was from time to time assigned to him by me. Through the many years of experience in the Museum, Mr. Thal's service is of the greatest value. Our taxidermist, Mr. George B. Turner, was always busy in mounting specimens for the collections. He mounted a large Buffalo Cow, two small Black Bears, one Jaguar, one Ocelot, a number of Monkeys, a Dwarf

Elephant, finished a group of Canada Porcupines, and a large number of smaller mammals and birds.

Miss Fanny Rauterberg resigned her position in August, and Miss Lydia Nehrling was appointed in her place. Both have printed a large number of labels, and attended to the visitors in the afternoon.

INVENTORY.

*Approximate Statement of the Contents and Value of the
Various Departments of the Museum.*

113,959 zoological specimens.............................	$25,856 50
15,739 botanical specimens.............................	944 90
8,586 anthropological specimens.......................	6,525 20
11,026 palaeontological specimens.......................	5,167 00
4,035 mineralogical and lithological specimens..........	3,767 14
5,036 books, pamphlets, catalogues, atlases and charts....	5,074 19
3,035 birds' eggs and nests.............................	10,000 00
Furniture, tools, jars, vessels, conservation supplies and stationery.............................	11,776 52
Upham collection held in trust....................	350 00
Aggregate value of the contents of the Museum......	$69,461 45

FINANCIAL TRANSACTIONS OF THE MUSEUM.

Debit.

Balance in Museum fund Sept. 1st, 1892....................	$7,201 12
Appropriation to Museum fund Jan. 31st, 1893..............	11,367 51
Refunded insurance premium, Feb. 28th, 1893..............	61 50
Refunded insurance premium, March 1st, 1893.............	60 00
Refunded insurance premium, April 18th, 1893.............	15 90
Refunded insurance premium, June 27th, 1893..............	9 50
	$18,715 53

Credit.

Amounts paid by warrants on the city treasurer since the last
annual statement was rendered:

Permanent improvements......................	$82 00	
Pay roll.....................................	5,880 00	
Fuel and light	602 85	
Repairs......................................	29 46	
Postage and freight..........................	30 75	
Stationery and printing......................	171 45	
Furniture....................................	459 43	
Anthropology and Ethnology..................	565 00	
Mammals....................................	84 56	
Birds..	57 83	
Crustaceans and insects......................	8 10	
Minerals and rocks...........................	25 00	
Fossils and casts............................	56 35	
Wages.......................................	284 91	
Insurance....................................	946 82	
Rent and Tax...............................	850 00	
Miscellaneous................................	393 53	
Library......................................	195 06	
Conservation supplies........................	22 23	
		$10,745 33
Balance in Museum fund Sept. 1st, 1893..............		$7,970 20

INSURANCE.

Security Insurance Co., of New Haven, Conn...............	$1,500 00
Fireman's Fund Insurance Co., of San Francisco, Cal.......	2,500 00
British America Assurance Co., Toronto, Ont..............	1,000 00
Fire Insurance Co., of the County of Philadelphia.........	1,000 00
Phenix Insurance Co., of Brooklyn......................	1,500 00
State Insurance Co., of Des Moines, Ia...................	1,500 00
Queen Insurance Co., of America, N. Y..................	2,500 00
Royal Insurance Co., of Liverpool, England..............	1,000 00
German Insurance Co., of Quincy, Ill.....	1,000 00
Oakland Home Insurance Co., of Oakland, Cal............	1,500 00
Saint Paul Fire and Marine Insurance Co., of St. Paul, Minn.	1,500 00
Grand Rapids Fire Insurance Co., of Grand Rapids, Mich...	1,500 00
Citizens' Insurance Co., of Pittsburg, Pa.................	1,000 00
Norwich Union Fire Insurance Society, England	2,500 00
Rockford Insurance Co., of Rockford, Ill.................	2,500 00
American Insurance Co., of Newark, N. Y................	1,500 00
Commonwealth Insurance Co., of New York..............	1,500 00
Rutger's Fire Insurance Co., of New York...............	1,500 00
Pacific Fire Insurance Co., of the City of New York........	1,500 00
Citizens' Insurance Co., of Cincinnati, Ohio..............	1,500 00
Germania Insurance Co., of New Orleans, La.............	1,500 00
Allemannia Fire Insurance Co., of Pittsburg, Pa...........	1,500 00
Orient Insurance Co., of Hartford, Conn.................	2,000 00
Phenix Insurance Co., of Brooklyn, N. Y................	1,000 00
Rockford Insurance Co., of Rockford, Ill.................	2,500 00
Rhode Island Underwriters Association, Providence, R. I...	2,000 00
Farmers' Fire Insurance Co., of York, Pa.................	2,500 00
Oakland Home Insurance Co., of Oakland, Cal............	2,500 00
Liverpool & London and Globe Ins. Co., of Liverpool, Eng.	2,000 00
Commercial Union Assurance Co., Limited, of London, Eng.	2,500 00
Total...	$51,500 00

VISITORS.

	1892 Sept.	1892 Oct.	1892 Nov.	1892 Dec.	1893 Jan.	1893 Feb.	1893 Mar.	1893 April.	1893 May.	1893 June.	1893 July.	1893 Aug.	1892-93 Whole year.
Average daily attendance...	1,487	683	39	42	40	58	83	99	54	59	82	79	230
Greatest daily attendance...	6,572	4,845	183	130	103	172	210	231	144	121	390	153	
Least daily attendance	99	13	10	6	10	11	17	26	15	5	20	39	
Av. attendance on Sundays.	125	558	98	72	75	139	178	199	94	81	70	74	
Total attendance............	44,607	20,492	1,148	1,259	1,215	1,562	2,581	2,980	1,682	1,787	2,551	2,447	84,311

All the above is respectfully submitted,

HY. NEHRLING,

Secretary and Custodian.

APPENDIX.

ZOOLOGY.

C. J. Allen, Milwaukee, Wis.

1 Pigeon Hawk,	Fox Point, Milwaukee Co., Wis.			
1 Cooper's Hawk,	"	"	"	
1 Vesper Sparrow,	"	"	"	
1 American Hawk Owl,	"	"	"	
1 Chickadee,	"	"	"	
1 Screech Owl,	"	"	"	
1 Yellow-legs,	"	"	"	
1 Downy Woodpecker,	"	"	"	
2 Blue Jays,	"	"	"	
2 Snowflakes,	"	"	"	
1 Mourning Dove,	"	"	"	
1 Northern Shrike,	"	"	"	
1 Barred Owl,	"	"	"	
1 Short-eared Owl,	"	"	"	

Jos. Caspari, Milwaukee, Wis.

1 Cormorant, Fox River, Wis.

1 American Long-eared Owl, Fox River, Wis.

Hugo Dennhardt, Milwaukee, Wis.

1 Fish, Mississippi River.

James Garbade, Milwaukee, Wis.

1 Fox Squirrel (Albino), West Bend, Wis.

Carl Hagenbeck, Hamburg, Germany.

2 Pair of horns of Gazella Soemmeringi, East Africa.

1 Pair of horns of Lithocranius Walleri, Somoliland, E. Africa.

1 Pair of horns of Strepsiceras Kudu, East Africa.

1 Pair of horns of Alcelaphus Swaynei, Somoliland, E. Africa.

1 Pair of horns of Tragelaphus imberbis, Somoliland, E. Africa.

1 Skin and skeleton of Dwarf Elephant "Lilly," Sumatra.

H. Hirsch, Milwaukee, Wis.

1 Red-tailed Hawk, West Bend, Wis.

1 Saw-whet Owl, "   "

1 Screech Owl, Sussex, Wis.

Miss Louise Hoffmann, Hustisford, Wis.

    1 Humming Bird's nest.

Fred. Krempel, Milwaukee, Wis.

    1 Coral, Santa Ana, Cal.

    1 Lizard,   "   "

A. E. Kurth, Milwaukee, Wis.

    1 Snake, Hustisford, Wis.

Adolph Meinecke, Milwaukee, Wis.

    2 Sponges, Sarasota Keys, Fla.

    1 Crab,   "   "

    6 Snakes, Gotha, Orange County, Fla.

    1 Sandhill Crane,   "   "

    59 Tropical Beetles.

George Orth, Jr., Milwaukee, Wis.

    1 Fox Squirrel, Wisconsin.

Miss Fanny Rauterberg, Milwaukee, Wis.

    1 Yellow-bellied Sapsucker, Milwaukee, Wis.

J. Seefeld & Son, Milwaukee, Wis.

    1 Common Land Crab, West Indies.

August Stirn, Milwaukee, Wis.

    1 Gray Sandpiper, Europe.

    4 White Rice-birds (Munia oryzivora, var. alba.), Japan.

    4 White and Variegated Bengalese (Urolancha acuticauda, var.), Japan.

    6 Humming-birds.

Ch. Preusser, Milwaukee, Wis.

    2 Western Fox Squirrels, Wisconsin.

    1 Red Squirrel, Wisconsin.

    1 Canada Jay, Hurley, Wis.

    2 White Rabbits, Minnesota.

    1 American Merganser, Milwaukee Market.

    2 Hooded Mergansers,   "   "

    2 Bonaparte's Gulls, Fox Point, Milwaukee Co., Wis.

    1 Woodchuck, Fox Point, Milwaukee Co., Wis.

    1 Green Heron, Wisconsin.

Oscar Widule, Milwaukee, Wis.

    1 Night-hawk, Milwaukee Co., Wis.

ACQUIRED BY PURCHASE.

    2 Scissor-tailed Flycatchers, Cameron Co., Tex.

    2 Cardinals, Augusta, Ga.

1 Cardinal, Keokuk, Ia.

2 Androglossa guatemalensis, San Pedro Sula, Honduras, C. A.

2 Ceryle torquata, Rio Blanco, Brazil.

2 Eumomota superciliaris, San Pedro Sula,   "

1 Momotus lessoni, San Pedro Sula,   "

2 Prionirhynchus carinatus, San Pedro Sula,   "

2 Trogons, San Pedro Sula,   "

2 Chrysotis albifrons, San Pedro Sula   "

1 Pionias semilis,   "   "

1 Grallaria guatemalensis   "   "

1 Calliste larvata, Rio Almenta   "

1 Chlorophonia occipitalis, San Pedro,   "

1 Chlorophanes spiea guatemalensis, Rio Almenta,   "

1 Abycodynastes luteiventris, Rio Almenta   "

1 Dromococcyx phasianellus, Chasniguas,   "

1 Leucopternis ghiesbrechti, San Pedro Sula   "

1 Thrasaetus, San Pedro Sula,   "

2 Kinkajous,   "
1 Ocelot,   "

1 Armadillo,   "

1 Porcupine,   "

1 American Buffalo, Montana.

2 Limpkins, Bird Island.

1 Gila Woodpecker, Camp Lowell, Arizona.

1 Broad-billed Hummingbird, Huachuca Mountains, Arizona.

2 Thurber's Juncos, Cala.

2 Blue Grosbeaks, Cameron Co., Tex.

1 Jaguar, San Pedro Sula, Honduras.

1 Bicolored Blackbird, Marin Co., Cala.

1 Sycamore Warbler, Cameron Co., Tex.

1 Gray Vireo, San Bernardino, Cala.

1 Lawrence's Goldfinch, San Bernardino, Cala.

1 Henslow's Sparrow, Quincy, Ill.

1 Calliope Hummingbird, San Diego Co., Cala.

1 Bachman's Sparrow, Georgia.

1 Red Fox, Gogebic, Mich.

1 Beaver, Gogebic, Mich.

1 American Bittern, Gogebic, Mich.

1 Zebu Cow, East India.

2 Loons, Gogebic, Mich.

1 Boat-tailed Grackle, Hillsborough Co., Fla.

1 Gray Kingbird,   "   "

1 Cerulean Warbler, Tampa, Fla.
1 Sycamore Warbler, Helena Isl.
1 Pine-woods Sparrow, Hillsborough Co., Fla.

MINERALOGY AND LITHOLOGY.

DONATIONS.

Ad. Meinecke, Milwaukee, Wis.

1 Barite, Hungary.
1 " Germany.
1 Fluorite, England.
1 Alunite, Germany.
1 Copper, "
1 Calcite, Wurtemberg.
1 Chabazite, Nova Scotia.
1 Lepidolite, Bohemia.
1 Pyrite, Colorado.
1 Tourmaline, Isle of Elba.
1 Antimon, Germany.
1 Quartz, Italy.
1 Wood Opal, Hungary.
1 Zeolite, Nova Scotia.
1 Pyroxene, Germany.
1 Dolomite, "
1 Malachite, Chile.
1 Magnetite, Lake Superior.
1 Chabazite, Bohemia.
1 Orthoclase, Switzerland.
1 Pyromorphite, Tyrol.
1 Zeolite, Tyrol.
1 Pyroxene, California.
1 Hematite, Wurtemberg.
1 Quartz, Germany.
1 Aluminite, England.
1 Baryte, England.
1 Augite, Tyrol.
1 Rhodonite, Germany.
3 Aragonite, Bohemia.
1 Pyrosmalite, Sweden.
1 Rutile, Hungary.
1 Indigo Copper, Chile.

1 Cassitarite, Saxony.
1 Wolframite, Bohemia.
1 Jasper, Germany.
1 Bismuth, Saxony.
1 Hagemannite, Saxony.
1 Scheelite, Saxony.
1 Tourmaline, New York.
3 Boracite, Lueneburg.
1 Mica, New York.
1 Stannite, Germany.
1 Calcite, Germany.
1 Strontianite, England.
1 Bismuth, Saxony.
1 Magnesite, Texas.
1 Calcite, Germany.
1 Quartz,   "
1 Specular Iron, Germany.
1 Alvite, Switzerland.
1 Augite, Tyrol.
1 Cryolite, France.
1 Calcite, Canada.
1 Tourmaline, Maine.
1 Amphibole, Tyrol.
1 Copper Ore, Chile.
1 Dolomite, Germany.
1 Zeolite, Nova Scotia.
1 Wismuth, Silesia.
1 Wulfenite, Austria.
1 Melanite, India.
1 Garnet, Tyrol.
1 Heliotrope, Saxony.
1 Gersdorffite, Saxony.
1 Hematite, Germany.
1 Amblygonite, Paris.
1 Emplectite, Saxony.
1 Azurite, Russia.
1 Azurite,   "
1 Siderite,   "
1 Bismuth, Saxony.
1 Cuprite, Chile.
1 Stilbite, Tyrol.

1 Corynite, Austria.
1 Nagyagite, Hungary.
1 Zincite, Germany.
1 Cuprite, Chile.
1 Cervantite, Germany.
1 Opal, Hungary.
1 Calcite, Germany.
1 Celadonite, Tyrol. .
7 Strontianite, Germany.
1 Gypsum, Wurtemberg.
1 Chabazite, Nova Scotia.
1 Magnetite, Germany.
1 Spinel, Asia.
1 Copper, Chile.
1 Amphibole, Norway.
1 Pyrosmalite, Sweden.
1 Chalcedony, France.
1 Andalusite, Switzerland.
1 Chabazite, Tyrol.
1 Lead, Germany.
1 Kyanite, Maine.
1 Chalcocite, Chile.
1 Gypsum, Germany.
1 Cuprite, Chile.
1 Bismuth, Saxony.
1 Alunite, Hungary.
1 Malachite, Arizona.
1 Amphibole, Germany.
1 Acadialite, Nova Scotia.
1 Bronzite, Saxony.
1 Bismuth,   "
1 Zeolite, Nova Scotia.
1 Cassiterite, Bohemia.
1 Amblygonite,   "
1 Pyroxene, Germany.
1 Iron Ore   "
1 Opal, Hungary.
1 Serpentine, Saxony.
1 Cobalt, Saxony.
1 Calcite, Michigan.
1 Bismuth, Germany.

1 Chabazite, Nova Scotia.
1 Calcite, Germany.
1 Heulandite, Nova Scotia.
1 Magnesite, Texas.
1 Zeolite, Tyrol.
1 Laumonite, Işle Royale, B. S.
7 Rutiles, Switzerland.
1 Beryl, New Brunswick.
1 Coal, New Brunswick.
1 Scheelite, Saxony.
1 Zinc-blende, Germany.
1 Dolomite,   "
1 Wulfenite, Austria.
1 Nagyagite, Hungary.
1 Gypsum, Germany.
1 Topaz, Saxony.
1 Cassiterite, Saxony.
1 Hematite,   "
1 Cuprite, Chile.
1 Analcite, Bohemia.
1 Coal, New Brunswick.
1 Augite, Saxony.
1 Rutile, Switzerland.
1 Fluorite,
1 Garnet, Tyrol.
1 Wulfenite, Austria.
1 Cassiterite, Silesia.
1 Emplectite, Saxony.
1 Stilbite, Nova Scotia.
1 Celestite, Sicily.
1 Iron Ore, Wurtemberg.
1 Zincite, Germany.
1 Chalcedony, Iceland.
1 Vesuvian, Hungary.
1 Cobalt, Cuba.
1 Cobalt, Hungary.
1 Manganite, Germany.
1 Trachyte, Hungary.
1 Trachyte, Italy.
1 Basalt, Saxony.
1 Quartz, Germany.

1 Scheelite, Saxony.
24 Cuprite, France,
1 Covellite, Chile.
1 Molybdenite, New Hampshire.
1 Talc, Tyrol.
1 Flint, France.
1 Obsidian, California.
1 Garnet, Tyrol.
1 Beryl, Bavaria.
1 Analcime, Bohemia.
1 Chabazite, Nova Scotia.
1 Stilbite, Tyrol.
1 Antimon, Germany.
2 Cobalts, Hessia.
1 Chabazite, Germany.
1 Ryacolite, Hungary.
1 Clintonite, New York.
1 Siderite, Wurtemberg.
1 Carbonate of Iron, Greenland.
1 Olivine, Saxony.
2 Fluor-spar, Greenland.
1 Graphite, New York.
1 Fluorite, England.
16 Pyroxene, Baden.
1 Zircon, Pennsylvania.
1 Cryolite, Greenland.
1 Wolfram, Germany.
1 Bismuth,   "
1 Black Mica, Tyrol.
1 Franklinite, New Jersey.
1 Beryl, Germany.
1 Pyromorphite, Saxony.
1 Wolfram, Saxony.
1 Pyrite of Iron, Germany.
1 Gypsum, Germany.
1 Wulfenite, Saxony.
1 Wismuth, Saxony.
1 Nickel,   "
1 Bismuth   "
1 Pisolite, Bohemia.
1 Copper Pyrites, Chile.

1 Indigo Copper, Chile.
5 Gypsum, Ohio.
1 Opal, Saxony.
1 Albite, Switzerland.
1 Sulphur, Hungary.
1 Magnelite, Germany.
1 Calcite, Pennsylvania.
1 Roselite, Saxony.
1 Cassiterite, Saxony.
1 Erythrite, New Hampshire.
1 Bismuth, Saxony.
1 Talc, Germany.
1 Garnet, Tyrol.
1 Scheelite, Traversella.
1 Chalcedony, Arizona.
1 Vesuvian, Hungary.
1 Gold Quartz, Virginia.
1 Tellur Wismuth, Hungary.
1 Buratite, Germany.
1 Calcite,   "
1 Apophyllite, Nova Scotia.
1 Rutile, Switzerland.
1 Zincite, Pennsylvania.
1 Horolite, Nova Scotia.
1 Calcite, Bohemia.
1 Cassiterite, New South Wales.
1 Chalcedony, Germany.
1 Sphalerite,   "
1 Cobalt, Nova Scotia.
1 Azurite, Chile.
1 Stilbite, Tyrol.
1 Pyromorphite, Tochopan.
1 Cobalt, Baden.
1 Tellur Wismuth, Hungary.
1 Cassiterite, Germany.
1 Vesuvian, Hungary.
1 Calcite, Saxony.
1 Trilomite,   "
1 Chalcedony, Germany.
1 Zeolite, Tyrol.
1 Bismuth, Colorado.

1 Calcite, Wurtemberg.
1 Cuprite, Chile.
1 Rutile, Norway.
1 Albite, 	Germany.
1 Manganese, 	"
1 Cassiterite, 	"
1 Andalusite, 	"
1 Nagyagite, Hungary.
1 Amphibole, Tyrol.
1 Datolite, Lake Superior.
1 Quartz, Germany!
1 Sphalarite, Germany.
1 Andalusite, Bavaria.
1 Cassiterite, Saxony.
1 Lead, Germany.
1 Opal, Hungary.
1 Witherite, England.
1 Opal, Hungary.
1 Arsenic, Hungary.
1 Calcite, Germany.
1 Howlite, Nova Scotia.
1 Cobalt, Germany,
1 Quartz, 	"
1 Scapolite. Hessia.
1 Cassiterite, Bohemia.
1 Scheelite, Saxony.
1 Calcite, Germany.
1 Cobalt, Wurtemberg.
1 Chalcedony, Germany.
1 Bismuth, Saxony.
1 Garnet, 	"
1 Grammatite, Switzerland.
1 Bismuth, Saxony.
1 Analcim, 	"
1 Cryolite, Greenland.
1 Specular Iron. Elba.
4 Limonites, Wurtemberg.
1 Calcite, Germany.
1 Chabazite, Austria.
1 Cobalt, 	Saxony.
1 Cassiterite, 	"

1 Chrysocolla, Chile.
1 Cornwallite, Cornwall.
1 Malachite, Chile.
1 Chrysocolla, "
1 Vesuvian, Naples.
1 Cryolite, Greenland.
1 Arsenic, Germany.
1 Specular Iron, Elba.
1 Cassiterite, New South Wales.
1 Vesuvian, Naples, Italy.
1 Manganese, Germany.
1 Kyanite, Switzerland.
1 Scheelite, Saxony.
1 Strontianite, Sicily.
1 Cryolite, Greenland.
1 Quartz, Germany.
1 Lava, Italy.
1 Jasper, Germany.
1 Analcite, Iceland.
2 Topaz, Brazil.

ACQUIRED BY PURCHASE.

1 Silver and Copper, Quincy Mine, Mich.
5 Pyrites, Cementville, Wis.
1 Geode, containing Calcite, Cement Quarry, Milw. Co., Wis.
1 Barite, Cementville, Wis.

PALÆONTOLOGY.

DONATIONS.

Adolph Meinecke, Milwaukee, Wis.

SPECIMENS FROM EUROPE.

5 Pleurotoma rotata.
2 Ostraea undata.
2 Corbula resoluta.
7 Venus Bosteroti.
7 Corbula gibba.
7 Arca barbata.
2 Ostrea flabellula.

Specimens from Europe—Continued.

9 Tellina proxima.

26 Astarte Laurentiana.

100 Limnaeus socialis.

1 Ammonites polygyratus.

3 Olenus gibbosus.

1 Chætetes mammulatus.

1 Calceola.

2 Palæoniscus Freiesleberi.

1 Trogus patella.

1 Favosites cervicanus.

1 Gastrosacus Wetzleri.

1 Gryphæa calceola.

3 Trinucleus Goldfussi.

1 Pleurotomaria.

1 Pileopsis haliotus.

1 Mæandrina.

1 Pinna mitis.

1 Impression of rain drops.

1 Medley of Fossils.

3 Cypraea Lyncoides.

1 Helix aquensis.

1 Arca incerta.

25 Cardita affinis.

2 Strombus Bonelli.

4 Natica mutabilis.

4 Astarte incrassata.

3 Terebra acuminata.

47 Cerithium scabrum.

9 Pleurotoma interrupta.

2 Melanopsis Dufouri.

5 Neritina.

2 Siliquari anguina.

10 Cardium solitarium.

5 Cardium Andracæ.

5 Murex alveolatus.

2 Natica patula.

7 Buccinum serraticostatum.

1 Helix turensis.

10 Helix depressa.

1 Anomia tellinoides.

1 Cornus Diyardini.

Specimens from Europe—Continued.

2 Cardita Bazini.
1 Pyrula reticulata.
5 Lucina columbella.
1 Cerithium cornucopiæ.
3 Cerithium tricinctum.
1 Concellaria buccinula.
2 Mursa aquitanicus.
4 Nassa Thiolliersi.
4 Nassa clathrata.
2 Arca barbata.
2 Turitella.
31 Cerithium plicatum.
8 Cerithium trochleare.
6 Rostellaria—Chenopus pespelicani.
12 Clausilia turricula.
2 Cerithium papaveraceum.
1 Fusus longævus.
5 Fusus Turonensis.
7 Oliva plicaria.
4 Mitra scoobiculata.
7 Anomia argentea.
2 Ostræa angusta.
3 Pleurotoma granulata cincta.
8 Pleurotoma dimidiata.
2 Pleurotoma asperulata.
6 Buccinum Gossardi.
7 Turitella terebralis.
3 Ampullaria Willemeti.
1 Conus.
1 Conus fusco cingulatus.
4 Conus ventricosus.
3 Conus Mercati.
4 Calyptræa tabillata.
2 Pecten cypris.
5 Arca umbonata.
28 "   turonica.
6 "   diluvii.
14 Turitella multisulcata.
2 "   carinifera.
1 "   vermicularis.
1 Vermetus.

4 Cerithium papale.
6   "   lapidum.
3   "   subacutum.
7   "   tuberculosum.
4   "   echinoides.
1 Dentalium entalis.
2 Helix Ramondi.
7   "   turonensis.
1 Pyrula condita.
10 Cardium sociale.
3 Voluta nodosa.
3 Ostræa gregaria.
1 Venerupsis Gumbeli.
1 Natica cæpacea.
2 Pectunculus.
3 Tapas Partschii.
2 Planorbis pseudoammonius.
6 Athyris Royssii.
3 Venus turonensis.
8 Murex sublavatus.
6   "   spirillus.
2 Pectunculus pulvinatus.
3 Cerithium.
4 Trochus crenularis.
3 Paludina aspera.
8 Operculina complanata.
8 Planorbis corniculum.
6 Rostellaria fissurella.
26 Pecten.
4 Pectunculus.
5 Natica mutabilis.
4 Natica sigaretina.
10 Maetra substriaetella.
3 Turitella turruss.
6 Turitella abbreviata.
2 Fusus rugosa.
2   "   Burdigalensis.
1   "   politus.
4 Murex spinicosta.
3 Pleurotoma granulatocincta.
14   "   spiralis.

Specimens from Europe—Continued.

16 Corbula carinata.

23 Cerithium serratum.

2 " plicaria.

5 Pleurotoma monilis.

2 Cellepora globularis.

8 Cyclostoma bisulcatum.

85 Valvata multiformis turbiniformis.

4 Natica epiglottina.

13 " helicina.

1 Unio Eseri.

1 Rissoa Michaudi.

1 Mitra cupressina.

5 Lymnaeus cuspidatus.

1 Tapes Ulmensis.

2 Balanus tintinabulum.

12 Buccinum semistriatum.

3 Astarte Burdinii.

6 Natica Parisiensis.

1 " sphaerica.

2 Cassis saburon.

4 Ostræa lanceolata.

2 Crassatella bellovarina.

2 Venericardia acuticosta.

2 Fusus subcarinatus.

2 Voluta rarispinosa.

21 Corbulomya complanata.

20 Cardium obliguum.

10 Lucina undulata.

2 Helix Steinheimensis.

1 " Ehingensis.

2 Paludina varicosa.

8 Diastoma costellata.

5 Lucina concentrica.

99 Valvate multiformis var. trochiformis.

13 Lucina saxorum.

2 Trochus milliaris.

3 Planorbis subovatus.

2 Ancillaria dubia.

10 Cardium.

2 Turiballa echta.

Specimens from Europe—Continued.

5 Turiballa edita.

3 Glossus.

3 Cerithium biserialis.

3 Cerithium biserialis.

1 Clausilia Terverii.

13 Cerithium scalaroides.

3 Fusus polygonus.

2 Fusus tuberculosus.

3 Fusus longirostris.

10 Fusus bilineatus.

2 Melania.

1 Spirobis vitrus.

1 Columbella curta.

5 Buccinum Rosthorni.

1 Natica redempta.

8 Helix osculum.

3 Arca.

2 Cardium Vindobonense.

4 Conus.

2 Cardita caliculata.

8 Cardita scalaris.

19 Pectunculus turonicus.

1 Cytherea splendens.

8 Natica clausa.

7 Pectunculus.

6 Ancillaria glandiformis.

15 Scutellina nummularia.

10 Cytheria semisulcata.

7 Paludina globulus.

8 Rissonia pusilla.

1 Conus fusco-cingulatus.

2 Astarte.

1 Buccinum baccatum.

2 Helix pachystoma.

3 Helix subnitens.

1 Succinea minima.

1 Phorus Parisiensis.

204 Melania horducea.

5 Melania inquinata.

1 Veritina obtusangula.

Specimens from Europe—Continued.

1 Conus.
14 Cyclostoma conicum.
1 Astarte pumila.
51 Nummulites planulatus.
3 Nummulites planulatus.
27 Valvata multiformis var. intermedia.
1 Natica patula.
4 Strombus decussatus.
14 Cytherea elegans.
30 Cytherea distans.
7 Bulla coronata.
1 Voluta rarispina.
2 Terebratula insignis.
103 Valvata multiformis planorbiformis.
16 Helix.
1 Venericardia costata.
6 Pleurotoma pustulata.
6   "   interrupta.
2   "   ramosa.
2   "   cataphracta.
6   "   coronata.
18 Rissoina decussata.
3 Mitra striatula.
11 Caliptrea Sinesis.
1 Astarte porrecta.
1 Cyrena (Tapes) Ulmensis.
14 Lucina columbella.
2 Cancellaria inermis.
3 Turbinella subreticulata.
3 Fusus Ligniarius.
8 Cerithium rubigunosum.
8   "   Bronnii.
79   "   crenulatum.
2 Cardita intermedia.
1   "
3 Pleurotoma asperulata.
2 Mya.
8 Calyptraea deformis.
2 Crepidula unquiformis. ·
2 Trigonia clavellata.

3 Plicatula tubifera.
5 Mya truncata.
1 Ostraea ungulata.
1 Arca diluvii.
30 Rhynchonella pectunculoides.
1 Lima proboscidea.
1 Turitella terebralis.
8 Turitella fasciata.
3 Cardium.
13 Pleurotoma cataphracta.
2 Pleurotoma Brochii.
10 Venus laevigata.
5 Cytherea nitidula.
9 Hipponyx cornucopiae.
31 Marginella cypreola.
9 Nassa termistriata.
5 Nassa reticulata.
2 Melania lactea.
3 Palaeomeryx.
13 Planorbis erassus.
18 Cerithium pictum.
4 Neritodsis radula.
9 Buccinum cosmatum.
2 Fusus semirugosus.
9 Fusus subcarinatus.
21 Trichotropis borealis.
10 Voluta harpula.
2 Natica millepunctata.
4 " Josephina.
3 " tigrina.
2 Dentalium Badense.
3 " Bouéi.
16 Pleurotoma obeliscus.
3 " semi-marginata.
1 Vermetus.
13 Turitella subangulata.
1 " terebralis.
2 Nassa elegans.
5 Buccinum costulatum.
3 Delphinula striata.

1 Terebratula antiplecta.
1   "   vicinalis.
2 Cerithium multigramum.
4   "   crassum.
3   "   lignitarum.
4 Voluta nodosa.
2 Pecten Sowerbyi.
2 Ranella marginata.
1 Cassadaria carinata.
1 Fasciolaria modifera.
15 Fusus rostratus.
1 Pyrula rustica.
3 Pecten Besori.
2   "   Beudanti.
2 Cardita planirostra.
9 Fasciolaria Burdigalensis.
7 Turitella archimedis.
6 Melania grossecostata.
7 Turitella bicarinata.
8   "
5 Voluta cythara.
7   "   spinosa.
2 Murex aquitanica.
5 Fusus.
8 Arca diluvii.
5 Corbis.
6   "   lamellosa.
4 Cytherea erycinoides.
1 Pectunculus pilosus.
2   "   glycimeris.
8 Chama.
13 Helix.
9   "   sylvestrina.
2   "   globulosa.
1 Pecten palmatus.
6 Turitella imbricataria.
9 Pectunculus obovatus.
1 Crassatella ponderosa.
6 Conus deperditus.
5 Natica Parisiensis.

Specimens from Europe—Continued.

2 Fusus longævus.

2 Pleurotoma rustica.

4 Cerithium minutum.

1 Nassa prismatica.

2 Arca reticulata.

6 Cidarites conoideus.

2 Plagiostoma notatum.

2 Strophodus reticulatus.

1 Rhynchonella Badensis.

3 Spirifer rostratus.

2 Venericardia.

3 Lamna elegans.

1 Venus suevica.

1 Astræa helianthoides.

1 Ammonites hecticus.

1 Terebratula.

1   "   pala.

1   "   Bouéi.

1   "   quadrifida.

1 Cytherea Terverii.

1 Venus Brochii.

1 Pectunculus pilosus.

7   "   varians.

1 Pecten palmatus.

1 Tapes (Venus) helvetica.

5 Cardita crana.

18 Saxicava rugosa.

3 Natica sigaretina.

5 Platyostoma niagarense.

6 Fusus tornatus.

4   "   corneus.

4 Pleurotoma asperulata.

2 Terebratula belemnitica.

1   "   resupinata.

2   "

1   "   subdigonæ.

15   "   varians.

1 Chama sublamellosa.

2 Cardita scalaris.

2 Galeus aduncus.

Specimens from Europe—Continued.

3 Congeria amygdaloides.
1 Fragment of a Turtle.
1 Metamorphic Clay Slate.
4 Ammonites lingulatus.
1 Spondylus.
1 Spondyluscys alpinus.
1 Paludina tentaculata.
10 Orthis Mickelini.
9 Pecten cypris.
3 Congeria (Dreissena) elevaeformis.
6 Oxyrhina hastalis.
18 Ammonites Lamberti.
11   "   annularis.
9   "   hecticus laevigatus.
1 Ancylus.
1 Cassidulus.
5 Terebratula actoplicata.
8   "   resupinata.
4   "   gutta.
1 Gasteropod.
1 Ammonites Parkinsoni.
7   "   opalinus.
12   "   lingulatus.
2   "   flexuosus.
1 Inoceramus.
2 Thamnastræa suevica.
1 Pecten.
1   " undatus.
1 Cyprina ligeriensis.
2 Pteroceras Oceani.
1 Leuciscus Steinheimensis.
1 Pectunculus.
3 Arca turonica.
1 Fusus.
17 Venus Casinoides.
2 Crassatella.
18 Cerithium plicatum.
1 Exogyra.
1 Vertebræ.
2 Trochosmilia complanata.

Specimens from Europe—Continued.

1 Nautilus ovatus.
6 Spirifer striatus.
1 Sæpia hastiformis.
29 Encrinus liliiformis,
3 Terebratula gutta.
5   "   nucleata.
3   "   Bouéi.
3   "   Vilsensis.
1 Palæomeryx Schenchzeri.
1 Lamna oxyrhina.
2 Helix subverticillus.
1 Dendrites.
1 Anthophyllum sessile.
1 Modiola modiolata.
3 Terebratula triplicata.
1   "   insignis.
28   "
1   "   quinqueplicata.
1   "
1   ."   cornuta.
3   "   insignis.
1 Ciderites.
5   "   spinosus.
3   "   glandarius.
7 Spirifer verrucosus.
1 Nucula suevica.
5   "   pectinata.
1 Rostellaria bicarinata.
1 Crinoid.
8 Arca Cottaldina.
1 Congeria subglobosa.
2 Nucula.
4 Rhynchonella.
3 Terebratula floridana.
1 Nerinea.
1 Unio.
1 Prosopon grande.
3 Turbinolia.
1 Ostrea calceola.
1 Placenticeras placenta.

Specimens from Europe—Continued.

2 Antophyllum.
1 Hemicidaris.
1 Cidarites psilonoti.
1 Cnemidium stellatum.
1 Arca Gabrielis.
1 Baculites.
3 Natica Ceres.
3 Echinus sulcatus.
2 Venus Robinaldina.
3 Terebratula omalogastyr.
1 Trigonia Barrensis.
1 Ammonites bifurcatus.
1 Dendrophyllia irregularis.
2 Terebratula.
1 Pecten palmatus.
3 Actinocrinus Indianensis.
7 Cyprina Brogniarti.
3 Waldheimia aequivalvis.
9 Astræa cristata.
3   "   limbata.
35 Atrypa reticularis.
1 Ammonites lingulatus.
1   "   planulatus.
1   "   convolvulus.
1   "   Lamberti.
2 Cirthium hexagonum.
8 Marginella ovulata.
1 Ammonite.
5 Ammonites plicatiles.
5   "   biplex.
13   "   dentatus.
2   "   Parkinsoni.
15   "   Jason.
1   "   torulosus.
1 Pecten cingulatus.
1 Astræa reticulata.
3 Cardiomorpha missouriensis.
6 Palæocyclus porpila.
2 Cones.
4 Rhynchonella bidentata.

Specimens from Europe—Continued.

1 Ammonites lunula.
1   "   flexuosus.
8   "   canaliculatus.
21   "   fonticula.
13   "   concolutus.
22   "   Parkinsoni.
2 Glandina antiqua.
6 Rhynchonella Fürstenbergensis.
3   "   loxia.
6 Terebratula pentagonalis.
2   "   lacunosa.
3 Terebra lampæ.
2 Spatangus.
4 Actobatis armatus.
2 Terebratulina gracilis.
11 Terebratula striocinta.
12   "   pectunculoides.
3   "   loricata.
8   "   substriata.
1   "   difformis.
3   "   bisinuata.
2 Cyrena tellinella.
1 Venus vetula.
1 Pecten.
1 Pyrula reticulata.
15 Ancillaria buccinoides.
4 Trochus crenulatus.
13 Cyprina affinis.
6 Cardiata scalaris.
2 Rostellaria.
2 Cardita multicostata.
2 Crassatella trigona.
6 Pectunculus terebratularis.
11 Turitella terebra.
24 Melania turita.
2 Natica cæparea.
2   "   patula.
4   "   sphærica.
10 Cytherea cuneata.
10 Cyrene desperdita.

Specimens from Europe—Continued.

5 Lucina undulata.

3 Murchisonia cingulata.

24 Terebratula lacunosa.

1 Janira asquicostatus.

6 Rhynchonella borealis.

4 Streptelasma hemiplicata.

1 Cnemidium.

1   "   rimulosum.

2 Ammonites discus.

1   "   convolutus.

1   "   opalinus.

7   "   gracilis.

1   "   biplex.

9 Heterocrinus heterodactylus.

1 Prosopon.

1 Astræa.

1 Spatangus.

1 Pecten æquistriatus.

2 Turbo limosus.

1 Ostræa Roemeri.

3 Terebratula bisuffarcinata.

3   "   triplicata.

1   "   strioplicata.

1 Spongites radiciformis.

1 Micrastis minimus.

19 Cidarites propinquus.

13   "   filogramus.

1 Verinea Mandelslopi.

5 Rhynchonella curviceps.

8 Terebratula caliecosta.

3   "   plicatissima.

4 Disasler silicius.

1 Cueinidium corallinum.

1 Diadema subangularia.

1 Astræa Perastræa grandiflora.

2 Teeth of Mosaurus.

1 Arca.

1 Turitella.

2 Cidarites coronatus.

13   "   tripterus.

Specimens from Europe—Continued.

1 Anomia spalina.
1 Spatangus parastatus.
2 Aptychus lamellasus.
1 Hemicidaris crenularis.
6 Batocrinus subæqualis.
16 Melocrinus decadaclylus.
1 Astraca gracilis.
1 " calceola.
1 Ammonites flexuosus.
1 " Murchisoni.
1 " Woolgari.
4 " Lamberti.
1 " polygyratus.
19 Cidaris Blumenbachii.
2 Cyathophyllum nitratum.
1 " turbinatum.
4 Myacetes elongatus.
4 Echinopsis Nattheimensis.
3 Cardium semipunctatum.
11 Rhynchonella lacumosa, var. dichotoma.
10 Ammonites flexuosus.
7 Nummulites lævigatus.
1 Ammonites hecticus.
4 " inflatus.
1 Turbinolia cretaceous.
2 Cidarites alternatum.
1 " elegans.
9 " trilaterus.
2 Baculites acuarius.
4 Terebratula bifrons.
3 Lithodendron plicatilis.
4 Serpula.
2 Lucina.
5 Spirifer Walcotti.
3 Lucina ceta.
1 Cardita tenuicosta.
1 Ostrea gregares.
12 Rhynchonella quadriplicata.
2 Ammonites biplex.
4 " Parkinsonii dubius.

Specimens from Europe—Continued.

15 Ammonites hecticus lumila.
 6   "   alternatus.
 1   "   polyplœus.
 5 Terebratula scalpellum.
 4   "   striocincta.
 8 Serpula limosa.
 1 Fungia elliptica.
 2 Astarte ceta.
 2   "   Beaumontii.
 1 Trigonia muricata.
 3   "   costata.
 1   "   carinata.
 9 Ammonites Lamberti.
 4 Belemnites acutus.
 8 Terebratula impressa.
 2 Cidarites elegans.
 6   "   tnberculosus.
54   "   marginatus.
 1 Spondylus pygmaeus.
 1 Spondylus aculeatus.
 2 Nucula suevica.
 2 Modiola modiolaris.
 1 Venus suevica.
 1   "   trigonelaris.
 4 Cytherea.
 3 Trochus ornatus.
 1 Plagiostoma acuticosta.
 7 Typodus splendens.
 1 Pholadomya glabra.
 1 Natica abyssinus.
 1 Terebratula difformis.
 4 Astarte pulla.
 1 Astarte.
 1 Diana.
 4 Serpula socialis.
 1 Trigonia.
 2 Lima gibbosa.
10 Pecten.
 1 Corbula.
 1 Pleuromya.

Specimens from Europe—Continued.

6 Terebella lapilloides.

1 Cardium pesolinum.

2 Terebratula pectunculus.

7 Belemnites semihastatus depressus.

9 " pervus.

1 Terebratula lænuosa multicostata.

11 Belemnites fussiformis.

9 Terebratula pala.

2 Aucella mosquensis.

1 Voluta volutilithes nasuta.

2 Nucula claviformis.

1 Isocardia minima.

2 Lucina plebeia.

1 "

7 Teeth.

9 Astarte socialis.

2 Disaster carinatus.

6 Terebratula acuticosta.

11 Cidarites maximus.

1 Turitella sinicarinata.

2 Hemicidaris Wrighti.

2 Pecten monarius.

1 Trigonia longa.

1 Pholadomya costata.

1 Plagiostoma acuticosta.

5 Mytilus fureatus.

2 Isoarea transversa.

4 Terebratula.

2 Nolidanus Muensteri.

8 Ammonites hecticus compressus.

2 Cressatella vadosa.

2 Cardium acuteatum.

1 Plagiostoma tenuistriata.

2 Venus suevica.

4 Arca carinata.

1 Astarte.

4 " pulla.

11 " semile.

5 " pacifæ.

2 " minima.

Specimens from Europe—Continued.

5 Helix subrugulosa.
1 Trigonia navis.
1 Spondylus.
2 Pholadomya glabra.
1 Posidonia ornati.
1 Spondylus aculeatus.
3 Inoceramus.
1 Pecten demissus.
2 Ostræ.
1 Trochus glaber.
6 Ammonites pictus.
2 Nautilus.
1 Ammonites Murchisoni.
1   "   polygyratus.
1   "   Parkinsoni.
1 Pecten.
1 Pteroceras oceani.
2 Nerinea podolica.
1 Vertebræ.
1 Serpula.
2 Belemnites parvus.
1 Pholadomya fidicula.
2 Spondylus aculiferus.
1 Lunatia obliquata.
1 Perna quadrata.
1 Littorinella acuta.
2 Astarte purnila.
2 Posidonia ornati.
1 Pyropsis Richardsonii.
1 Cyprina cordiformis.
1 Cardium aculeatum.
1 Inoceramus Barabini.
3 Trigonia.
1 Lingula zeta.
5 Terebratula trigonella.
2 Diceras arietina.
2 Lucina aliena.
3 Rhynchonella lacunosa.
2 Aptychus planulatus lævis.
6 Terebratula biplicata.

Specimens from Europe—Continued.

2 Terebratula insignis.
5 Serpula.
6   "   quadristriata.
1 Cidarites alternatus.
2   "   coronatus.
1   "   elegans.
1 Astarte excavata.
6 Nucula ornati.
8 Disaster granulosus.
1 Cidarites.
13 Terebratula subsella.
1 Dendrites.
1 Crab.
1 Ammonites.
1 Orbicula papyracea.
2 Pleuromya.
1 Ostræa.
8 Cidarites nobilis.
1   "   maximus.
1 Ammonites polyplocus.
3   "   flexuosus,
1 Astarte.
1 Berenicea diluviana.
1 Verinea.
3 Rhynchonella spatica.
3 Ostræa Roemeri.
5 Hemicidaris crenularis.
1 Inoceramus.
1 Nummulitic Limestone.
1 Anodonta anatinoides.
3 Pholadomya fidicula.
4   "   donacina.
8 Ostræa virgula.
3 Pectunculus laevis.
1 Prosopon.
3 Pholadomya Protei.
1   "   glabra.
3 Cucullaea.
1 Cyclolites elliptica.
4 Myacites jurassi.

Specimens from Europe—Continued.

1 Melania.

1 Trigonia costata.

2 Terebratula lamnosa var. rostrata.

5 " loricata.

2 Nucula.

1 Terebratula numismalis.

10 Rhynctronella strioplicata.

1 Siderastræa radians.

2 Inoceramus.

1 Pecten æquietriatus.

1 Inoceramus Barabini.

2 Corbis subchlaprata.

4 Terebratula bullata.

1 Terebratula lacunosa.

1 Spiriferina Walcotti.

3 Terebratula indentata.

5 Trochus bilincatus.

2 Ammonites hecticus.

3 Rhynchonella multicosta.

6 Echinopsis.

1 Euomphalus funatus.

1 Terebratula insignis.

1 Pholadomya caudata.

2 Nerinea.

1 Exogyra virgula.

1 Pteroceras lævis.

1 Gervillia aviculoides.

5 Nodiola gibbosa.

4 Pecten demissus.

1 Plagiostoma notatum.

7 Cassidulus florealis.

1 Tinna mitis.

3 Lunatia obliquata.

5 Ostræa ponda.

5 " molassicula.

16 Terebratula insignis.

2 Inoceramus.

1 Ostræa.

2 Diceras.

1 Pleurotomaria.

1 Nerinea.
1 Favosites hemisphericus.
1 Murchisonia.
1 Ammonites polyplocus.
2 Inoceramus.
1 Natica.
1 Natica abyssinus.
1 Anomalodonta alata.
1 Limnaeus ovatus.
1 Ammonites.
3 Ranella marginata.
1 Inoceramus problematicus.
1 Productus punctatus.
6 Pholadomya Protei.
1 Inoceramus.
6 Myacites.
3   "   gregarius.
1 Venus æqualis.
1 Spirifer radiatus.
1 Conocardium trigonale.
1 Modiolopsis.
1 Aulopora.
10 Gasteropoda.
4 Belemnitella quadrata.
2 Cassidulus subquadratus.
1 Eucalyptocrinus.
1 Medley of Fossils.
3 Plagiostoma gibbosa.
1 Goniatites rotatorius.
1 Ambonychia radiata.
1 Conocardium trigonale.
1 Stromatepora.
1 Ammonites polygyratus.
1 Polypora.
1 Chætetes.
1 Strophomena alternata.
1 Unio Wetzleri.
1 Anodonta anatinoides.
1 Ostræa pratensis.
1 Trigonia navis.

Specimens from Europe—Continued.

1 Tragos.
1 Strotocrinus regularis.
1 Stringocephalus Burtini.
9 Nerinea.
1 Trigonia suevica.
1 Astræa helianthoides.
7 Terebratula acuticosta.
12 Rhynchonella Steinbeisi.
5 Cidarites curvatus.
19 Lamia denticulata.
2 Helix orbicularis.
2 Actinocrinus turbinatus.
1 Serpula.
1 Scaphiocrinus aequalis.
1 Cucullæa Muensteri.
1 Conocardium trigonale.
4 Favosites.
1 Unio.
5 Crania velata.
6 Terebratula perovalis.
3 Cerithium Bouchardia.
2 Helix pulchella.
1 Astarta Sibylla.
17 Crania Ponsorti.
2 Cerithium.
9 Pupa Bartelii.
6 Linum.
4 Turbo ranellatus.
1 Paludina.
1 Lutraria.
1 Tapes heloetica.
1 Trochus.
1 Orthis testudinaria.
10 Rhynchonella obsoleta.
3 Cardium Gresseri.
4 Donacites Aldirini.
4 Terebratula bullata.
4 Pholadomya clathrata.
1 Naticopsis.
1 Cidarites nobilis.

Specimens from Europe—Continued.

1 Chætetes gracilis.
1 Ambonychia.
2 Euomphalus costatus.
1 Murchisonia.
3 Belemnites, elongatus.
1   "   hastatus.
1 Pectunculus.
1 Lepidotus giganteus.
1 Belemnites mucronatus.
1   " .   oxyconus.
1   "   paxillosus.
1   "   acuminatus.
4 Cyprina regularis.
1 Chama.
4 Terebratula omalogastyr.
10 Dorycrinus unicornis.
16 Pentremites Norwoodii.
1 Strophomena alternata.
1 Goniatites rotatorius.
1 Cellepora orbiculata.
1 Orthoceratites.
3 Aptychus latus.
4 Crinoids.
5 Gryphaea.
5 Belemnites bipartitus.
3 Goniatites Oweni.
1 Cyrena.
1 Murchisonia.
1 Pentamerus oblongus.
11 Terebratula biplicata.
1 Chama gryphoides.
2 Amblyptherus.
4 Nummulites laevigata.
1 Chætetes.
1 Ambonychia radiata.
3 Pentremites pyriformis.
3 Modiola modiolaris.
1 Phasianella striata.
1 Myacites.
3 Plagiostoma acuticosta.

Specimens from Europe—Continued.

8 Astarte bipartita.

1 Strotocrinus regalis.

5 Actinocrinus Verneuilianus.

1 Spongites.

3 Dentalium cinetum.

3 Pholadomya.

1 Spirifer radiatus.

5 Granatocrinus melo.

2 Cyathophyllum.

4 Rhynchenella Astieriana.

3 Zaphrentis.

6 Terebratula marginata.

2 Theonoidea Ulmensis.

1 Nummulites.

1 Strombus Fortisii.

1 Trematocrinus.

3 Turitella scalata.

3 Dictyocrinus proboscidialis.

1 Belemnites digitalis acutus.

1 Trigonia suevica.

1 Hemispatangus ornatus.

7 Rhynchonella aculicosta.

4 Bellarophon bilobatus.

5 Delphinula.

5 Terebratula ornithocephala.

1 Terebratula reticulata.

48 Terebrotula substriata.

9 Terebratula triloboides.

2 Terebratula insignis.

3 Nucula ornati.

1 Rhynchonella.

18 Rhynchonella conoinnoides.

1 Astrea reticulata.

2 Turbo clathratus.

13 Crinoids.

2 Corinya alta.

3 Panopaea peregrina.

1 Vernulites trigonellaris.

1 Cardium aculeatum.

1 Pholadomya clathrasula.

Specimens from Europe—Continued.

1 Natica capacea.

2 Trigonia crenulata.

2 Trochus speciosus.

1 Trigonia tuberculata.

7 Prosopon.

1 Turitella.

3 Cucullæ masquivalvis.

2 Pecten.

7 Terebratula Endesi.

1 Calymene.

1 Isocardia.

2 Rhynchonella quadriplicata.

1 Spongites cylindrica.

1 Terebratula lagenalis.

1 " ornithocephala.

5 " cornuta.

4 " perovalis.

4 " biplicatæ.

7 " dichotomae.

8 " nummismalis.

4 " emarginata.

5 " intermedia.

1 Nassa globosa.

3 Productus semireticulatus.

1 Cardium multicostatum.

1 Pteroceras laevis.

36 Natica.

3 Helix Kleinii.

3 Helix coarctata.

1 Kirkbya permiana.

2 Myacites depressus.

1 Lucina plana.

16 Encrinus liliformis.

1 Cidarites triaculeatus.

4 Trochrus duplicatus.

53 Cidarites.

1 Apiocrinitis Milleri.

1 Pecten monareus.

1 Cidarites trispinatus.

10 Diadema sulcatum.

Specimens from Europe—Continued.

  1 Monotis lamnose.
  1 Pleurotomaria Quenstedti.
  1 Ceriopora ramulosa.
  1 Heliolites porosa.
  1 Spondylus areatus.
  1 Limna.
  2 Terebratula lamnore var. multiplicata.
  7 Nucula.
  2 Rhynchonella lacunosa.
  1 Pinna mites.
  3 Terebratula nummismalis.
  2 Amplexus ibicinus.
  1 Heliolites porosa.
  1 Alveolites suborbicularis.
  1 Pinna mites.
  1 Pseudomelania affinis. ·
  1 Astraea confluens.
  1 Pseudomelania gigantea.
  1 Spatangus.
  1 Trigonia Constantii.
  4 Nucula pectinata.
  1 Trochus bijugatus.
  1 Cypraea affinis.
 15 Terebratula Bangerii.
 11 Crinoid Stems.
  3 Belemnites Aalensis.
  1   "   acutus.
  7   "   brevirostris.
  3   "
  1   "   digitalis.
  1   '   acuarius.
  1   "   hastatus.
  I   "   oxyconus.
  1   "   amarius.
  2   "   mucronatus.
  3 Euomphalus tuberculatus.
  8 Melanopsis impressa.
  1 Astraea confluens.
  5 Cidaris tuberculosus.
  2 Trochus ornatus.

Specimens from Europe—Continued.

3 Cidaris elegans.
3 Dictyocrinus proboscidialis.
3 Actinocrinus longirostris.
1 Terebratula insignis.
3   "   carinata.
2   "   nucleata.
1 Venus.
1 Trigonia costata.
1 Spirifer pinnatus.
8 Terebratula inconstans.
19 Actinocrinus.
13 Rhynchonella concinna.
56 Terebratula varians.
13 Terebratula perovalis.
7 Turbonella scalata.
3 Prosopon æquum.
5 Michelina favosa.
1 Clypeaster conoideus.
1 Asaphus.
1 Rhinoceros tichorhinus.
2 Hippurites.
2 Terebratula insignis.
2 Astarte Kemmeridge.
1 Cardium acuticosta.
5 Posidonia alpine.
6 Batocrinus Christyi.
1 Nautilus cretanons.
1 Strombus Fortisii.
1 Sphærulites.
6 Goniatites Lyoni.
3 Terebratula impressa.
2 Terebratula bisuffarcinata.
1 Scaphiscrinus æqualis.
1 Terebratula pervalis.
1 Bellerophon bilobasus.
1 Ammonites annularis.
1 Lingula.
7 Pileopsis haliotus.
23 Pleurotomaria Ysanii.
1 Pteroceras Oceani.

Specimens from Europe—Continued.

5 Myalina melineformis.

1 Ammonites inflatus.

5 Astarte depressa.

1 Batrocrinus turbinatus.

4 Venus Rothomagensis.

2 Streptorhynchus crenistia.

1 Trigonia caudata.

1 Pholidophyllum.

10 Batocrinus formosus.

14 Heterocrinus heterodactylus.

12 Crinoids.

9 Terebratula globata.

3 Ammonites opalinus.

1 Plagiostoma.

2 Neritina conoidea.

1 Ceratites nodosus.

1 Crania velata.

1 Clypeaster.

1 Sphaerulites Beaumontii.

1 Pterinea ventricosa.

1 Belemnites triplicatus.

1 Belemnites acuarius.

8 Terebratula trilobata.

10 Acroculia.

1 Maeandrina.

1 Productus semireticulatus.

1 Amblyptorus macropterus.

1 Orthoceras.

18 Terebratula vulgaris.

1 Orthis Keokuk.

5 Chemnitzia Lefeberii.

4 Cyatophyllum.

1 Taegonia costata.

4 Athyris lamellosa.

1 Natica.

1 Belcompressus.

3 Trochocyathus cornutus.

1 Fish scale.

1 Arca triasina.

9 Belemnites digitalis.

Specimens from Europe—Continued.

1 Belemnites elongatus.
6   "   amarius.
3   "   paxillosus.
2   "   compressus.
1   "   giganteus.
3   "   acutus.
1   "   gracilis.
1   "   hastatus.
1 Nerinia.
3 Echinids.
1 Fish Tooth.
7 Batocrinus papillatus.
1 Spirifer cultrijugatus.
1 Chonetes sarcinulata.
1 Pleurotomaria crenalostricta.
3 Hysterolithus vulva.
1 Pleurodictyun problematicum.
1 Orthis.
1 Strophomena tæniolata.
1 Murchisonia bellicincta.
5 Trigonia aliformis.
4 Heliophyllums.
4 Stringocephalus Burtini.
3 Orthoceras Ludensis.
2 Cyathophyllum.
1 Spirifer Sowerbyi.
1 Cardita planicosta.
4 Bellerophon bicarenus.
1 Pileopsis haliotus.
6 Cyprina regularis.
8 Bellerophon tenuifascia.
3 Kirkbya permiana.
7 Pleurotomaria helicina.
3 Favosites.
3 Encrinites liliiformis.
4 Actinocrinus multiradiatus.
4 Heleropora conifera.
1 .Orthis testudinaria.
2 Palæoniscus Freieslebeni.
1 Crinoidal Limestone.

Fred. Krempel, Milwaukee, Wis.

    1 part of petrified tree, California.

Frank W. Suelflow, Milwaukee, Wis.

    5 Gyroceras eryx, Humboldt, Wis.

    2 Gomphoceras, Humboldt, Wis.

    2 Spirifera.

Horace Beach.

    1 Foot Print on Slab, Colorado Springs, Colorado.   (Cast.)

ACQUIRED BY PURCHASE.

   1 Medley of Fossils, Hawthorne, Ill.
   1 Amplexus,   "   "
   1 Ceraurus niagarensis,   "   "
   1 Cladopora,   "   "
   1 Saccocrinus,   "   "
   9 Illaenus insignis,   "   "
 15 Othoceras Wauwatonense, Wauwatosa, Wis.
   2 Phragmoceras,   "   "
 14 Phragmoceras parvum,   "   "
   9 Strophodonta,   "   "
   8 Trochoceras desplainense,   "   "
   1 Cyrtoceras dardanum.   "   "
   2 Cyrtoceras,   "   "
   7 Pentamerus ventricosus,   "   "
   2 Orthoceras,   "   "
 22 Illaenus coniculus,   "   "
   9 Illaenus insignis,   "   "
   2 Gomphoceras scrinium,   "   "
   1 Ceraurus niagarensis,   "   "
   2 Subulites ventricosus,   "   "
   3 Amphicœlia Leidyi.   "   "
   9 Ambonychia acutirostra,   "   "
 37 Sphoerexosus Romingeri,   "   "
   5 Calymene niagarensis,   "   "
   3 Pleurotomaria Laphami,   "   "
   2 Triplecia,   "   "
   2 Eucalyptocrinns cornutus, Bridgeport, Ill.
   6   "   "
   1 Euomphalus, Hawthorne, Ill.
 18 Crinoid stems, Bridgeport, Ill.

2 Orthoceras annulatum, Hawthorne, Ill.
1 " scammoni, "
4 " "
5 Gomphocystites, "
3 " Bridgeport, Ill.
16 Monomorella prisca, Hawthorne, Ill.
6 " "
4 Siphonocrinus, Bridgeport, Ill.
1 Platyceras, Hawthorne, Ill.
1 Illænus insignis, Hawthorne, Ill.
8 Pleurotomaria, "
5 Ichthyocrinus corbis, Bridgeport, Ill.
5 Saccocrinus "
4 " Christyi, Hawthorne, Ill.
1 " Egani, "
2 " urniformis, "
1 " Marcuarius, Bridgeport, Ill.
1 Raphistoma, Hawthorne, Ill.
1 Gomphoceras marcyæ, "
6 Spirifera radiata var. plicatella, Bridgeport, Ill.
3 Melocrinus, "
9 Glyptocrinus, "
3 Strombodes pentagonus, Hawthorne, Ill.
16 Meristina maria, "
1 Medley of Fossils, Hawthorne, Ill.
26 Atrypa reticularis, Cementville, Wis.
13 Spirifer, "
10 Orthis impressa, "
11 Spirifera medialis, "
5 " granulifera, "
69 Pieces of Fish Bone, "
7 Gomphoceras, "
7 Gyroceras erix, "
1 Nautilus, Hawthorne, Ill.
1 Orthoceras, Cementville, Wis.
1 Conularia, "
16 Atrypa reticularis, "
2 Spirifera, "
4 " granulifera, "
9 " medialis, "
6 Orthis impressa, "

5 Bryozoæ, Cementville, Wis.
1 Fenestella, "
1 Gomphoceras, "
2 Illænus insignis, Hawthorne, Ill.
1 Ceraurus niagarensis "
1 Calymene " "
9 Spirifera niagarensis, Wauwatosa, Wis.
9 Illænus insignis, Hawthorne, Ill-
10 " armatus, "
1 Pentamerus pergibbosus, "
7 " "
8 Calymene niagarensis, Bridgeport, Ill.
7 Ceraurus niagarensis, "
1 Trochonema fatua, "
2 Hemicosmites, "
1 Trochoceras desplainense, Hawthorne, Ill.
5 Amplexus, "
7 Bucania chicagoensis "
1 Actinocrinus, Bridgeport, Ill.
3 Ambonychia acutirostra "
1 Amphicoelia Leidyi, Hawthorne, Ill.
I " "
3 " Leidyi, Bridgeport, Ill.
2 Apiocystites imago, "
6 Corals, "
5 Caryocrinus ornatus "
5 Cyathocrinus waukoma, "
9 Cyathocrinus corax, Hawthorne, Ill.
1 Syringopora, Bridgeport, Ill.
1 Fenestella, Hawthorne, Ill.
1 Halysites, "
3 Heliolites, "
6 Favosites, "
16 Eucalyptocrinus, "

ETHNOLOGY.

DONATIONS.

Martin Berliner, Milwaukee, Wis.

1 Warrant for £20, to David Hillhouse, contractor, for furnishing supplies at the treaty with the Creek Indians, June 25th, 1789.

Hy. Fischer, Milwaukee, Wis.

    1 Confederate States Note ($1.00).

    1   "   "   " ($1.00).

    1 Newspaper, "Boston Evening Post," Sept. 3, 1765.

    1   "   "New Hampshire Gazette," Oct. 11, 1765.

R. Loewenthal, Milwaukee, Wis.

    1 Hand-twisted Brass Basket.

Nic. Lorénz, Milwaukee, Wis.

    1 Silver Goblet, thoroughly gilded, etc.

Ad. Meinecke, Milwaukee, Wis.

    1 Spanish Iron Sword, Gotha, Orange Co., Fla.

    1 Spanish Iron Hatchet, Gotha, Orange Co., Fla.

Dr. Hugo Tilsner, Milwaukee, Wis.

    1 Drinking Glass, made in 1787 at Berlin, Germany, and containing engravings of the secret signs of the order of "Free Masons," which order was instituted at Berlin in the 15th century.

Wyoming Historical and Geological Society.

    1 Wyoming Memorial Medal, struck in commemoration of the "one hundredth anniversary of the battle and massacre of Wyoming, July 3, 1778,–July 3, 1878."

ACQUIRED BY PURCHASE.

5 Iron locks,   Germany.

1 Pewter lamp,   "

1 Shade lamp,   "   made of tin.

1 Candle stick,   "   "   brass.

1 Pair of snuffers, "   "   brass.

1   "   "   "   steel.

1 Small war club. "   Sioux Indian.

1 Necklace made of eagle claws, elk teeth and beads, Arapahoe Indian.

1 Necklace made of beads, Arapahoe Indian.

ARCHÆOLOGY.

DONATIONS.

Mrs. William Frankfurth, Milwaukee, Wis.

    1 Baptizing Font, Hettenheim, Germany.

    1 Earthen Water Urn.

William Orth, Milwaukee, Wis.

    1 Fragment of Stone Implement, Milwaukee Co., Wis.

C. A. Read, Milwaukee, Wis.

    7 Copper Implements, found at Christ. Wahl's farm on the Kinnickinnic.

ACQUIRED BY PURCHASE.

4,000 Flint arrowheads of all shapes and sizes.

  200 Polished stone hatchets, stone axes, hoes, digging tools, agricultural implements and tomahawks.

  200 Leaf-shaped spearheads and spades.

   20 Copper implements.

    6 Pipes of Peace.

    1 Skull taken from a mound at Atztalan.

   12 Discoidal stone.

   11 Pieces of iron implements from Black Hawk War.

LIBRARY.

DONATIONS.

Academy of Science, St. Louis.

    Transactions, Nos. 6, 7 and 8.

Americann Museum of Natural History, New York.

    Bulletin, Vol. IV, 1892.

    Annual Report, 1892.

Australian Museum, Sidney.

    Report of the Trustees, 1891.

    Records 2-4.

Belfast Natural History and Philosophical Society, Belfast.

    Report and Proceedings.

Blackburn Free Public Library and Museum, Blackburn.

    Report, 1892.

Bureau of Ethnology, Washington, D. C.

    Bibliography of the Athapascan Languages.

    Seventh Annual Report of the Bureau of Ethnology, 1885-86.

    Contributions to North American Ethnology, Vol. VII.

Cincinnati Museum Association, Cincinnati.

    12th Annual Report, 1892.

Cincinnati Society of Natural History, Cincinnati, O.
> The Journal of Natural History, Vol. XIV, Nos. 3, 4.
> "   "   "   "   Vol. VI, Nos. 3, 4.

Connecticut Historical Society, Hartford, Conn.
> Papers and Reports.

Denison Scientific Association, Granville, O.
> Journal of Comparative Neurology, Vol. II, 1892.
> Bulletin of the Scientific Laboratory.
> Journal of Comparative Neurology, Vol. III, Pages 1-34.

Department of the Interior, Washington, D. C.
> 3 Vols. Compendium of the Eleventh Census, 1890.

Deutsch Wissenschaftlichler Verein, Santiago, Chile.
> Verhandlungen, II Bd., III Heft.

Elisha Mitchell Scientific Association, Raleigh, N. C.
> Journal, Vol. IX, Part I and II.

Essex Institute, Salem, Mass.
> Bulletins, Vol. 24Nos. 4-12.

Free Public Library, Museum and Walker Art Gallery, Liverpool, Eng.
> 40 Annual Reports.

Gesellschaft zur Beförderung der gesammten Naturwissenschaften, Marburg, Germany.
> Sitzungsberichte, 1892.

Gesellschaft fur Natur- und Heilkunde, Dresden, Germany.
> Jahresbericht, 1891-1892.

Government Central Museum, Madras, India.
> Administration Report, 1891-1892.

Grossherzogliches Museum zu Darmstadt, Germany.
> Ueber naturgeschichtliche Sammlungen.

International Entomologcial Society Zuerich-Hottigen, Switzerland.
> Societas entomologica, VII Jahrg, Nos. 11-24.
> "   "   VIII Jahrg, Nos. 1, 2, 4, 5, 7, 9.

Instituto Fisico Geographico Ydel Museo Nacional de Costa Rica.
> Anales, 1892.

John Hopkins University, Baltimore, Md.
> Circulars, Vol. XII, No. 106.

Journal of Comparative Neurology, Granville, O.
> Journal, Vol. II, Page 89-136.

Kgl. Akademie gemeinnütziger Wissenschaften zu Erfurt, Germany.
> Jahrbücher, Neue Folge, Heft XVIII.

K. K. Geologische Reichsanstalt, Wien, Austria.
      Jahrbuch, XLII Bd, Heft 3 und 4.
      Verhandlungen Nos. 11, 12, 13, 14, 17, 18, 1892.
          "   Nos, 1, 2, 3, 4, 5, 1893.

K. K. Naturhistorisches Hofmuseum, Wien, Austria.
      Annalen, Bd. VII, Nro. 1, 2, 3, 4.
      Jahresbericht, 1892.

Kgl. Sächsische Gesellschaft der Wissenschaften, Leipzig, Germany.
      Berichte über die Verhandlungen, II, III, IV, V, VI, 1892.
        "   "   "   "   I, II, III, 1893.

Marine Biological Laboratory, Boston, Mass.
      Fifth Annual Report, 1892.

Milwaukee Public Library, Milwaukee.
      Quarterly Index of Additions, Vol. IV, No. 29.

Missouri Botanical Garden, St. Louis.
      III Annual Report, 1892.

Museum Carolino Augusteum, Salzburg, Austria.
      Jahresberichl, 1891.

Museum of Comparative Zoology, Cambridge, Mass.
      Annual Report, 1891–1892.

National Academy of Sciences, Philadelphia, Pa.
      Fourth Memoir, Vol. 5.

Nassauischer Verein für Naturkunde, Wiesbaden, Germany.
      Jahrbücher, Jahg. 45.

Naturforschende Gesellschaft, Bern, Switzerland.
      Mittheilungen, No. 1265–1278.

Naturforschende Gesellschaft zu Görlitz, Germany.
      Abhandlungen, 20. Vol.

Naturforschende Gesellschaft, Emden, Germany.
      76. Jahresbericht, 1890–1891.

Naturforschende Gesellschaft des Osterlandes, Altenburg, Germany.
      Mittheilungen, Neue Folge, V. Bd.

Naturhistorische Gesellschaft, Nürnberg, Germany.
      Abhandlungen, IX. Bd.

Naturhistorischer Verein der preussischen Rheinlande in Westfalens,
    Bonn, Germany.
      Vorhandlungen, 49. Jahg., I. und II. Heft.

Naturwissenschaftliche Gesellschaft " Isis," Dresden, Germany.
      Sitzungsberichte, Jahrg. 1892, Januar bis Juni.
        "   "   " Juli bis Dezember.

Naturwissenschaftlicher Verein zu Osnabrück, Germany.
      9. Jahresbericht, 1891–1892.

Naturwissenschaftlicher Verein für Steiermark, Graz, Austria.
    Mittheilungen, Jahg. 1892, 29. Heft.

Naturwissenschaftlicher Verein für das Fürstentum, Lüneburg, Germany.
    Jahreshefte.

Naturwissenschaftlich-Medizinischer Verein in Innsbruck, Austria.
    Berichte, 1892.

Naturwissenschaftlicher Verein, Regensburg, Germany.
    Berichte, 1892.

Naturwissenschaftlicher Verein für Schleswig-Holstein, Kiel, Germany.
    Schriften, Bd. IX, Heft II.

Naturwissenschaftlicher Verein " Polichia " Dürkheim, Germany.
    Festschrift, 1892.

Nova Scotian Institute of Natural Science, Halifax, N. S.
    Proceedings, Vol. VII, Part IV.

Observatorio Astronomico National de Tacubaya, Mexico.
    Boletin, Tomo I, V. 11–13.

Offenbacher Verein für Naturkunde, Offenbach, Germany.
    29, 30, 31 und 32. Bericht, 1887–1891.

Physikalisch-Oekonomische Gesellschaft, Königsberg, Germany.
    Schriften, 32. Jahrg.

Physikalischer Verein, Frankfurt, a. M., Germany.
    Jahresbericht, 1890–1891.

Rijks Museum van Oudheden, Leiden, Holland.
    Verslag van den Directeur.

Rochester Academy of Science, Rochester, N. Y.
    Proceedings, Vol. II, pages 1–112.

Royal Irish Academy, Dublin, G. B.
    Transactions, Vol. XXX, Parts I and II.
    Proceedings, III Ser., Vol. II, No. 3.

Schlesische Gesellschaft für vaterländische Cultur, Breslau, Germany.
    69. Jahresbericht.
      I. Heft der Literatur der Landes- und Volkskunde der Provinz Schlesien.

Senckenbergische Naturforschende Gesellschaft, Frankfurt, a. M., Germany.
    Bericht fuer 1892.
    Katalog der Batrachier Sammlung in dieser Gesellschaft.

Smithsonian Institution, Washington, D. C.
    Circular concerning the Hodgkins Fund Priess.
    Annual Report for 1890.
      Dahl, W. H. Instructions for Collecting Mollusks and other useful Hints for the Concologist.

Riley, C. V.   Directions for Collecting and Preserving Insects.

Stejneger, L.   Directions for Collecting Reptiles and Batrachians.

Bendire, Chas.   Directions for Collecting, Preparing and Preserving Bird's Eggs and Nests.

Lucas, Fred. C.   Notes on the Preparation of rough Skeletons.

Knowlton, F. H.   Directions for Collecting Recent and Fossil Plants.

Ridgeway, Robert.   Directions for Collecting Birds.

Montandon, A. L.   Notes on American Hemiptera–Heteroptera.

Smyth, Bernh. B.
Check List of the Plants of Kansas, 1892.

Sociètè Helvétique des Sciences Naturelles, Fribourg, Switzerland.
Actes de la Sociètè Helvetique des Sciences Naturelles.

Société Imperiale des Naturalistes, Moscow, Russia.
Bulletin No. 2, 3, 4.

Sociètè de Physique Et D' Histoire Naturelle, Geneve, Switzerland.
Compte Rendu de Séances de la Sociètè de Physiques et d' Histoire Naturelle de Geneve.

Sociètè Scientifique du Chili, Santiago, Chile.
Actes de la Society, Tomo II, 1892.

State Agricultural College, Lansing, Mich.
Bulletin No. 49.

State Historical Society, Madison, Wis.
II Triennial Catalogue of the Portrait Gallery.
Proceedings, 1892.
Bibliography of Wisconsin Authors, Class List No. 2.

Stavanger Museum, Stavanger, Norway.
Aarsberetning, 1891.

Thurgauische Naturforschende Gesellschaft, Frauenfeld, Switzerland.
Mittheilungen, X Heft.

U. S. Department of Agriculture, Washington, D. C.
Fisher, A. K.   The Hawks and Owls of the U. S. in their relation to Agriculture.
North American Fauna, No. 7.

U. S. Geological Survey, Washington, D. C.
Mineral Resources of the U. S., 1890.
"   "   "   "   1891.
Bulletins 65–96.
Monographs, XVII, XVIII, XX.

U. S. National Museum, Washington, D. C.
> Howard, L. O. Insects of the Subfamily Encyrtinæ with Branched Antennæ.
> 2 Bulletins, No. 40.
> Proceedings, Vol. XIV, 1891.

U. S. War Department, Washington, D. C.
> The War of the Rebellion, Vol. I to V.
> " " " " Vol XXXIX, Part II and III.
> " " " " Vol. XL and XLI.

Verein der Aerzte in Steiermark, Austria.
> Mittheilungen, 29 Vereinsjahr.

Verein fuer Erdkunde zu Darmstadt, Germany.
> Notizblatt, 1892.

Verein fuer Erdkunde, Leipzig, Germany.
> Mittheilungen, 1892.

Verein der Freunde der Naturgeschichte in Mecklenburg, Guestrow, Germany.
> Archiv., 46. Jahrg, I. und II. Abthlg.

Verein Luxemburger Naturfreunde, Luxemburg.
> "Fauna," Jahrg. 1893, Heft I und II.

Yerein fuer Naturkunde zu Kassel, Germany.
> Bericht, 1891-1892.

Zoological Society of Philadelphia, Pa.
> 21st Annual Report.

Dr. Wilhelm Mueller, Charlottenburg, near Berlin.
> Die Mineralien-Sammlung des Rittergutsbesitzers.
> A. v. Janson, auf Schloss Gerdauen, Ostpreussen.

ACQUIRED BY PURCHASE.

Jardine, Sir William, Bart. Hummingbirds, Vols. I, II.
Schimper, A. F. W. Die epiphytische Vegetation Americas.
Reichenbach, H. G. Ludwig. Die ausländischen Singvögel.
> " " " Canores exotici.
> " " " Trochilinæ.

Finsch, Otto. Die Papageien, Bd I, II.
Sharpe, Bowdler R. Catalogue of the Passeriformes or Perching Birds in the Collection of the British Museum, Vols. III–XV.

Edwards, W. H.   The Butterflies of North America, III Series, Pt. XIII.

Garman, S.   On the Reptiles and Batrachians.

Goode, Brown G.   American Fishes.

Brockhaus Konversations Lexicon, Bd I–VI.

Bulletin of the Nuttall Ornithological Club, Vols. I–VI.

The "Auk."   A quarterly journal of Ornithology.
>
        Vol. IX, No. 3.

        Vol. X, Nos. 1–3.

The "American Naturalist," Vol. XXVI, Nos. 310–312.

    "   "   "   Vol. XXVII, Nos. 313–319.

Neumayr, Melchior Dr.   Erdgeschichte, Bd I, Heft 1–14.

Engler and Prantl.   Die natuerlichen Pflanzenfamilien, Lief. 1–86.

Laws of Wisconsin Concerning the Public Museum.

(330, A.)   (Published April 13, 1882.)

CHAPTER 329.

AN ACT relating to the Natural History Society of the city of Milwaukee.

The People of the State of Wisconsin, represented in senate and assembly, do enact as follows:

SECTION 1.   The board of directors of the Natural History Society of the city of Milwaukee is hereby authorized and empowered, in the name of said association or society, to assign, transfer and convey to the city of Milwaukee, all and singular, the natural historical collections of every kind constituting the Museum belonging to said Natural History Society, in trust, to be kept, supported and maintained by said city, as a free Museum for the benefit and use of all citizens of said city, provided, the said city shall accept the trust and assume the care and maintenance of such. Museum.

SEC. 2.   This act shall take effect and be in force from and after its passage and publication.

Approved March 31, 1882.

(No. 329, A.)   (Published April 14, 1882.)

CHAPTER 328.

AN ACT to authorize the city of Milwaukee to establish
and maintain a Public Museum in said city.

*The people of the State of Wisconsin, represented in senate
and assembly, do enact as follows:*

SECTION 1.   The city of Milwaukee is hereby authorized
to receive and accept from "The Natural History Society
of Wisconsin"—a corporation located in the said city of
Milwaukee—a donation of its collection of objects in Natural
History and Ethnology, or of the greater part thereof, upon
such conditions as may be agreed upon by and between said
city and said society, subject, however, to the provisions of
this act.

SEC. 2.   In case of such donation and acceptance, said
city of Milwaukee is hereby authorized and empowered to
establish and maintain in said city a free, Public Museum,
exhibitions of objects in Natural History and Ethnology,
and for that purpose to receive, hold and manage the collection so donated, and any devise, bequest or donation
that may be made to said city for the increase and maintenance of such Museum under such regulations and conditions as are herein contained, or may be agreed upon by
and between the donors and said city, or as may be hereafter provided in this act.

SEC. 3.   The Museum established and maintained under
this act shall be under the general management, control and
supervision of a board of nine trustees, who shall be styled
"The Board of Trustees of the Public Museum of the City of
Milwaukee." Said Board of Trustees shall consist of the president of the school board and the superintendent of schools

of said city, ex-officio, of three members of the common council of said city, designated and appointed by the mayor thereof, and of four residents and tax-payers of said city, to be appointed by the mayor as herein provided. The first appointments of trustees by the mayor under this act shall be made within ten days after the formal acceptance by the common council of said city, of a donation by said Natural History Society, as authorized in the first section of this act. Of the first three trustees appointed from the members of the common council of said city, one shall be appointed from the three-year class, one from the two-year class, and one from the one-year class of aldermen, and they shall serve as such trustees during their respective terms as such aldermen. And annually on the third Tuesday of April thereafter, at the expiration of the term of any such trustee, the mayor shall appoint his successor for three years, from the aldermen then having three years to serve. In case any such trustee shall vacate the office of alderman before the expiration of his term, he shall at the same time cease to be a trustee under this act, and the mayor shall appoint some other member of the common council of his class in his place for the balance of his term. In the appointment of the four remaining trustees and their successors, the mayor shall prefer such persons as may be recommended for such appointment by said Natural History Society. Such four trustees first appointed shall, at the first meeting of the board after their appointment, determine by lot their term of service, so that one of their number shall serve for one year, one for two years, one for three years, and one for four years from the third Tuesday of May next after the organization of such board. And all vacancies shall be filled by like appointment of the mayor for the remainder of the term, and annually on the third Tuesday of April a trustee shall be appointed by said mayor in like manner for the term of four years, in place of the trustee whose term shall expire the following May. None of said trustees shall receive any compensation from the city treasury, or otherwise, for their services as such trustees. And no member of said Board of Trustees shall become, or cause himself to become interested, directly or indirectly, in any contract or job for the purchase of any matter pertaining to the Museum, or of fuel, furniture, stationery or things necessary for the increase and maintenance of the Museum. Said trustees shall take the official oath, and be subject to the restrictions, disabilities, liabilities, punishments and limitations prescribed by law as to aldermen in the said city of Milwaukee.

Sec. 4. The first meeting of said Board of Trustees for the purpose of organizing, shall be held on the third Tuesday of the month next following their appointment, and the city clerk shall give at least one week's previous notice of the time and place of such meeting to each member of such board in writing. At such first meeting said board shall organize by the choice of one of their number as president to serve until the third Tuesday of May next following, and until his successor shall be chosen. The annual meeting of said board shall be held on the third Tuesday of May in each year, and at such meeting a president shall be chosen from their number to serve for one year and until his successor shall be chosen.

Sec. 5. The Board of Trustees shall have general care, control and supervision of the Public Museum, its appurtenances, fixtures and furniture, and of the selection, arrangement and disposition of the specimens and objects appertaining to said Museum, and also of the disbursements of all the moneys appropriated for and belonging to the

Museum fund, in the manner hereinafter provided. And the said board shall adopt, and at their discretion modify, amend or repeal by-laws, rules and regulations for the management, care and use of the Public Museum, and fix and enforce penalties for their violation, and generally shall adopt such measures as shall promote the public utility of the Museum; provided, that such by-laws, rules and regulations shall not conflict with the provisions of this act.

SEC. 6. The Board of Trustees shall, at their first meeting, or thereafter, as soon as practicable and every five years thereafter, at an annual meeting, elect by ballot a person of suitable scientific attainments, ability and experience for custodian, who shall so act and be ex-officio secretary of said Board of Trustees. The custodian first appointed shall hold his office for five years from the time of the first annual meeting, unless previously removed, and thereafter the term of appointment shall be for the term of five years, and the compensation of the custodian shall be fixed by said Board of Trustees. Said Board of Trustees shall also appoint such assistants and employes for said Museum as they may deem necessary and expedient, and shall fix their compensation. All vacancies in the office of custodian, assistants and other employes, shall be filled by said Board of Trustees, and the person so elected or appointed shall hold for the unexpired term.

SEC. 7. The custodian elected under this act may be removed from office for misdemeanor, incompetency or inattention to the duties of his office, by a vote of two-thirds of the Board of Trustees; the assistants and other employes may be removed by the board for incompetency, or for any other cause.

SEC. 8. It shall be the duty of the Board of Trustees, within ten days after the appointment of the custodian and other salaried employes, to report and file with the city comptroller a duly certified list of the persons so appointed, with the salary allowed to each, and the time or times fixed for the payment thereof, and they shall also furnish such comptroller with a list of all accounts and bills which may be allowed by said Board of Trustees, stating the character of the materials or service for which the same were rendered, immediately after the meeting of said board at which such allowance shall be made. And said Board of Trustees shall also, on or before the first day of October in each year, make to the common council a report, made up to and including the 31st day of August of the said year, containing a statement of the condition of the Museum and of the additions thereto during the year, together with such information and suggestions as they may deem important, and such report shall also contain an account of the moneys credited to the Museum fund, and expended on account of the same during the year.

SEC. 9. From and after the organization of the Board of Trustees under this act, the common council of said city shall levy and collect annually upon all the taxable property of the said city, at the same time and in the same manner as other city taxes are levied and collected by law, a special tax not exceeding one-tenth of a mill upon each dollar of the assessed value of said taxable property, the amount of which shall be determined by said board of trustees, and certified to the common council at the time of making their annual report to said council, and the entire amount of said special tax shall be paid into, and held in, the city treasury, as a separate and distinct fund, to be known as the Museum fund, and shall not be used or appropriated, directly or indirectly, in any other purpose than for the maintenance and for the increase of the Public Museum, the payment of the salaries of the custodian, assistant and other employes of the Museum, the purchase of furniture, fixtures, supplies and fuel, and the incidental expenses of the Museum.

SEC. 10. The board of trustees shall erect, purchase, hire or lease buildings, lots, rooms and furniture, for the use and accommodation of said Public Museum, and shall improve, enlarge and repair such buildings, rooms and furniture ; but no lot or building shall be purchased, erected or enlarged for the purpose herein mentioned, without an ordinance or resolution of the common council of said city, and deeds of conveyance and leases shall run to the city of Milwaukee.

SEC. 11. All moneys received by or raised in the city of Milwaukee for Museum purposes shall be paid over to the city treasurer, to be disbursed by him on the orders of the president and secretary of the said Board of Trustees, countersigned by the city comptroller. Such orders shall be made payable to the order of the persons in whose favor they shall have been issued, and shall be the only voucher of the city treasurer for the payments from the Museum fund. The said Board of Trustees shall provide for the purchase of specimens, supplies, fuel and other matters necessary or useful for the maintenance of the Museum ; provided, however, that it shall not be lawful for said Board of Trustees to expend or contract a liability for any sum in excess of the amount levied in any one year for the Museum fund, on account of such fund.

SEC. 12. All moneys, books, specimens and other property received by the city of Milwaukee by device, bequest or gift, from any person or corporation, for Public Museum purposes, shall, unless otherwise directed by the donors, be under the management and control of said Board of Trustees ; and all moneys derived from fines and penalties for violations of the rules of the Museum, or from any other source in the course of the administration of the Museum, including all moneys which may be paid to the city upon any policy or policies of insurance, or other obligation or liability, or on account of loss or damage to any property pertaining to the Museum, shall belong to the Museum fund in the city treasury, to be disbursed on the orders of the said Board of Trustees, countersigned by the city comptroller, for Museum purposes in addition to the amount levied and raised by taxation for such fund.

Sec. 13. This act shall take effect and be in force from and after its passage and publication.

Approved March 31, 1882.

(No. 895, A.)　　　　　　　　(Published April 15, 1887.)

CHAPTER 521.

AN ACT to amend chapter 328 of the laws of 1882, authorizing the city of Milwaukee to establish and maintain a Public Museum, and Chapter 7, of the laws of 1878, to establish a Public Library in the city of Milwaukee.

The people of the State of Wisconsin, represented in senate and assembly, do enact as follows:

*　　*　　*　　*　　*　　*　　*　　*

Section 2. Hereafter all appointments of members from the Common Council for the Board of Trustees of the Public Museum of the city of Milwaukee, made by the mayor of said city on the third Tuesday in April, shall be made from aldermen having two years to serve, and in case any person so appointed shall vacate his office of alderman before the expiration of his term, he shall thereupon cease to be a member of said Board of Trustees, and the mayor shall appoint some other alderman of his class in his place to be such trustee for the remainder of his term. Each alderman appointed shall serve as such trustee during his term as alderman. It shall be the duty of the mayor on the third Tuesday in April in each year to appoint a sufficient number of aldermen having two years to serve to be members of such Board of Trustees of the Public Museum to keep the number of members of such board from the Common Council, always three.

All provisions of Chapter 328, of the laws of 1882, which in any way conflict with the provisions of this section, are hereby amended accordingly.

SEC. 3. This act shall take effect and be in force from and after its passage and publication.

Approved April 14, 1887.

(No. 614, A.)   (Published April 20, 1887.)

CHAPTER 433.

AN ACT to amend Chapter 328, of the laws of 1882, entitled, "An act to authorize the city of Milwaukee to establish and maintain a Public Museum in said city."

The people of the State of Wisconsin, represented in senate and assembly, do enact as follows:

SECTION 1. The Board of Trustees of the Milwaukee Public Museum are hereby authorized to appoint an acting custodian whenever the proper service of the Museum shall require it, and for such time and on such terms as they may deem proper. Such acting custodian shall be ex-officio the acting secretary of said Board of Trustees, and his acts as such shall receive full credit. Said Board of Trustees are also authorized to appoint from time to time honorary curators, who shall perform ·such duties and have such special privileges as may be provided in the by-laws of the Museum, but shall receive no pecuniary compensation. Such appointments shall be made of persons who have manifested a special interest in the Museum or some particular department thereof.

SEC. 2. This act shall be in force from and after its passage and publication.

Approved April 12, 1887.

RULES GOVERNING THE MUSEUM.

I. MEETINGS.

ART. 1. The regular meetings of the board shall be held at the Museum rooms on the third Tuesday of each month at 4:30 P. M.

ART. 2. The annual meeting of the board shall be held on the third Tuesday of May at 4 P. M.

ART. 3. Special meetings shall be called by the secretary upon the written request of the president, or any three members of the board, but the object for which the special meeting is called must be stated in the notice, and no business other than the special business shall be transacted at such meeting, unless all the members of the board are present, and unanimous consent is obtained.

ART. 4. Five members of the board shall constitute a quorum.

II. OFFICERS AND EMPLOYES.

ART. 5. At the annual meeting in May, the board shall elect by ballot a president, whose duty it shall be to preside at all meetings of the board, to sign all warrants drawn on the city treasurer by order of the board, to appoint the standing committees for the year, and prepare for the consideration and approval of the board, the annual report of the Board of Trustees, required by section eight of the "Public Museum Act."

ART. 6. The duties of the custodian shall be as follows:

To take charge of and exercise control over the museum and library, and to see that the regulations relating thereto are properly carried out.

To exercise control over all employes of the board and the work allotted to them respectively.

To receive all specimens intended for the Museum, and with the advice and assistance of specialists to classify, label, catalogue and arrange them as soon as possible.

To receive all books and other articles intended for the library, and to label and catalogue them.

To take all precautions necessary for the good preservation of the collections, according to the most approved methods within the means of the institution.

To keep running records, containing all necessary particulars, concerning articles received or disposed of.

To purchase specimens, books and other matter under the general direction of the board.

To inaugurate a system of exchanges with other natural history museums as soon as possible.

To correspond with scientific societies and public authorities for the purpose of obtaining reports and other documents containing information relating to natural history.

To submit from time to time to the board or to the respective committees, measures for the efficient management and increase of the museum, and such other matters as he may deem advisable.

To prepare and submit to the board a monthly report in writing of the work done, stating the number of visitors, and other matter of interest to the board.

To prepare and submit at the annual meeting in September an annual report of like contents for the preceding year ending Aug. 31st, said report to accompany the annual report of the board, required by Section 8 of the "Public Museum Act."

To discharge such other duties as usually belong to the office of the custodian and from time to time be prescribed by the board.

But in the performance of his duties, no debt or liability of any kind shall be incurred by him without authority from the board.

The custodian shall be required to give bonds in the sum of one thousand dollars, with two or more sureties, to be approved by the board, for the faithful performance of his duties.

ART. 7. It shall be the duty of the custodian as secretary of the board of trustees to be present at all meetings of the board and of the committee and to keep full and correct records of their proceedings, except when otherwise directed.

To keep exact and detailed accounts of all moneys received from fines and other sources, to report the same monthly to the board at the regular meetings, and to pay over all moneys so received promptly to the city treasurer as directed by the board.

To keep books of account in which all the money transactions of the board shall be set forth accurately in detail, and to make out and sign all warrants drawn on the city treasurer by order of the board.

To take care of all business papers of the board and keep the same neatly filed for convenient reference.

To prepare and submit a monthly statement of the finances of the Museum at the regular monthly meetings.

To give notice of all meetings of the board, and of committees, at least 24 hours before the time of meeting.

To receive all documents, letters and other communications addressed to the Board or Museum, and to see to their proper disposal by the proper officer or committee.

To transact all such other business as may be required of him by the board and its committees in his capacity as secretary thereof.

ART. 8. The janitor shall, under the direction of the custodian, attend to the heating, ventilation and cleaning of the Museum in all its parts, and perform such other work as may be assigned to him at any time by the custodian. The other assistants shall also work under the direction of the custodian and perform such work as the custodian may assign to them.

ART. 9. Engagements of employes or assistants shall be made by the executive committee, subject to approval by the board.

III. COMMITTEES.

ART. 10. The standing committees shall be:

1. The Executive Committee, consisting of the president ex-officio, and four other members of the board.

2. The Finance Committee, consisting of three members of the board.

3. The Committee on Exchanges, consisting of three members of the board, to whom, with the custodian, all applications for exchanges shall be referred for recommendation to the board.

4. The Committee on Furniture, consisting of three members of the board.

5. The Committee on Purchase, consisting of three members of the board, to whom all matters of purchasing

specimens shall be referred for recommendation to the board. The committee on purchase shall have authority to expend from month to month in the interest of the Museum a sum not exceeding $50.

Art. 11. The Natural History Society of Wisconsin shall be invited to appoint five scientific persons from among their members to act in an advisory capacity as a joint counsel, in conferences with the Executive Committee ; such conferences to take place at such times as the Executive Committee may desire.

Art. 12. The Executive Committee shall have supervision of all matters relating to the purchasing, construction, leasing, repairing and heating of the buildings or rooms occupied by the Museum, and of insurance, the furnishing, order and cleanliness of the rooms and collections ; the selection, purchase, preparation, arrangement, exchange, sale or other disposal of specimens, books or other articles ; the acceptance or rejection of donations ; the preparation, printing, sale or other disposal of catalogues and guides ; provided that in all such matters no action be taken involving an expenditure or liability greater than authorized by the board. This Committee shall assign a suitable room to the Natural History Society of Wisconsin for holding their meetings and receiving their library. It shall be the duty of the committee to see that all persons employed in the service of the Museum are faithful and prompt in the performance of their duties, and that the regulations of the Museum are enforced.

Art. 13. The Finance Committee shall have the supervision of all matters pertaining to the accounts and account books of the board. It shall be their duty to prepare the annual budget of the board, to direct the manner of keeping and to examine all the account books ; to examine the

monthly and other financial statements of the secretary and
custodian and certify the correctness of the same to the
board; to examine and audit all vouchers and accounts
against the Museum, to report to the board upon the correctness of the same, and to make such suggestions from
time to time concerning the finances of the museum as they
may deem advisable. Said committee shall also at the
regular meeting in September each year, submit an estimate
of the amount that will be needed for maintaining the
Museum during the following year, and the action of the
board upon such estimates shall be forthwith certified by
the secretary to the comptroller of the city of Milwaukee.

ART. 14. A majority of any committee shall constitute
a quorum.

ART. 15. The standing committees shall prepare and
submit to the board at the annual meeting in May, a report
of all matters subject to their supervision.

ART. 16. The reports of all standing committees shall
be in writing.

IV. MUSEUM AND LIBRARY.

ART. 17. The Museum shall be conducted, according to
the intention of the "Public Museum Act" and the conditions made by the Natural History Society of Wisconsin in
donating the "Engelmann Museum" with the following
aims in view.

The exhibition of natural history and ethnology, so as
to provide material and help for scientific investigation and
public instruction.

The collection therein contained are to represent and
illustrate as far as possible the natural history and the
natural resources of the city and county of Milwaukee and

state of Wisconsin in the first order, and then of the United States and remainder of our planet for purposes of comparison and generalization.

The Museum shall be placed in a building reasonably fireproof, and kept insured for at least five-sixths of its value.

No objects in the collection can be loaned, and the removal of specimens from the rooms cannot be permitted, except if sold or for the purpose of exchange or identification and under proper authority from the Executive Committee. All matters relating to the arrangement, preservation and use of the collection are under the immediate direction of the custodian, subject to the supervision of the Executive Committee, who will give more detailed instructions if needed.

ART. 18. The library is to be considered a reference and working library. Its contents cannot be loaned, but may be used for study or reference in the rooms during museum hours under necessary restrictions.

V. MISCELLANEOUS.

ART. 19. It shall be the duty of every member of the board to frequently visit the Museum and of the members of the Executive Committee to do so at least once every week, for the purpose of general superintendence and direction.

ART. 20. The term of service of all the employes of the Museum except the custodian shall be during good behavior. They shall only be removed for cause of which the board shall be the exclusive judge.

ART. 21. The records of the proceedings of the board of trustees and its committees and the books of account, shall be kept in the secretary's office, and shall be open at all times to inspection and examination by any member of the board.

ART. 22. The order of business of the board of trustees, except at special meetings, shall be as follows:

1. Calling the roll.
2. Reading minutes of previous meeting.
3. Report of custodian and secretary.
4. Report of standing committees.
5. Report of special committees.
6. Reading of communications.
7. Unfinished business.
8. Election of officers.
9. New business.

ART. 23. All resolutions and amendments before the board or any committee shall be presented in writing.

ART. 24. All persons employed at the Museum must be promptly at their posts, as directed, and must remain there during the hours of their regular duty. They will remember that their time, while in the Museum, should constantly be occupied in its service, and it is the duty of the custodian and Executive Committee to enforce this rule.

ART. 25. No amendments to the rules of the board, or the regulations of the Museum shall be acted upon until the next regular meeting after the same shall have been proposed.

REGULATIONS.

The Museum will be open:

On Sundays, from 1:30 to 5 P. M.

Saturdays, from 9 to 12 A. M. and 1 to 5:30 P. M.

On all other days, from 1 to 5:30 P. M.

Visitors are admitted on condition that they observe the following regulations:

SECTION 1. Any person of good deportment can be admitted during the above named hours. Children less than fourteen years of age will be admitted only if accompanied by parents, teachers or other responsible adults. Dogs or other live animals will not be admitted.

SEC. 2. Admission is free. Employes of the Museum are forbidden under penalty of discharge, to receive fees from visitors.

SEC. 3. The removal of books, specimens, or any other objects belonging to the Museum from any of its rooms, is strictly prohibited.

SEC. 4. The use of tobacco, and all other conduct not consistent with the quiet and orderly use of the Museum, are prohibited.

SEC. 5. Visitors are not allowed to touch any object.

SEC. 6. Visitors will be held responsible for any mutilation or other injury to specimens, books, furniture, or other property of the Museum caused by them.

SEC. 7. The time for closing will be announced by three bell signals ten minutes previous to the appointed hour.

OFFICE HOURS OF EMPLOYES.

Custodian, from 9 to 12 A. M. and 1 to 4 P. M.

Assistant Custodian, from 8:30 to 11:30 A. M. and 1 to 5 P. M.

Taxidermist, from 8 to 12 A. M. and 1 to 5 P. M.

First Assistant, from 8:30 to 11:30 A. M. and 1 to 5:00 P. M.

Janitor, from 7 to 11:30 A. M. and 1 to 5:30 P. M.

In Memoriam.

—

Benjamin F. Goss,

Died July 6, 1893.

—

By

H. Nehrling.

It was always a very pleasant time when the late Mr. Benjamin F. Goss, Honorary Curator of Oology and Ornithology of the Public Museum of Milwaukee, visited the institution. His kindness to all the employes, his congeniality, his good humor, his interesting conversation made him a very delightful and always welcome visitor. I have spent many happy hours with him in the Museum, and I must say that I rarely have met a man who was so upright, so true and kind and friendly than Mr. Goss. Like all those who really know anything he was very modest. A boundless love for nature and her beauties and a never-ceasing enthusiasm for the birds of our country and their nesting habits characterized him.

Benjamin F. Goss was born in Lancaster, N. H., April 24, 1823. In 1841 he came with his brother, the late Colonel N. S. Goss, to Wisconsin, spending the fourteen succeeding years on a farm near Pewaukee Lake. In 1854 he was elected to the Assembly of the State of Wisconsin for the northeast district of Waukesha Co. In the spring, 1855, he left Wisconsin, and after a brief sojourn in Iowa he settled in Neosho Falls, Kansas. During that time Mr. Goss was very active in politics, and when the war broke out in 1861 he enlisted a company for three years' service in the Union Army, and as captain of Company F, Ninth Kansas

Cavalry, served the full term. "The constant guerilla warfare which was maintained in the border states rendered the service very dangerous, and Mr. Goss had many narrow escapes and took part in many battles and skirmishes." At the close of the war Captain Goss returned to Pewaukee, and there he spent the remainder of his life, while his brother, Col. N. S. Goss, made Kansas his home.

Although Mr. Goss had been a student of nature, especially of bird-life, since his boyhood, it was not until he returned to Wisconsin in 1866 that he began to collect the eggs and nests of North American birds in a scientific way, with a view of acquiring a private collection. This work he followed with all the devotion, energy and enthusiasm which were so eminenty characteristic of him. Since 1866 he made extensive and successful journeys to different parts of the country, mostly in company with his brother. A trip to the Gulf Coast of Texas was especially fruitful, and excursions in the mountains of Colorado and California were of great value to him, as he everywhere made new discoveries in the line of rare bird's eggs. In the winter of 1891 he made a trip to Florida for the special purpose to look for the still undiscovered eggs of the Carolina Paroquet (Conuropsis carolinensis A. O. U.) When he returned home he told me that the only places where these once common birds of the United States could be found in Florida were the extensive cypress swamps, and that before long this Paroquet would be placed on the list of extinct American birds. Although he had visited many places in Florida he had been unable to obtain any reliable information on the breeding habits of this Paroquet.

His last ornithological excursion was made to Oconto County of this State. He reached the home of his friend, Mr. A. J. Schoenebeck, on June 7, 1892, and left again on the 13th of the same month. Mr. Schoenebeck writes me that he and Mr. Goss made excursions in all directions, visiting the beautiful evergreen woods of that region as well as the extensive swamps. That Mr. Goss was a trained field ornithologist, was proved by his finding the nest of a large number of birds, among them Picoides arcticus, Loxia curvirostra minor, Zonotrichia albicollis, Vireo solitarius, Dendroica macculosa and Troglodytes hiemalis.

Although Captain Goss has published almost nothing, he is well known to almost all the American ornithologists as an enthusiastic and careful collector, and through his extensive correspondence with the leading publishing ornithologists many of his valuable observations have long since found their way into the ornithological literature. He was an old correspondent of the late Dr. T. M. Brewer. Capt. Chas.

Bendire has acknowledged frequent contributions from his pen to his great work, "Life Histories of North American Birds." The late Col. N. S. Goss, in his "Birds of Kansas," also quotes many valuable observations of his brother. In 1892 he was again elected to the Assembly of Wisconsin.

In the spring of 1893 his health began to fail, and he repeatedly suffered attacks of neuralgia of the heart, and on the 6th of July died suddenly at his beautiful home in Pewaukee, aged 70 years.

His collection of eggs of North American birds, consisting of 721 species, and 3,015 specimens was presented by him a few years before his death, to the Public Museum of the city of Milwaukee. It is one of the best, if not the best collection of bird's eggs on exhibition in this country.

TWELFTH

ANNUAL REPORT

———— OF THE ————

BOARD OF TRUSTEES

———— OF THE ————

PUBLIC · MUSEUM

——— OF THE ——— —— ——

CITY OF MILWAUKEE.

———————

September 1st, 1893, to August 31st, 1894.

———————

OCTOBER 1st, 1894.

———————

MILWAUKEE:
ED. KEOGH, PRINTER, 386 AND 388 BROADWAY.
1894.

MUSEUM SERVICE.

HY. NEHRLING, - - - - - - Custodian.

CARL THAL, - - - - - - Assistant Custodian.

GEO. B. TURNER, - - - - - Taxidermist.

ALEXANDER GOETHEL, - - - - Assistant Taxidermist.

LYDIA NEHRLING, - - - - - Assistant.

LINA SPANKUS, - - - - - - Assistant.

CARL BINDRICH, - - - - - Janitor.

*To the Honorable, the Common Council of the City of Mil-
waukee:*

GENTLEMEN:—The Board of Trustees of the Public
Museum, in accordance with Section 8, Chapter 328, of the
laws of 1882, presents herewith its annual report as required
by law. It respectfully refers to the annual report of Mr. H.
Nehrling, the custodian of the Museum, for such details and
information as are not contained in this report.

There are at present in the Museum:

116,164 Zoological specimens, valued at..................	$32,040 54
15,744 Botanical specimens, valued at...................	975 00
14,253 Anthropological specimens, valued at.............	7,957 60
11,036 Palaeontological specimens, valued at............	5,168 80
4,076 Mineralogical and Lithological specimens, valued at.	3,788 84
5,560 Books, pamphlets, catalogues, atlasses, etc., valued at	5,479 84
3,035 Bird's eggs and nests, valued at..................	10,000 00
Total..	$65,410 62

The number of visitors during the year was 27,234, a
decrease of 57,077 as compared with the attendance of last
year, which decrease was due to the fact that the Industrial
Exposition was not held during the year.

The insurance on the property of the Museum is now
$63,000, against $50,000 of the preceding year.

The financial statement of the Board is as follows:

Balance in Museum fund on September 1, 1893............	$7,970 20
Appropriation to Museum fund on December 1, 1893.......	12,392 91
From other sources........................	6 75
Total...	$20,369 86
Total expenditures during last year.....................	16,582 13
Unexpended balance in Museum fund Sept. 1, 1894..	$3,787 73

My thanks are due the members of the Board and the officers of the Museum for their cordial assistance in furthering the best interests of the Museum.

Respectfully submitted,

GEO. W. PECKHAM,

President.

REPORT OF THE CUSTODIAN.

MILWAUKEE, WIS., September 18th, 1894.

*To the Board of Trustees of the Public Museum of the City
of Milwaukee:*

GENTLEMEN:—In compliance with Article 6 of your Rules
and Regulations, I herewith submit to you my fourth annual
report, being the twelfth in the series of reports since the
establishment of the Museum.

The present museum year has been still more successful
and important than the preceding one.

Soon after my last annual report was submitted to your
honorable body, I had the opportunity of making selections
of great value from a number of exhibits at the World's Fair
in Chicago. Most specimens of the valuable collection of
bird-skins from British Guiana were purchased by me for a
very low price, and the cream of the large collection exhibited
by the U. S. of Colombia was also obtained. From Ward's
natural history exhibit in the Anthropological Building, the
very best mounted specimens of rare mammals and birds were
bought. Of the $2,000 allowed me by the Board of Trustees
for purchasing specimens only about $1,450 have been
expended. Much valuable material has been donated by the
World's Fair Commissioners, Mr. J. J. Quelch from British
Guiana and Mr. Roundsevelle Wildman of Johore, Malayan
Peninsula.

The space in the cases of the third hall of the Museum has entirely been taken up by specimens bought at the World's Fair or such which were donated to us. For the Wisconsin Forestry Exhibit from the World's Fair, which was donated to the Museum by the State Board of Directors, it was necessary to procure additional room from the Milwaukee Industrial Exposition Association. The room which contains the collection of Wisconsin woods contains 3,860 square feet. We have now 12,000 square feet for exhibition purposes, against 5,736 square feet two years ago.

The Museum has been open to the public daily, from 1 to 5:30 p. m., and on Sundays from 1:30 to 5 p. m. The number of visitors was 27,234. The total number of persons who visited the Museum during the year shows a considerable decrease compared with the previous year, but this is due to the fact that there was no exposition held last year. On forenoons the Museum, although closed to the public, has been accessible to students and sometimes to schools for teaching purposes. Although many classes of our schools have visited the Museum during the regular hours, not so many have availed themselves of the privilege to see the collections as could be expected. It is frequently combined with much trouble and annoyance for a teacher to take a large class to the Museum, especially at present in our crowded halls.

But there is another way to make use of the Museum collections. The teachers should influence their pupils to visit the Museum alone for the purpose of carefully studying the objects in one department at a time. If they come with their classes many of the children are bewildered by the cases filled with apparently similar kinds of birds' eggs, shells, mammals and birds. They aimlessly stray around, often without taking with them any new impressions and ideas, especially when the teachers themselves are not sufficiently interested in natural history to make the visit delightful to their classes. If the children come with enthusiasm and take their time in looking over the collections they will certainly visit the Museum with profit.

In reading about the Catbird, Bluebird, Song Sparrow, Chipping Bird, Baltimore Oriole, etc., of the Bear, Raccoon, Skunk, Badger, Woodchuck, Opossum, etc., they should know that excellent specimens of all these animals can be seen in the Museum.

In United States history, in talking about the Indians, they should be instructed to go to the Museum, where they can see Indian war-shirts, tomahawks, scalps, bows and arrows, copper and stone implements, pipes of peace, etc.

The rapid developments of modern arts and illustrations, says a recent writer, and the conspicuous use of these methods in books, magazines, and even the daily papers, attest the power of the pictorial art, barbarous as it may be in many cases, in imparting information quickly and clearly. If illustrations are so important in modern publications—and to do without them would seem well-nigh impossible—how far more important is it to see on exhibition objects of scientific and historic interest in the Museum, correctly labeled and well prepared. There are no better object lessons for our school children than to see our native animals mounted in their natural position. In this way they learn to see, to observe, to compare and to find the differences in specimens which appear alike to the eye of the layman.

To any one who knows something about the habits and names of our native birds, mammals, etc., the ignorance displayed by many of his friends concerning their very names, size, color, etc., is often astounding.

I frequently meet educated people who do not know, for instance, the difference between a Blue Jay and a Bluebird, between a Blackbird and a Martin, between a Yellow Warbler and a Goldfinch, between a Cardinal Redbird and a Scarlet Tanager; they ask whether a certain animal in the collection is a Badger or a Woodchuck, a Raccoon or a Wolverine. The same ignorance extends to the animal kingdom in general. This is certainly not as it should be. "The remedy is extremely simple," says Mr. G. M. Minchin, of the Royal Indian Engineering College. "Introduce among the school books a short manual of natural history, dealing rather with the interesting characteristics of animals than with the science of their structure—just those things which interest you without producing a strain on the intellect—and the result will be a far more widely spread knowledge of the inhabitants of our fields, streams and woods than that which now prevails. Another result will be a greater sympathy with the non-human portion of life. Indeed, the omission of the teaching of natural history in an easy and interesting shape in our schools fits ill with the vast importance now attained by biology, a science of immense possibilities and one which is advancing by leaps and bounds."

That this can be done, and it is done in several schools, I have sometimes observed.

Since our honorable president, Dr. Geo. W. Peckham, —himself a well-known naturalist and a great friend of nature—has taken charge of the schools of the city, the teaching of natural history in a pleasant and attractive way has been inaugurated. The result is already a most noticeable one.

There are quite a number of children coming to the Museum with the special purpose of seeing the objects they have read about. The names of these objects usually have been jotted down on a piece of paper. Some come to see the Buffalos and Bears, others the Muskrats, Beavers, Porcupines, etc.; others have a list of the more familiar native birds, and still others are anxious to compare their botanical specimens with specimens in our herbarium.

Since my taking charge of the institution as custodian, it has always been my aim to arrange special collections for our schools and for all those interested in the geographical distribution of animals. Owing to our crowded halls, I succeeded thus far in completing only a case of characteristic animals of Australia.

The Museum of the future cannot be satisfied with well arranged systematic collections only. It must also show something of the life-history of the specimens exhibited. The bird must be shown with its nest and eggs and the quaint appearance of the young. The collection of shells is valuable, but usually they are shown with no inkling of the kind of life associated with them. Every Museum, if it is to be of use to the people at large, must contain something for everybody. We have already a beginning in this line, as the groups of Muskrats, Porcupines, Beavers, Opossums, Badgers, Skunks, Orang-Outans, Otters, and Foxes show, and although it takes much consideration, much time, a large amount of patience and much money, we have to keep in the track which only leads to success. We will by no means neglect the systematic collections of North American forms, but our main work in the future will lie in the composition of life-like groups of native mammals and birds, and in this respect even domestic forms, such as Pigeons, Chickens, Ducks, Dogs, etc., will be utilized to show the visitor the variations an animal is capable of under domestication.

With the increase of the collections, which have more than doubled since I took charge of the Museum four years ago, the work has increased in proportion. Much has been accomplished during the past year. My own time has been taken up in arranging, looking up and correcting old labels in accordance with the advancement of science. The "Catalogue of the British Museum," as far as it is in our hands, has served to good purpose. Several thousand old labels have been replaced by new ones, printed on our hand press in the Museum. Large collections of plants have been looked over and provided with labels. The scientific papers and pamphlets, many hundreds in number, have been examined and marked for our

·card catalogue. Only articles of special interest will in future find a place therein. I had frequently to confer with Mr. Turner as to the arrangement of the groups and the positions of the individual specimens that were to be mounted by him. Besides this I had to attend to the minor details of all the work done, and much time was spent in corresponding with scientific men and collectors, and in showing visitors around in the Museum.

Our taxidermist, Mr. Geo. B. Turner, mounted a large number of birds and mammals. He especially succeeded in forming a very fine life-like group of Black Bears, an old and three young ones. He is now engaged in making up a group of Bisons or American Buffalos. Since we received a fine Buffalo calf and a heifer from Montana, we have all the material for such a group on hand. After this is completed, a group of Prairie Wolves, or Coyotes, will be made up. Through the kindness of Mr. Gustav Preusser we received all the specimens necessary for such a group.

To make it possible to mount also the many specimens of tropical birds purchased at the World's Columbian Exposition, the Board found it necessary to employ an assistant to the taxidermist.

Mr. Alexander Goethel, a promising young man, was engaged for this position.

The work of the janitor increased so much that it was impossible for him to keep all the glass cases clean. The Board therefore employed Miss L. Spankus, whose duty it is to help the janitor in cleaning the cases in the morning and to attend to visitors in the afternoon.

As several insurance agents insisted to have the records of the Museum copied and stored in a fire-proof vault outside of the Museum, the Board, after having considered the matter thoroughly, employed Mr. Paul Dachsel for this work.

The routine work, i. e., the keeping of the record books, the type-writing, a large part of the correspondence, the monthly statements, etc., etc., has been done by the assistant custodian, Mr. Carl Thal. He also did such Museum work as was from time to time assigned to him by me. With Mr. Dachsel he compared the duplicates of the record books as far as they have been copied. In all this various work of the Museum I have always found that I could depend on Mr. Thal's hearty assistance.

The four years' work in the Museum have been too brief a time for me to give my attention to the development of all the departments that the Museum is intended to represent. Still I think that all the departments have been considerably increased and improved in the number of specimens as well as in the condition of their preservation.

I. ZOOLOGY.

A.—MAMMALS.

The department of mammals has been enriched by many new and valuable specimens. I can mention only the most important donations and purchases. For the rest I refer the reader to the appendix.

Near his winter home at De Funiak Springs, Fla., Mr. Ernst von Baumbach procured a Water Hare (Lepus aquaticus, Bach.), which he donated to the Museum.

Through Mr. Christian Wahl, president of the Park Commission, I had the good fortune of obtaining a fine specimen of Wapiti (Cervus canadensis, Erxl.) for the Museum, which had been killed in one of the city parks. This specimen will enter into a fine group which will be constructed by our taxidermist as soon as we have the necessary material together.

From Mr. Carl Hagenbeck, Hamburg, Germany, two Baboons and four other valuable monkeys were received. These monkeys died during the World's Fair in Hagenbeck's Arena and Animal Show, Midway Plaisance, and were sent to the Museum immediately after their death. They were all mounted and are now on exhibtion in the southeast hall.

From one of his hunting trips to Gogebic, Mich., Mr. Christian Preusser brought back two Porcupines (Erethizon dorsatus), one Mink (Putorius vison), etc. Although these animals are by no means uncommon in the northern parts of our state and in our collection, they will be of value in making up groups.

Mr. Gustav Preusser especially endeavors to obtain for the Museum such North American mammals and birds as are not yet represented in our collection. He lately donated two Jack Rabbits (Lepus campestris), one Western Fox Squirrel (Sciurus niger, var. ludovicianus) and two old Coyotes or Prairie Wolves (Canis latrans, Say.). Mr. Preusser several weeks ago, has procured a litter of five young Coyotes of which with the old ones a group will be formed. All these mammals come from Missoula, Mont.

By purchase the Museum obtained one old and three young Black Bears (Ursus americanus), of which a beautiful group has been formed by our taxidermist, Mr. Geo. B. Turner.

An old and two young Pumas or Mountain Lions, also known as American Panther and Cougar (Felis concolor), were purchased and the three made up into an attractive group.

On recommendation of trustee Ch. Preusser, the following four cases of mammals, $100 each, were bought from Mr. T. H. Storey, Duluth, Minn. They were on exhibition in the Minnesota State Building, World's Fair:

1. A group of Skunks, an old one and seven young.
2. A group of three American Badgers, an old one and two young.
3. A group of one old and two young Red Foxes.
4. A group of one old and two young Otters.

The following mammals which I selected from Ward's Natural History Exhibit in the Anthropological Building are especially interesting and valuable.

1.   A group of one old and six young Opossums (Didelphis virginiana) from the Southern States.

2.   A Monkey Bear or Koala (Phascolarctus cinereus) with its young on the back, from New South Wales. Like the Opossums it belongs to the order of Marsupialia, though it is quite unlike the foregoing in appearance, in manners and food habits.   The short, thick head is somewhat bear-like. The fur is very thick, soft and woolly and of an ashy-gray color, which changes into a paler color on the lower parts. The tail is wanting.   The ears, which are blackish in color, are very hairy.   The female is much attached to her young, which is carried about on her back long after it is able to leave the pouch.   In this position both animals are mounted and are displayed in the case containing the characteristic mammals and birds of Australia.   The Koalas live on the leaves and shoots of the trees on which they climb.

3.   A fine specimen of Phalanger, (Phalangista fuliginosa), also a native of New South Wales.   As it has a prehensile tail it reminds us of our Opossum.

4.   A specimen of Dasyurus maculatus, related to the Tasmanian Devil (Dasyurus ursinus) from Van Diemensland.

5.   The Bandicoat (Perameles nasuta) from Australia is found in the mountain regions, living in burrows.   In general form these animals resemble rats and are almost as troublesome where they are abundant.

6.   Of the Giant Kangaroo (Macropus major) a fine female, with two young in the pouch, was purchased.   As these Kangeroos are becoming rarer from year to year, this is a valuable acquisition.   All these animals are members of the order Marsupialia.

7.   An Aard Wolf (Proteles lalandi) from the Cape Colony, related to the Hyenas.

8.   A good specimen of the Yaguarandi (Felis yaguarandi), which belongs to the Cat family and occurs from Mexico to Paraguay.

9. The Raccoon Dog (Canis procynonoides), from Japan.

10. The so-called Raccoon Fox (Bassaris astua) a native of Texas, California, Mexico, etc., was also added to our collection. This animal is often tamed in Texas and Mexico.

11. The Guerza (Guerza rueppeli), one of the most beautiful monkeys. The prevailing color is a deep black, which contrasts strongly with the long white hair on the sides and tail. These monkeys frequent the high trees, jumping from branch to branch; the silvery fringe flapping out from the sides gives them almost the appearance of being winged. They are natives of tropical Africa.

12. A fine specimen of the Central American two-toed Sloth (Chlolopus hofmanni), and a number of less common mammals.

Mr. Erich Wittkugel, of San Pedro Sula, Honduras, has sent us two Deer (species not yet determined), a Nosebear or Mexican Coati (Nasua narica), a very interesting species, related to our Raccoon, and a few species of other mammals.

B.—BIRDS.

The ornithological collection has increased considerably. Though the systematic collection of North American birds is still lacking many of the rarer species and forms, we have nevertheless succeeded in obtaining much valuable material. Old and poorly mounted specimens have been substituted by new and nicely mounted ones, showing the natural position of the birds.

Mr. Clarence J. Allen, of this city, as in former years, has donated several birds of prey, among them a Broad-winged Hawk, a Pigeon Hawk and two American Long-eared Owls.

Mr. Christian Preusser donated a number of the more common native birds, and Mr. Gustav Preusser presented a fine specimen of the American Magpie (Pica pica hudsonica), and Woodhouse's Jay (Aphelocoma woodhousei).

Among a number of tropical birds Mr. August Stirn donated four Pagoda Starlings (Temenuchus pagodarum) which are especially worthy of mentioning. They come from India.

While visiting the California Midwinter Fair, Mr. Wm. Vogel purchased a female of the Road Runner or Chapparal Cock (Geococcyx californicus) which he donated to our collection.

From Mr. Carl Hagenbeck we received five rare Parrots which died in captivity during the World's Fair.

Through the kindness of Mr. Rounsevelle Wildman, U. S. Commissioner of Straits, Settlements and Borneo, and now editor-in-chief of the "Overland Monthly," San Francisco, Cal., we received twenty-two rare birds collected in Johore, Malayan Peninsula, all correctly labeled.

Mr. Louis Wöltersdorf, of Chicago, donated an Australian Zebrafinch (Stagonopleura castanotis), which he had raised in confinement.

Of the birds purchased only a few can be mentioned.

From February 1st, 1892, to January 19th, 1893, Mr. Chas. W. Richmond, of Washington, D. C., collected a large number of birds in Nicaragua, which were offered to the Museum for a reasonable price. Owing to our slow way of making purchases, the whole collection was sent to England, and we had only the chance to buy the rest, about 138 specimens, representing about fifty species. All these birds were collected in Nicaragua, near Bluefields and on the Escondido River, and all are correctly labeled. Mr. Richmond has laid down his observations in a paper "On a Collection of Birds from Eastern Nicaragua, etc." (Proceedings of the U. S. National Museum, Vol. 16, Pages 479 to 532.)

From Mr. G. E. Mitchell, of Herndon, Va., we bought a fine pair of Carpodectes nitidus, which were also collected on the Escondido River, Nicaragua.

While looking around in the different state buildings for natural history objects, during the World's Fair, I became acquainted with Mr. Henry Rowan Lemly, Commissioner for the U. S. of Colombia. He called my attention to a large collection of birds that were stored in an out-of-the-way place in the building, which had been made by the Colombian Government for the World's Fair in the Andes, near Bogota, and on the Magdalena River. He promised me to let me have as many specimens as I would select at the end of the World's Fair for a low price. I made a selection of 132 specimens, the cream of the entire collection.

The finest and most valuable collection of tropical birds was exhibited by British Guiana in the Agricultural Building. Dr. J. J. Quelch, Commissioner of that country, and at the same time director of the Museum at Georgetown, B. G., promised me already in August to let me have, with a few exceptions, the whole collection for our Museum. The specimens purchased from Mr. Quelch number 207 and are in the best possible condition. In addition to these skins Mr. Quelch donated a very large number of other natural history specimens.

From Ward's Natural History exhibit I selected the following mounted birds: Lady Amherst's Pheasant (Thaumalea amherstii), a rare and beautiful bird from Yunan, East Setchuan, Tibet, etc., where it inhabits the mountain regions. The color of this Pheasant is strikingly beautiful. Its crimson, white-tipped crest, pure white ruff, margined with deep green, metallic green breast, pure white underparts, and the greatly lengthened tail with bars of green and black mottlings attract the attention of every one who beholds it.

The most valuable purchase is a pair of white-tailed Pheasants (Lobiophasis bulweri). This species was discovered on the Lawas River, Borneo. In many particulars this elegant Pheasant is unique and beheld with great interest by the visitors of the Museum. The dark brownish plumage, showing various metallic hues, contrasts strongly with the long pure white tail.

A fine specimen of the Satyr Pheasant or Crimson Tragopan (Ceriornis satyra) and the Black-headed Tragopan (Ceriornis melanocephala) were also obtained. These beautiful birds are dwellers of the higher ranges of the Himalayas, being found at heights ranging from 8,000 to 11,000 feet.

Another valuable addition is the Vulture Guinea Fowl (Acryllium vulturinum), a native of Africa, a very beautiful bird, the prevailing color being blue, which is relieved by black and white. These birds live in large flocks, are very noisy and swift on foot, wild and wary.

Penelope jacutinga, an American member of the order Gallinae, is a very interesting bird. Its true home is to be found in the tropical forests of Brazil. There were quite a number of other birds purchased, among them several Pittas, Toucans, Pigeons, Parrots, Birds of Paradise, etc.

C.—ICHTHYOLOGY.

Several specimens of fishes were donated to the Museum, but they are not yet determined. Through my friend, Dr. Sigmund Graenicher, this department will receive special care in the future. The aforesaid gentleman has promised me to collect, determine and preserve all the fishes living in the rivers and lakes of Wisconsin which he will be able to obtain. He will also give his attention to the Batrachians and Reptiles.

D.—CONCHOLOGY.

Mr. Chas. P. Dadman of National City, Cal., a former citizen of Milwaukee, presented to the Museum 722 shells collected by him on the shore of the Pacific Ocean. Mr. John Erickson of this city donated 212 shells, found at the sea-shore of Hayti, West Indies.

E.—ENTOMOLOGY.

Mr. Carl Miller donated 115 Butterflies and 54 Beetles, collected by him on the Gold Coast, West Africa.

A very valuable collection of 112 Butterflies and 70 Moths was donated by Mr. Wm. Vogel, who collected them partly in and near Belize, British Honduras, and partly in San Pedro Sula, Republic of Honduras.

II. BOTANY.

A.—PLANTS.

The principal addition to the botanical department consists of a very fine herbarium donated by Mr. Charles E. Monroe. The plants are better preserved than any I have seen heretofore, and each one is a very fine specimen. This collection is rich in Compositae and Ferns, not only in species but also in forms. Most of the plants were collected in this vicinity, but the flora of Niagara Falls, Mount Washington and the Dells of the Wisconsin is also represented.

Mr. Reuben Strong has donated a large number of plants, collected in Milwaukee County.

Prof. Emil Dapprich, Director of the German-English Academy and Teachers' Seminary, donated a fine herbarium of plants collected by him in summer 1893 in the mountain regions of Colorado.

All these plants will be recorded in our next annual report.

B—WOODS, ETC.

Dr. J. J. Quelch, Commissioner for British Guiana, donated four palm-logs, each representing a different species, blocks of wood, bark of tropical trees and samples of tropical woody twining plants.

The State Board of Directors of the World's Fair presented to the Museum their entire collection of woods, which was exhibited in the Forestry Building. As the collection lacks scientific correctness in labeling, it will take some time before we are able to enter the specimens into our books.

III.—MINERALOGY.

The specimens registered in this department were acquired as follows: By purchase 12, by donation 27.

IV.—PALAEONTOLOGY.

The most important donations consist of one Halysites, from Mr. August Fiebelkorn, Cascade, Wis., of a conglomerate of shells, found by Mr. August Stirn near Pine Lake, Wis., and a piece of petrified wood, found at Freistadt, Wis., and donated by Assemblyman Frank W. Suelflow.

V.—ETHNOLOGY.

The additions to this department are very numerous. The most important donation comes from Mr. Carl Miller of this city. While holding a position on the Gold Coast, West Africa, this gentleman brought together an exceedingly fine and valuable collection of weapons, household goods, garments, personal ornaments, and interesting articles used by the natives in their tribal operations and rites. The collection, in itself very large, is accompanied by maps, and numerous larger and smaller photographs. It is displayed in three wall cases in the new hall of the institution.

Mr. August Muenzenberger, of Sabinal, Mexico, donated several ethnological specimens made by Mexican Indians.

Mr. Rounsevelle Wildman presented quite a number of specimens, mostly household utensils, used by the natives of Johore, Malayan Peninsula. He also donated two models of houses. These objects were exhibited in the Johore Bungalows, Midway Plaisance, World's Fair.

By purchase thirty-one specimens of Indian relics were obtained.

VI.—ARCHAEOLOGY.

The thousands of specimens of the Haskell Collection, which was purchased last year and to which I alluded in my last year's report, have been entered and numbered. As almost all of the specimens have been found in Jefferson Co., near Aztalan, Wis., this collection has a great value.

Mr. H. C. Mansfield, Jefferson, Wis., donated twenty-one arrowheads, and Mr. Horace McElroy, Janesville, Wis., a number of fragments of a large stone knife. Several other objects came from Mr. August Fiebelkorn of Cascade, and Mr. Frank Sholes of this city.

Mr. Bernhard Heyn donated a very fine stone celt with a deer horn handle from the pile dwellings of Switzerland.

VII.—LIBRARY.

On account of the limited annual appropriation for the Museum the acquisition of scientific books has been curtailed and the purchase of costly illustrated works made impossible. Only a few of such works which were indispensible have been obtained.

From the various foreign and native scientific societies we have received a large number of reports, pamphlets and books in exchange. The Smithsonian Institution, the National Museum and the Agricultural Department have enriched our library with very valuable scientific books.

INVENTORY.

Approximate Statement of the Contents and Value of the Various Departments of the Museum.

116,164	Zoological specimens	$32,040 54
15,744	Botanical specimens	975 00
14,253	Anthropological specimens	7,957 60
11,036	Palaeontological specimens	5,168 80
4,076	Mineralogical and lithological specimens	3,788 84
5,560	Books, pamphlets, catalogues, atlases and charts	5,479 84
3,035	Birds' eggs and nests	10,000 00
	Furniture, tools, jars, vessels, conservation supplies and stationery	13,974 05
	Upham collection held in trust	350 00
	Aggregate value of the contents of the Museum	$79,734 67

FINANCIAL TRANSACTIONS OF THE MUSEUM.

Debit.

Balance in Museum fund Sept. 1st, 1893....................	$7,970 20
Appropriation to Museum fund Dec. 1st, 1893..............	12,392 91
Refunded insurance premium Dec. 1st, 1893................	6 75
	$20,369 86

Credit.

Amounts paid by warrants on the city treasurer since the last annual statement was rendered:

Permanent improvements	$154 60	
Fuel and light...............................	264 01	
Repairs	37 84	
Postage and freight	168 59	
Stationery and printing	157 62	
Furniture	2,197 53	
Anthropology and ethnology..................	578 85	
Mammals....................................	1,311 85	
Birds..	770 25	
Minerals and rocks...........................	23 25	
Botany......................................	595 32	
Insurance....................................	1,684 92	
Rent.	1,275 00	
Miscellaneous	484 27	
Library	244 05	
Pay roll	6,070 00	
Conservation supplies	36 37	
Wages.......................................	527 81	$16,582 13
Balance in Museum fund Sept. 1st, 1894..............		$3,787 73

INSURANCE.

Saint Paul Fire & Marine Insurance Co., St. Paul, Minn....	$1,500 00
Palatine Insurance Co., (Limited), Manchester, England....	1,500 00
Hamburg-Bremen Fire Insurance Co., Hamburg, Germany..	1,500 00
Norwich Union Fire Insurance Society, England..........	2,500 00
Reading Fire Insurance Co., Reading, Penn...............	1,000 00
Capital Fire Insurance Co., Concord, N. H	1,000 00
Citizens' Insurance Co., Pittsburgh, Pa..................	1,000 00
Grand Rapids Fire Insurance Co., Grand Rapids, Mich......	1,500 00
Oakland Home Insurance Co., California.................	1,500 00
Rhode Island Underwriters' Association, Providence, R. I...	2,000 00
Royal Insurance Co., Liverpool, England	1,000 00
Queen Insurance Co. of America, N. Y....................	2,500 00
Phenix Insurance Co. of Brooklyn, N. Y.......	1,500 00
British American Assurance Co., Toronto, Ont.............	1,000 00
Hanover Fire Insurance Co., New York...................	1,500 00
Security Insurance Co., New Haven, Conn	1,500 00
Commonwealth Insurance Co., New York.................	1,500 00
Rutger's Fire Insurance Co., New York.....	1,500 00
Isthmus Lloyds of the City of New York..................	2,500 00
New York Central Lloyds, New York.....................	2,500 00
Merchants Fire Lloyds, New York........................	2,500 00
Columbia Fire Lloyds, New York........................	2,500 00
Metropolitan Lloyds, New York.........................	7,500 00
Pacific Fire Insurance Co., New York....................	1,500 00
American Insurance Co., Newark, N. J.	1,500 00
Rockford Insurance Co., Rockford, Ill...................	2,500 00
Allemannia Fire Insurance Co., Pittsburgh................	1,500 00
Orient Insurance Co., Hartford, Conn....................	2,000 00
Germania Insurance Co., New Orleans...................	1,500 00
German Fire Insurance Co., Peoria, Ill...................	2,000 00
Manufacturers' and Merchants' Mutual Ins. Co., Rockford..	2,500 00
Phenix Insurance Co. of Brooklyn, N. Y.................	1,000 00
Commercial Union Assurance Co., (Limited), of London...	2,500 00
Total...	$63,000 00

VISITORS.

	1893 Sept.	1893 Oct.	1893 Nov.	1893 Dec.	1894 Jan.	1894 Feb.	1894 Mar.	1894 April.	1894 May.	1894 June.	1894 July.	1894 Aug.	1893-94 Whole year.
Average daily attendance......	96	82	72	54	68	115	104	70	60	64	73	75	74
Greatest daily attendance......	280	326	188	116	182	313	288	228	204	133	242	159	
Least daily attendance	42	26	13	16	15	11	24	12	10	13	23	41	
Av. attendance on Sundays.....	121	137	122	81	125	233	133	180	93	71	161	100	
Total attendance............	2,854	2,527	2,173	655	2,096	3,270	3,200	2,108	1,854	1,912	2,259	2,331	27,234

The Board of Trustees and the whole population of our city can point with pride to the Public Museum and its treasures. This is acknowledged by all the scientific men of this country and abroad who have had an opportunity of seeing the collections and examining them thoroughly. Natural history, in all its branches, has marked this century, and the progress made by mankind through natural science has never been, and will never be excelled. My sincere wish is that the people of this city, especially teachers and parents, may visit the Museum more frequently as it is done. Though we have achieved much with our limited means, it will perhaps not be out of place to mention, that those "blessed with the world's riches" in our beautiful city, could assist us more as it is done in purchasing specimens. The large Museums of New York, Philadelphia, Cambridge, Salem, Chicago, etc., are almost entirely maintained by contributions of wealthy citizens.

Respectfully submitted,

H. NEHRLING,

Secretary and Custodian.

APPENDIX.

ZOOLOGY.

DONATIONS.

C. J. Allen, Milwaukee, Wis.

    1 Broad-winged Hawk, Marinisco, Mich.

    1 Pigeon Hawk,   "   "

    2 American Long-eared Owls, Fox Point, Wis.

Ernst v. Baumbach, Milwaukee, Wis.

    1 Water Hare, De Funiak Springs, Fla.

Wm. Biersach, Milwaukee, Wis.

    1 Sora Rail, Milwaukee, Wis.

Board of City Park Commissioners.

    1 Wapiti, (Cervus canadensis) Captivity, City Parks.

Wm. F. Brummer, Milwaukee, Wis.

    1 Goldfish.

Chas. P. Dadman, National City, Cal.

    3 Shark's Eggs, National City, Cal.

722 Shells,   "   "   "

Dr. A. Duestrow, St. Louis, Mo.

    1 Bittern,   Elkhart, Wis.

    1 American Hawk Owl,   "   "

    1 Common Tern,   "   "

Ernst Ehlert, Milwaukee, Wis.

    1 Butterfly, Milwaukee, Wis.

John Ericsson, Milwaukee, Wis.

    212 Shells, Hayti, West Indies.

W. C. Fish, Milwaukee, Wis.

    1 English Setter, Milwaukee, Wis.

Otto Goethel, Milwaukee, Wis.

    1 Melopsittacus undulatus, Captivity, Milwaukee.

    1 Cardinal,   "   "

    2 Canary Birds,   "   "

Carl Hagenbeck, Hamburg, Germany.

    2 Baboons, India.

    5 Parrots.

    4 Monkeys.

H. Hirsch, Milwaukee, Wis.

    1 American Crow, Milwaukee Co., Wis.

    1 Short-eared Owl, Brookfield, Wis.

    1 Black-bellied Plover, Wisconsin.

    1 Barred Owl, Waukesha Co., Wis.

S. Kander, Milwaukee, Wis.

    1 Gorgonid, Anastasia Isl., Fla.

    4 Shells,   "   "   "

Adolph Meinecke, Milwaukee Wis.

    1 Saw-whet Owl, Milwaukee Wis.

    4 Turtles, Gotha, Orange Co., Fla.

    1 Frog,   "   "   "   "

    1 Rabbit,   "   "   "   "

    68 Beetles, Germany.

J. Middaugh, Janesville, Wis.

    1 Bat, Florida.

Carl Miller, Milwaukee, Wis.

    5 Gorgonids,   West Africa.

    2 Leopard's Teeth   "

    1 Antelope's Foot,   "

    2 Teeth of Saw-fish,   "

    2 Tusks of a young Elephant,   "

    4 Scorpions,   "

    3 Scolopendra,   "

    4 Locusts,   "

    2 Pteropus,   "

    2 Lizards,   "

    4 Snakes,   "

    1 Spider,   "

    115 Butterflies,   "

    54 Beetles,   "

Walter Nehrling, Milwaukee, Wis.

    1 Murex,

    1 Ovenbird, Milwaukee, Wis.

Geo. Orth, Jr., Milwaukee, Wis.

    1 Virginia Rail, Milwaukee, Wis.

Ch. Preusser, Milwaukee, Wis.

    2 Porcupines,   Gogebic, Mich.

    4 Broad-winged Hawks,   "

    1 Mink,   "

    1 White Rabbit,   "

1 Great Blue Heron,   Gogebic, Mich.
1 Least Bittern,   "
1 Sora Rail,   "
2 Red Squirrels,   "
1 Bonaparte's Gull,   "
1 Sharp-shinned Hawk,   "
1 Sora Rail, Milwaukee, Wis.

Gustav Preusser, Milwaukee, Wis.

1 Western Fox Squirrel, Carlton, Montana.
2 Jack Rabbits,   "   "
1 Magpie,   "   "
1 Jay,   "   "
2 Coyotes or Prairie Wolves, Missoula, Mont.

Dr. J. J. Quelch, Georgetown, B. G.

1 Ants' Nest, British Guiana.

J. Reinhold, Milwaukee, Wis.

1 Cedar Waxwing, Milwaukee, Wis.

August Stirn, Milwaukee, Wis.

1 Sora Rail,   Milwaukee Co., Wis.
1 American Sparrow Hawk,   "   "
1 Tropical Bird, Nicaragua, C. A.
1 Golden Eagle, North America.
4 Temenuchus pagodorum, India.
1 Wasps' Nest, Pine Lake, Wis.

Geo. B. Turner, Milwaukee, Wis.

1 Fox Sparrow, Milwaukee, Wis.
1 Snake, Milwaukee Co., Wis.
1 English Sparrow, Milwaukee, Wis,

Wm. Vogel, Milwaukee, Wis.

1 Road-runner, Santa Ana, Cal.
112 Tropical Butterflies.
70 Moths.

John Wegener, Milwaukee, Wis.

1 Sora Rail, Milwaukee, Wis.

Mrs. G. F. Weiss, Milwaukee, Wis.

1 Robin, Milwaukee, Wis.

R ounsevelle Wildman, World's Fair Commissioner for Johore.

1 Alophonerpes pulverulentus, Johore, Malayan Peninsula.
1 Ptilocichla leucogaster,   "   "   "
1 Arachnothera modesta,   "   "   "
1 Macronus ptilosus,   "   "   "

1 Cinnyris pectoralis,	Johore, Malayan Peninsula.
1 Megalema duvaucelli,	" " "
1 Callolophus malaccensis,	" " "
1 Osmotreon fulvicollis,	" " "
1 Palaeornis longicauda,	" " "
1 Halcyon pileata,	" " "
1 Pycnonotus plumosus,	" " "
1 Artamus leucogaster,	" " "
10 other tropical birdskins,	" " "

L. Woltersdorf, Chicago.

  1 Zebra Finch, Australia.

(?) Boa constrictor.

ACQUIRED BY PURCHASE.

1 Black Bear, Michigan.

3 Black Bears, Shawano, Wis.

2 Pine Martens, Gogebic, Mich.

1 Vertebrae of Whale, Milwaukee, Wis.

1 Otter Group

1 Skunk Group.

1 American Badger Group.

1 Red Fox Group.

2 Red Foxes, Glidden, Wis.

1 Ermine,   "

1 Puma,

1 Fisher, Gogebic, Mich.

1 Myrmecophaga tridactyla,   Honduras, C. A

1 Monkey,   "

1 Nose-bear or Mexican Coati (Nasua narica),   "

2 Deer,   "

1 Ermine, Gogebic, Mich.

1 Fisher,   "

1 Lynx,   "

1 Skunk, Glidden, Wis.

1 Skeleton with Muscular Areas.

2 Phascolarctos cinereus, Australia.

1 Cholopus hofmanni, Costa Rica.

7 Didelphys virginianus, Hancock Co., Miss.

1 Proteles lalandii, Cape Colony.

1 Felis yaguarandi, South America.

1 Canis procyonoides, Japan.

1 Sciurus malabaricus, Malabar, India.
1 Pteropus jubatus, Singapore.
1 Cyclothúrus didactylus, Trinidad.
1 Sciurus niger, Mt. Pleasant, S. C.
1 Phalangista fuliginosa, N. S. Wales.
1 Dasyurus maculatus, Van Diemansland.
1 Perameles nasuta, New South Wales.
1 Sciurus rafflesii, Borneo.
1 Bassaris astuta, Texas.
1 Guerza rueppeli, West Africa.
3 Macropus giganteus, Australia.
73 Tropical Butterflies.
1 Pileated Woodpecker, Gogebic, Mich.
10 Tyrannus melancholicus satrapa, Escondido River, Nicaragua.
2 Pitangus derbianus,   "   "   "
1 Megarhynchus pitangus,   "   "   "
3 Progne chalybea,   "   "   "
1 Tachycineta albilinea.   "   "   "
1 Phlogothraupis sanguineolenta,   "   "   "
2 Campephilus guatemalensis,   "   "   "
3 Piaya cayana mehleri,   "   .   "   "
4 Pteroglossus torquatus,   "   "   "
4 Crotophaga sulcirostris,   "   "   "
4 Ramphastos brevicarinatus,   "   "   "
2 Jacana spinosa,   "   "   "
3 Thamnophilus melanocrissus,   "   "   "
3 Melanerpes purcherani,   "   "   "
1 Ceryle amazona,   "   "   "
2 Saltator magnoides,   "   "   "
8 Myiozetetes texensis,   "   "   "
5   "   granadensis,   "   "   "
5 Myiarchus lawrencei nigricapillus,   "   "   "
4 Ramphocelus passerinii.   "   "   "
2 Manacus candaei,   "   "   "
2 Cercomacra tyrannica,   "   "   "
2 Chlorophanes spiza,   "   "   "
5 Arbelorhina lucida,   "   "   "
1 Coereba lucida,   "   "   "
6 Oryzoborus funereus,   "   "   "
7 Sporophila corvina,   "   "   "
1 Thamnophilus doliatus,   "   "   "

2 Tanagra cana,   Escondido River, Nicaragua.
1 Elainea pagana subpagana,   "   "   "
1 Synallaxis pudica,   "   "   "
1 Calliste larvata,   "   "   "
2 Chlorophanes spiza,   "   "   "
2 Pipra mentalis,   "   "   "
1 Coereba mexicana,   "   "   "
2 Euetheia lepida,   "   "   "
1 Euphonia hirundinacea,   "   "   "
1 Hylophilus decurtatus,   "   "   "
2 Formicivora boucardi,   "   "   "
3 Todirostrum cinereum,   "   "   "
1 Thaethornis longirostris, "   "   "
1 Melisuga minima,   "   "   "
1 Aithurus polytimus,   "   "   "
6 Amazilia fuscicauduata, •   "   "   "
2 Ardea coerulea,   "   "   "
1 Trogon atricollis tenellus, "   "   "
3 Phoenicothraupis salvini, "   "   "
1 Peristera cinerea,   "   "   "
2 Embernagra striaticeps,   "   "   "
7 Glyphorhynchus cuneatus, "   "   "
1 Ceophloeus pileatus, Gegebic, Mich.
1 White-necked Raven, Tombstone, Arizona.
1 Coppery-tailed Trogon, Ft. Huachuca, Arizona.
1 Broad-tailed Hummingbird, Huachuca Mts., Arizona.
1 Wilson's Warbler, Hamilton, Canada.
2 Juncos, Boulder, Colorado.
1 Arizona Junco, Ft. Huachuca, Arizona.
2 Townsend's Juncos, San Pedro Martir, Lower Cal.
2 Thurber's Juncos, San Diego Co., Cal.
2 White-naped Nuthatches, San Pedro Martir, Lower Cal.
132 Tropical Birdskins, U. S. of Colombia.
207   "   "   British Guiana.
2 Arizona Cardinals, Cameron Co., Texas.
2 Saint Lucas Cardinals, Lower Cal.
2 Broad-billed Hummingbirds, Nacosari, Sonora.
1 Florida Wren, Tarpon Springs, Fla.
1 Hermit Warbler, San Jose del Cabo, Lower Cal.
1 Centurus uropygialis, Triumfo, Lower Cal.
1 Heleodytes brunneicapillus, Mexico.

2 St. Lucas Thrashers, La Paz, Lower Cal.

1 St. Lucas Robin, Sierra de la Laguna, Lower Cal.

2 Aphelocoma hypotenea, National City, Cal.

2 Carpodectes nitidus, Escondido River, Nicaragua.

1 Lamprocolius splendida, Central Africa.

1 Rhamphocoelus nigrogularis, Brazil.

1 Merops rubricollis, Phillipines.

1 Megalaema versicolor, Malacca.

1 Phyllornis hardwickii, Hindostan.

1 Cinclostoma punctata, Tasmania.

1 Chalcites plagosus, Victoria.

1 Coracios indica, Malabar.

1 Pitta cyanoptera, Borneo.

1 Cymbirhynchus macrorhynchus, Malacca.

1 Procnias tersa, Brazil.

1 Epimachus maximus, New Guinea.

1 Seleucides nigricans,   "

1 Penelope jacutinga, Brazil.

1 Coereba cyanea,   "

1 Cinnirys afer, Cape Colony.

1 Rhamphocoelus brasilia, Brazil.

1   "   icteronotus, Ecuador.

1 Cissopis major, Rio Janeiro.

1 Ptilornis victoriae, Queensland.

1 Semioptera wallacii, Batchian.

1 Diphyllodes speciosa, New Guinea.

1 Ptilornis magnifica,   "

1 Querula cruentata, Venezuela.

1 Rhamphastos ariel, South America.

1 Thaumalea amherstiae, Thibet.

1 Rhamphastos toucardi, Costa Rica.

1 Turacus gigas, Sierra Leone.

2 Phasianus torquatus, China.

1 Temenuchus pagodarum, India.

1 Geopelia cuneata, Australia.

1 Aethopyga temminckii, Borneo.

1 Pericrocotus montanus, India.

1 Ptilornis paradisea, New South Wales.

1 Drepanornis albertisi, New Guinea.

1 Turacus albocristatus, S. Africa.

1 Acryllium vulturina, Africa.

1 Ceriornis satyra, Himalaya Mountains.

1 Cotinga amabilis alba, Demerara.

1 Garrulax ocellatus, Nepal.

1 Mimeta viridis, Sydney.

1 Treron olax, Mt. Kalulong, Sarawak.

1 Paradigalla carunculata, New Guinea.

1 Pitta maxima, Batchian.

2 Lobiophasis bulweri, Baram River, Borneo.

1 Polyplectron bicalcaratum, India.

1 Ceriornis melanocephala, Himalaya Mountains.

1 Calyptorhynchus banksii, Queensland.

1 Scythrops novae hollandiae, Australia.

1 Apteryx mantelli, New Zealand.

BOTANY.

DONATIONS.

J. J. Quelch, Georgetown, B. G.
  1 Caoutchouc from Ballata Tree, British Guiana.
  4 Palm Logs,   "

MINERALOGY.

DONATIONS.

E. N. Bacon, Milwaukee, Wis.
  10 Minerals, Michigan.
Jos. Crunican, Butte City, Montana.
  3 Minerals, Butte City, Mont.
S. Kander, Milwaukee, Wis.
  1 Calcite, Williams Canon, Colorado.
J. J. Kinrade, Milwaukee, Wis.
  1 Schist, Marion Co., Cal.
  3 Calcites, Kern Co., Cal.
  1 Jasper, San Mateo Co., Cal.
  1 Pectolite, New Zealand,
  1 Actinolite, Humboldt, Cal.
Hy. Klunder, Milwaukee, Wis.
  1 Mineral, Miles City, Montana.
Adolph Meinecke, Milwaukee, Wis.
  1 Pyrite, Milwaukee Co., Wis.

Hy. Nehrling, Milwaukee, Wis.

    1 Raw Asphalt, Pitch Lake, at La Brea, Trinidad.

    1 Glance Asphalt, Montserrat, Trinidad.

    1 Copal, Johore.

L. N. Skinner, Milwaukee, Wis.

    1 Asbestos, Elsinor, Cal.

ACQUIRED BY PURCHASE.

1 Fluorite, Cumberland, England.

6 Calcites,   "   "

1 Tin Ore, Black Hills, D. T.

1 Zinc Blende,   Cumberland, England.

2 Barites,   "   "

1 Zinc and Fluorite,   "   "

PALÆONTOLOGY.

DONATIONS.

E. N. Bacon, Milwaukee, Wis.

    1 Orthoceras annulatum, Wisconsin.

August Fiebelkorn, Cascade, Wis.

    1 Halysites, Cascade, Wis.

S. Kander, Milwaukee, Wis.

    1 Coral, Milwaukee, Wis.

    1 Coquina, Anastasia Isl., Fla.

C. M. Odell, Milwaukee, Wis.

    1 Medley of Fossils, Milwaukee, Wis.

Frank Sholes, Milwaukee, Wis.

    3 Fossil Shells.

August Stirn, Milwaukee, Wis.

    1 Conglomerate of Shells, Pine Lake, Wis.

Frank W. Suelflow, Milwaukee, Wis.

    1 Petrified Wood, Freistadt, Wis.

ETHNOLOGY.

DONATIONS.

Alexander Goethel, Milwaukee, Wis.

    1 Snuff-box, made of Brass, with engravings, about 100 years old.

Edward E. Harris, Milwaukee, Wis.

    Old Newspaper, called "Hampshire Herold," No. 165 of 1785.

Carl Miller, Milwaukee, Wis.

1 Mohammedan Gown, embellished with Woolen Embroidery, West Africa.

2 Household Baskets, twisted of Banana Fibres, Upper Niger River, West Africa.

1 Household Basket, twisted of Reed, Gold Coast, West Africa.

4 Table Cloths, West Africa.

5 Calabashes and Covers, embellished with Allegoric Figures, Gold Coast, West Africa.

2 Ornamented Calabashes, Gold Coast, West Africa.

3 Covers of Ornamented Calabashes, " "

2 Calabashes with Allegoric Figures, " "

3 Household Baskets, made of Reed and Banana Fibres, Gold Coast, West Africa.

1 Basket, made of Banana Fibres, Gold Coast, West Africa.

3 Trays, twisted of Banana Fibres, " "

4 Trays, twisted of Reed, " "

1 Tray-like Fan, twisted of Reed and trimmed with Leather, Gold Coast, West Africa.

1 Table Cloth, Gold Coast, West Africa.

3 Caps, twisted of Reed, " "

3 Caps, twisted of Banana Fibres, " "

1 Mohammedan Hat, twisted of Reed and ornamented with Leather, Gold Coast, West Africa.

1 Basket, twisted of Reed, Gold Coast, West Africa.

1 Fan, twisted of Palm Leaves, Akem, West Africa.

1 Hunting Bag, twisted of Reed, Salaga, West Africa.

1 Shield, made of Elephant Skin, Gold Coast, West Africa.

2 Battle Axes of Achantee Warriors, " "

1 Chief's Sword with Metal Handle, ornamented Scabbard and Pendants, Salaga, West Africa.

2 Swords with Leather Scabbards and Pendants, West Africa.

3 Quivers and Arrows, "

1 Violin and Bow, constructed of a Calabash and covered with Snake skin, West Africa.

1 Achantee Chief's Spear, "

1 Achantee Chief's Spear, with wooden Shaft, "

1 Achantee Chief's Spear, with iron Shaft, "

1 Warrior's Spear, with wooden Shaft, "

1 Chief's Bow, with Bast String, "

2 Warriors' Bows, with Leather String, "

1 Chief's Weapon with Leather Handle, made of Antelope Horn, West Africa.

2 Knives, with Scabbard,   Salaga, West Africa.

1 Dagger, with Leather Scabbard,   "   "

1 Dagger, with Scabbard,   "   "

1 Money-bag, of Leather,   "   "

2 Soup Ladles of Wood, with a carved gun-like handle, Gold Coast, West Africa.

1 Drum,   West Africa.

1 King's Seat,   "

3 Achantee Pipes, made of black Clay,   "

1 Pair of Boots, made of Kid Leather, ornamented with straw-work,   West Africa.

1 Pair of Warrior' Sandals,   "

1 Pair of Shoes, of Kid Leather,   "

2 Pairs of ornamented Shoes, with single Soles,   "

1 Pair of Chief's Shoes,   "

5 Achantee Pipes of red Clay,   "

2 Combs, made of Wood,   "

1 Knitting Machine,   "

4 Wooden Bracelets with Copper and Zinc Decorations, Salaga, West Africa.

2 Ivory Bracelets, Salaga, West Africa.

4 Copper Bracelets,   "   "

1 Barbed Spear, made of Brass, West Africa.

1 Dress of Negro, woven of Reed and colored with Indigo, West Africa.

1 Allegoric Figure, made of Brass, representing a warrior sitting in a chair, holding his gun, West Africa.

1 Allegoric Figure, made of Brass, representing a musician, playing upon his instrument,   West Africa.

1 Bird Cage, made of Brass,   "

1 Achantee's Seat, made of Brass,   "

1 King's Seat, made of Brass,   "

1 Allegoric Figure, made of Brass, representing two Achantees, greeting each other,   West Africa.

1 Duck, made of Brass,   "

1 Bird-trap, made of Brass,   "

1 Cannon, made of Brass,   "

1 Bird, made of Brass,   "

1 Quadruped, made of Brass,   "

1 Turtle and Young, made of Brass,   West Africa.

1 Allegoric Figure, made of Brass, representing a woman, nursing her child,   West Africa.

1 Weapon, made of Brass   "

1 Shield, made of Brass,   "

1 Allegoric Figure, made of Brass,   "

5 Gold-weights, made of Brass,   "

1 Shield, made of Brass, used for weighing Gold,   "

2 Scoops, made of Brass, used for weighing Gold,   "

1 Casket, made of Brass, used for weighing Gold,   "

1 Hand, made of Brass, and holding a pistol,   "

1 Bird, make of Brass, taking Food,   "

1 Scale, made of Brass, used for weighing Gold,   "

Adolph Muenzenberger, Sabinal, Mexico.

1 Wooden Bowl, Pacific Coast.

1 piece of Guadalajara Pottery, Mexico.

1 piece of Pottery of Ancient Design, near Village of San Juan de Testihuacan.

1 Necklace, Casas Grandes, Chihuahua, Mexico.

Peter Weber, Milwaukee, Wis.

1 Certificate of Membership of the Milwaukee Fire Department, issued to Mr. Weber in 1854.

Rounsevelle Wildman.

4 Brass Cake Moulds,   Johore, Malayan Peninsula.

4 Pitties' or Tin Coins,   "   "   "

8 Cake Forms, made of Brass,   "   "   "

3 Wooden Stirring Ladles,   "   "   "

1 Rattan Broom,   "   "   "

1 Cocoanut Broom,   "   "   "

2 Brass Cooking Bowls,   "   "   "

1 Three-legged Iron Stool for Fire,   "   "   "

1 Vessel for Cooking,   "   "   "

1 Copper Cooking Pot,   "   "   "

1 Dry Measure for the Household,   "   "   "

2 Earthen Cooking Pots with Rattan Basket Receiver, Johore, Malayan Peninsula.

1 Earthen Urn,   Johore, Malayan Peninsula.

1 Basket with Top for straining Cocoanut, for making Curry, Johore, Malayan Peninsula.

1 Betel Nut Case,   Johore, Malayan Peninsula.

1 Sieve,   "   "   "

1 Drying Basket,	Johore, Malayan Peninsula.		
1 Kneading Board,	"	"	"
1 Green Clay Food Cover,	"	"	"
1 Copper Pan,	"	"	"
1 Brass Candlestick,	"	"	"
1 Chopping Knife,	"	"	"
1 Cocoanut Grater,	"	"	"
1 Cocoanut shell Dipper,	"	"	"
1 Cooking Utensil,	"	"	"
1 Cover of Cooking Vessel,	"	"	"
1 Bali or Malayan Court House,	"	"	"

1 Campong or Village Mosque from Malayan Fishing Town, Johore, Malayan Peninsula.

ACQUIRED BY PURCHASE.

1 Medicine Man's Necklace from Big Road.   (Chamka Tanka.) Ogalalla Chief.

1 Pappoose Hood.

1 Knife Scabbard and Tail Ornament.

1 Necklace, made of Bone and Beads.

1 Medicine Man's Necklace.

1 Necklace.

1 Hair Ornament.

1 Moose-hair Ornament.

1 Feather Turban.

1 Hair Ornament.

1 Hair-brush.

2 Squaw Clubs.

1 War Club.

1 Tomahawk Pipe, probable of French origin.

2 Pipes.

1 War Club.

1 Medicine Man's Bone Mallet.

1 Fish-line.

1 Pair of Moccasins.

1 War Bonnet.

1 Ceremonial Spoon.

3 Spoons.

1 War Shirt with genuine Scalps.

1 Quirt, with horn Handle.

1 Bone Spoon and Mallet.

1 Dance Rattle, worn on right knee.

1 Halibut Hook for deep sea fishing.

1 Porcupine Quill Work.

ARCHÆOLOGY.

DONATIONS.

August Fiebelkorn, Cascade, Wis.

    3 Stone Arrowheads, Cascade, Wis.

Bernhard G. Heyn, Milwaukee, Wis.

    1 Stone Celt with Deer Horn Handle, Pile Dwellings, Switzerland

H. C. Mansfield, Jefferson, Wis.

    21 Flint Arrowheads, Jefferson, Wis.

Horace McElroy, Janesville, Wis.

    4 Fragments of Flint Implements, Janesville, Wis.

Frank Sholes, Milwaukee, Wis.

    1 Flint Scraper,   Wisconsin.

    8 Flint Arrowheads,   ''

Geo. B. Turner, Milwaukee, Wis.

    4 Wrought Flint Stones, Indian Mound near Mandan, Dak.

ACQUIRED BY PURCHASE.

5000 Stone Arrowheads and Spearheads,	Wisconsin.
39 Leaf-shaped Stone Implements,	"
101 Stone Celts,	"
4 Broken Flint Implements,	"
1 Stone Sinker,	"
186 Stone Axes,	"
35 Spherical Stone Implements,	"
4 Oval Stone Implements,	"
1 Cast of Pipe,	"
3 Biconcave disc-shaped Implements,	"
1 Pebble Stone Implement,	"
5 Indian War Club Stones,	"
2 Chisel-shaped Copper Implements,	"
9 Copper Spearheads with clasping Base,	"
3 Copper Spearheads with straight Base,	"
1 Copper Knife,	"
1 Copper Spike,	"

5 Indian Pipes,	Wisconsin.
3 Flat, drilled, polished Stone Implements,	"
2 Polished Stone Implements,	"
1 Stone Pipe,	"
1 Chisel-shaped Stone Implement,	"
1 Stone Implement,	"

LIBRARY.

Academy of Science, of St. Louis, Mo.
>Transactions, Vol. VI, Nos. 9–11, 17.
>The Academy of Science, of Saint Louis.

American Museum of Natural History, New York.
>Bulletin, 1893.
>Annual Report for 1893.

Annaberg-Buchholzer Verein fuer Naturkunde, Annaberg, Germany.
>IX. Bericht fuer 1888–1893.

Australian Museum, Sydney,
>Annual Report for 1892.
>Records of the Australian Museum, Vol. II, No. 5.
>Annual Progress Report of the Geol. Survey for 1891 and 1892.
>The Kangaroo Hills Silver and Tin Mines.
>Geol. Observations in British New Guinea, 1891.
>Report on Styx River Coal Field.
>Report on the Grass-tree Gold Field near Mackay.
>Geolog. Observations in the Cooktown District.

Bergens Museum, Bergen, Norway.
>Aarsberetning for 1891.
>Aarbog for 1892.

Blackburn Free Public Library, Blackburn.
>Report for 1893–1894.

F. Boettger, Peoria, Ill.
>Flora Peoriana, 1887.

Boston Society of Natural History, Boston, Mass.
>Proceedings, Vol. XXVI, Part I.

Botanischer Verein der Provinz Brandenburg, Berlin, Germany.
>33. und 34. Jahrg., 1891 und 1892.

Bureau of Education, Washington, D. C.
>Biological Teaching in the Colleges of the U. S., 1891.
>The History of higher Education in Ohio, 1891.
>Abnormal Man, etc.

Benjamin Franklin and the University of Pennsylvania, 1893.

Shorthand Instruction and Practice, 1893.

The History of Education in Delaware.

The Spelling Reform.

Catalogue of "A. L. A." Library, 5,000 Vols. for a popular library selected by the Am. Library Association.

Bureau of Ethnology, Washington, D. C.

Eighth Annual Report, 1886–1887.

Bibliography of the Chinookan Languages, 1893.

Ninth Annual Report, 1887–1888.

Bibliography of the Salishan Languages. 1893.

The Maya Year, 1894.

The Pamunka Indians of Virginia, 1894.

Bibliography of the Wakashan Languages, 1894.

Tenth Annual Report, 1888–1889.

Cincinnati Museum Association, Cincinnati, Ohio.

Thirteenth Annual Report, 1893.

Fourth Annual Exhibition of the Cincinnati Art Club, 1894.

Cincinnati Society of Natural History, Cincinnati, Ohio.

The Journal, Vol, XVI, Nos. 2, 3 and 4.

The Journal, Vol. XVII, No. 1.

Detroit Musenm of Art, Detroit, Mich.

Annual Report, 1893.

Deutsch Wissenschaftlicher Verein, Santiago, Chili.

Verhandlungen, 1893.

Geo. L. English & Co., New York City.

Price Lists of Minerals and Mineralogical Supplies, 16th Ed., 1894.

Essex Institute, Salem, Mass.

Bulletins, Vol. 25, Nos. 7, 8, 9, 10, 11, 12.

Free Public Library, Museum and Walker Art Gallery, Liverpool, England.

Forty-first Annual Report.

Gesellschaft für Natur-und Heilkunde zu Dresden, Germany.

Jahresbericht, 1892–1893.

Gesellschaft Naturforschender Freunde zu Berlin, Germany.

Sitzungsberichte, Jahrg. 1893.

Government Central Museum, Madras, India.

Administration Report for 1892–1893.

Historical and Philosophical Society of Ohio.

Annual Report, 1893.

Historical and Scientific Society of Manitoba, Winnipeg.
>Transactions, 45, 46, 47.
>Annual Report, 1893.

Instituto Fisico Geographico y Del Museo Nacional, Costa Rica.
>Anales, Tomo IV, 1891.

International Entomological Society, Zürich-Hottingen, Switzerland.
>Societas Entomologica, VIII Jahrg. 1893.

R. L. Jacks.
>Report on Mount Morgan Gold Deposits.

Journal of Comparative Neurology, Granville, Ohio.
>The Journal, Vol. IV, 1894.

Kansas Academy of Science, Topeka, Kansas.
>Transactions of the 24th and 25th Annual Meetings, Vol. XIII.

K. K. Geologische Reichsanstalt, Wien, Austria.
>Jahrbuch 1893, Bd. XLIII, Heft I, II, III, IV.
>Verhandlungen, No. 6–10, 1893.
>Verhandlungen, No. 1–4, 1894.
>Jahrbuch, XLIV Bd.

Kais. Leopoldino-Carolinische Deutsche Akademie der Naturforscher, Halle, Germany.
>Amtliches Organ, 1892.
>"Leopoldina," 29 Heft, 1893.

K. K. Naturhistorisches Hofmuseum, Wien, Austria.
>Annalen, Bd. VIII, No. 1, 2, 3, 4.
>Annalen, Bd. IX, No. 1.
>Jahresbericht für 1893.

Kgl. Akademie gemeinnütziger Wissenschaften, Erfurt, Germany.
>Jahrbücher, Neue Folge, Heft X1X, XX.

Kgl. Museum für Naturkunde zu Berlin, Germany.
>Die Insecten der Berglandschaft Adeli im Hinterlande von Togo, W. Africa.

Kgl. Preussische Academy der Wissenschaften zu Berlin, Germany.
>Ueber den Fang und die Verwerthung der Walfische in Japan.

Kgl. Sammlung für Kunst und Wissenschaft, Dresden.
>Bericht über die Verwaltung und Vermehrung, 1893.

Kgl. Sächsische Gesellschaft der Wissenschaften, Leipzig, Germany.
>Berichte über die Verhandlungen, IV, V, VI, VII, VIII, 1893; IX, 1894.

Kgl. Vitterheds Akademien, Stockholm, Sweden.
>Manadsblad, 1886–1891.

Kurländische Gesellschaft für Literatur und Kunst, Mitau, Russia.
Sitzungsberichte, 1893.
L'Institute Grand-Ducal de Luxembourg.
Publications, Tomo XXII.
Adolph Meinecke, Milwaukee, Wis.
Zeitschrift für Ethnologie, 25 Jahrg., 1893, Heft 3, 4.
Milwaukee Public Library, Milwaukee, Wis.
Quarterly Index of Additions, Vol. IV, No. 31.
Sixteenth Annual Report, 1893.
Missouri Botanical Garden, St. Louis, Mo.
Fifth Annual Report, 1893.
Missouri Historical Society, St. Louis, Mo.
President's Address for 1894.
Elisha Mitchell Scientific Society, Raleigh, N. C.
Journal for 1893, Part I.
John L. Mitchell, U. S. Senator, Milwaukee, Wis.
Report on Population and Resources of Alaska, 1893.
Abridgement of Message and Documents, 1891–1893.
Compendium of the Tenth Census, 1890, Part II.
Museum Francisco Carolinum, Linz, Austria.
51. Bericht. 1893.
52. Bericht, 1894.
Museo Nacional De Costa Rica.
Etnologica Centro Americana, 1893.
Museo Nacional de Rio Janeiro, Rio de Janeiro.
Archivos, Vol. VIII.
Museo Nacional de Montevideo, Montevideo.
Anales del Muses Nacional de Montevideo, I.
Museum für Naturkunde zu Berlin, Germany.
Beiträge zur Fanna des Togolandes, 1893.
Museum of the Illinois Wesleyan University, Bloomington, Ill.
First Annual Report, 1893.
Museum für Völkerkunde, Leipzig, Germany.
20. Bericht.
Museum of Zoology, Cambridge.
28. Annual Report.
Nassauischer Verein fuer Naturkunde, Wiesbaden, Germany.
Jahrbuecher, Jahrg., 46.
Natural History Society of Glasgow.
Proceedings and Transactions, Vol. III, Part III.

Natural Science Association of Staten Island, Brighton, N. Y.
>Proceedings, Vol. I, II, III, IV.

Naturhistorischer Verein der Preussischen Rheinlande und Westphalens, Bonn, Germany.
>Verhandlungen. 50. Jahrg. 5. Folge, I. Hälfte, II. Hälfte.

Naturhistorisch-Medicinischer Verein, Heidelberg, Germany.
>Verhandlungen, Neue Folge, V. Bd., II. Heft.

Naturforschende Gesellschaft zu Bamberg, Germany.
>XVI. Bericht.

Naturforschende Gesellschaft in Basel, Switzerland.
>Verhandlungen, Bd. X, Heft I.
>Verhandlungen, Bd. IX, Heft III.

Naturforschende Gesellschaft in Bern, Switzerland.
>Mittheilungen fuer 1892.
>Mittheilungen fuer 1893, No. 1305–1334.

Naturforschende Gesellschaft, Emden, Germany.
>77. Jahresbericht, 1891–92.

Naturforschende Gesellschaft des Osterlandes, Altenburg, Germany.
>Verzeichniss der Mitglieder, 1892.

Naturwissenschaftlicher Verein fuer Schleswig Holstein, Kiel.
>Schriften, Bd. 10, Heft I.

Naturwissenschaftlicher Verein des Regierungsbezirks Frankfurt a. M., Germany.
>"Helios," 11. Jahrg. 2–5, 1893.
>"Societatum," 7. Jahrg. 4–7, 1893.

Naturwissenschaftlicher Verein, Magdeburg, Germany.
>Jahresbericht und Abhandlungen, 1892.

Naturwissenschaftlicher Verein zu Bremen, Germany.
>Abhandlungen, XIII. Bd., I. Heft.
>Ueber Einheitlichkeit der botanisehen Kunstausdruecke und Abkuerzungen.

Naturwissenschaftliche Gesellschaft, St. Gallen, Switzerland.
>Bericht, 1891–1892.

Naturwissenschaftliche Gesellschaft "Isis," Dresden, Germany.
>Sitzungsberichte. Jahrg. 1893, Januar bis Juni.
>Sitzungsberichte, Jahrg. 1894.

Naturwissenschaftlicher Verein fuer Steiermark, Graz, Austria.
>Mittheilungen, Jahrg. 1893.

Naturwissenschaftlicher Verein fuer Schwaben und Neuburg, Augsburg.
>31. Bericht.

Henry Nehrling, Milwaukee, Wis.

  Catalogue of the Exhibit of Norway at the World's Columbian
  Exposition.

  Riggs, C. W., How we find Relics.

  Cook, A. J., Birds of Michigan.

New York State Museum, Albany, N. Y.

  Bulletin, Vol. 3, No. 11.

  45th and 46th Annual Report, 1891–1892.

New York Academy of Sciences, New York.

  Transactions, Vol. II, 1893.

  Annals, Vol. VIII, Nos. 1–4.

  Annals, Vol. VII, Nos. 6–12.

  Index of Vol. VI of the Annals.

Nova Scotian Institute of Natural Science, Halifax, N. S.

  Proceedings, Vol. I, Part II and III, Series II.

Oberhessische Gesellschaft fuer Natur-und Heilkunde, Giessen, Germany.

  29. Bericht, 1893.

Observatorio Astronomico Nacional, Tacubaya.

  Boletin, Tornf I.orns I, No. 14, 15, 16, 17.

  Annuario XIV, 1894.

Geo. W. Peckham, Milwaukee, Wis.

  Description des Brachi opodes, Bryozoaires, etc., des Terraines
  Crelaces de la Region Lud Des Aants, Plateaux de la
  Tunisii, 1885–86.

  Exploration Scientifique de la Tunisii.   Illustrations.

  Description de Quelgues Fossiles Nouveaux ou Criligues des
  Terraines, etc.

Physikalischer Verein zu Frankfurt, a. M., Germany.

  Jahresbericht, 1891–1892.

Physikalisch Medicinische Societät, Erlangen.

  Sitzungsberichte, 25. Heft, 1893.

Physik. Oekonomische Gesellschaft, Königsberg, Germany.

  Schriften, 33. Jahrg., 1892.

  Schriften, 34. Jahrg., 1893.

J. W. Rickert.

  Guide to the Museum of the Society in Taunton Castle.

Rochester Academy of Science, Rochester, N. Y.

  Proceedings, Vol. II, 1893.

Royal Irish Academy, Dublin, Ireland.

  Proceedings, III. Series, Vol. II, No. 4, 5.

  Proceedings, III. Series, Vol. III, No. 1, 2.

  Transactions, Vol. XXX, Part V–XII.

Schlesische Gesellschaft fuer vaterländische Cultur, Breslau, Germany.

    70. Jahresbericht, 1892.

    Ergänznngsheft zum 70. Jahresbericht.

Schweizerische Naturforschende Gesellschaft, Basel, Switzerland.

    Verhandlungen, 1892.

Schweizerische Naturforschende Gesellschaft, Lausanne, Switzerland.

    Verhandlungen, 1893.

Senckenbergische Naturforschende Gesellschaft, Frankfurt a. M., Germany.

    Katalog der Reptilien Sammlung, I. Theil.

    Bericht fuer 1892–93.

Smithsonian Institution, Washington, D. C.

    Annual Report for the year ending June 30, 1891.

    Contributions toward a Monograph of the Noctuidae of Boreal America.

    Notes on Myriapoda from Loanda, Africa.

    Annual Report to July, 1892.

Siebenbuergischer Verein fuer Naturwissenschaften, Hermannstadt.

    Verhandlungen und Mittheilungen, 1892.

Société Entomologique de France, Paris.

    Bulletins Nos. 1–9, 1894.

Sociéteé Imperiale des Naturalistes, Moscou Russia.

    Bulletin, 1893, No. 1, 2, 3,

Société De Physique et D'Histoire Naturelle De Genéve.

    Compte Rendu Des Séances de la Société de Physique et D'Histoire Naturelle.

Société Scientifique du Chili, Santiago.

    Actes de la Société Scientifique, Tomo III, 1893.

       "   "   "   "   " IV, 1894.

Stavanger Museum, Stavanger, Norway.

    Aarsberetning for 1892.

William Trelease, St. Louis, Mo.

    Sugar Maples, and Maples in Winter.

    The North American Species of Gayophytum und Boisduvalia.

    Leitneria Floridana.

Tufts College of Massachusetts.

    Studies No. 1.

U. S. Coast and Geodetic Survey, Washington, D. C.

    Report of the Superintendent for 1891, Part I, II.

U. S. Department of Agriculture, Washington, D. C.

    The Prairie Ground Squirrels, 1893.

Food Products, I, II, III.

Report of the Microscopist for 1892.

Report on Irrigation, 1893.

Report of the Statistician, New Series, Report 116.

Peach Yellows and Peach Rosette.

U. S. Department of the Interior, Washington, D. C.

Report of the Commissioner, 1889–90, Vol. I, II.

Report of the Secretary, being part of the Message and Documents to Congress, Vol. II.

U. S. Fish Commission, Washington, D. C.

Bulletin, Vol. XI for 1891.

U. S. Geological Survey, Washington, D. C.

Eleventh Annual Report, 1889–1890, Part I, II.

Twelfth Annual Report, 1890–1891, Part I, II.

Bulletins Nos. 85–86.

" Nos. 90–117.

Mineral Resources of the U. S., 1891–1892.

Monographs of the U. S. Geolog. Survey, Vols. XIX–XXII.

U. S. National Museum, Washington, D. C.

A Descriptive Catalogue of the Harvest Spiders.

Scientific Results of the U. S. Eclipse Expedition to West Africa.

Bulletin No. 43, 44, 45, 46.

Proceedings, Vol. XIV, 1891.

" Vol. XV, 1892.

Shufeldt, Dr. R. W. Scientific Taxidermy for Museums.

U. S. War Department, Washington, D. C.

The War of the Rebellion, Ser. I, Vol. XLI, Part IV.

" " " Ser. I, Vol. XLII, Part I to III.

" " " Ser. I, Vol. XLIII, Part I, II.

" " " Ser. I, Vol. XLIV.

" " " Ser. I, Vol. XLV, Part I, II.

Vassar Brothers Institute, Poughkeepsie, N. Y.

Transactions, 1891–93, Vol. VI.

Verein fuer Erdkunde zu Darmstadt, Germany.

Notizblatt, IV. Folge, 14. Heft.

Verein fuer Erdkunde zu Leipzig, Germany.

Mittheilungen, 1893.

Verein der Freunde der Naturgeschichte in Mecklenburg.

Archiv des Vereins, 47. Jahrg., 1893.

Verein fuer die Geschichte der Stadt Nuernberg, Germany.

    Mittheilungen, 10. Heft.

    Jahresbericht, 15. Vereinsjahr.

Verein fuer Geschichte und Naturgeschichte der Baar, Tuebingen.

    Schriften, 1893.

Verein Luxemburger Naturfreunde, Luxemburg.

    "Fauna," Jahrg. 1893, Heft 5, 6.

        "   "   1894, Heft 1, 2, 3.

Verein fuer das Museum Schlesischer Alterthuemer, Breslau

    Schlesiens Vorzeit in Bild und Schrift, Bd. VI, Heft I.

Verein fuer Naturkunde zu Kassel, Germany.

    39. Bericht, 1892–1894.

Vorarlberger Museums Verein, Bregenz, Austria.

    31. Jahresbericht, 1892.

Mrs. R. D. Whitehead, Milwaukee, Wis.

    Magnus Hippocrates Cous Prosperi Martiani of 1719.

Wisconsin Academy of Sciences, Arts and Letters, Madison, Wis.

    Transactions, Vol. IX, Part I, II.

Wyoming Commemorative Association, Wilkesbarre, Pa.

    Historical Address by Greenough Scott.

    Union Services at the Old Forty Fort Church on June 15, 1888.

Mrs. Sophie Zimmermann, Chino, Cal.

    "Zoe," a Biological Journal, Vol. II, No. 4, Jan. 1892.

Zoological Society of Philadelphia, Pa.

    Twenty-second Annual Report, 1894.

ACQUIRED BY PURCHASE.

The "American Naturalist." Vol. XXVII, 1893.

The "Auk." A Quarterly Journal of Ornithology.

    Vol. X, No. 4.

    Vol. XI, Nos. 1 to 3.

Sievers, Prof. Dr. Wilh. "Amerika," Eine allgemeine Landeskunde.

    "   "   "   "Asien,"   "   "   "

    "   "   "   "Africa,"   "   "   "

Zittel, Karl A., Handbuch der Palæontology, IV. Bd., II. und III. Lfg.

Keep, Josia. West Coast Shells.

Neumayer, Dr. M. Erdgeschickte.

Brockhaus, F. A. Konversation Lexicon, Bd. VII to X.

Moorehead, W. K. The Archaeologist, Vol. II, No. 1–8.

Engler and Prantl. Die natuerlichen Pflanzenfamilien, Lfg. 87 to 105.

Edwards, W. H.   The Butterflies of North America.
    III. Series, Part 14, 15.
Darwin, Chas.   The various Contrivances by which Orchids are fertilized
    by Insects.
Darwin, Chas.   Insectivorous Plants.
Duncan, James.   Beetles, British and Foreign.
Woodward, S. P.   A Manual of Mollusca.
Cooke and Berkeley.   Fungi, their Nature and Uses.
Foster, J. W.   Prehistoric Races of the U. S. of America.
Calwer, Dr. C. J.   Naturgeschichte der Käfer Europas.
Abbott, Chas. C.   Primitive Industry.
Knauber, Fried. Dr.   Handwörterbuch der Zoologie.
Eaton, D. C.   Ferns of North America, Vol. I, II.
Carus, Prof. J. Victor.   Zoologischer Anzeiger, Jahrg. I–XVI.
Cabanis, Prof. Dr. Jean.   Journal fuer Ornithologie, Jahrg. 1876.
    "   "   "   "   "   "   " 1879–1882.
    "   "   "   "   "   "   " 1884–1892.
    "   "   "   "   "   "   " 1893.
    "   "   "   "   "   "   " 1894, Heft I,
    II, III.
"Die Natur" fuer 1893.
Hornaday, Wm. T.   Taxidermy and Zoolog. Collection.
Davie, Oliver.   Methods in the Art of Taxidermy.
English, Geo. L. & Co., Catalogue of Minerals and Mineralogical
    Supplies.

Laws of Wisconsin Concerning the Public Museum.

(330, A.)   (Published April 13, 1882.)

CHAPTER 329.

AN ACT relating to the Natural History Society of the City of Milwaukee.

The People of the State of Wisconsin, represented in Senate and Assembly, do enact as follows:

SECTION 1. The board of directors of the Natural History Society of the City of Milwaukee is hereby authorized and empowered, in the name of said association or society, to assign, transfer and convey to the City of Milwaukee, all and singular, the natural historical collections of every kind constituting the Museum belonging to said Natural History Society, in trust, to be kept, supported and maintained by said city, as a free Museum for the benefit and use of all citizens of said city, provided, the said city shall accept the trust and assume the care and maintenance of such Museum.

SEC. 2. This act shall take effect and be in force from and after its passage and publication.

Approved March 31, 1882.

(No. 329, A.)   (Published April 14, 1882.)

CHAPTER 328.

AN ACT to authorize the City of Milwaukee to establish and maintain a Public Museum in said city.

The people of the State of Wisconsin, represented in Senate and Assembly, do enact as follows :

SECTION 1. The City of Milwaukee is hereby authorized to receive and accept from "The Natural History Society of Wisconsin"—a corporation located in the said City of Milwaukee—a donation of its collection of objects in Natural History and Ethnology, or of the greater part thereof, upon such conditions as may be agreed upon by and between said city and said society, subject, however, to the provisions of this act.

SEC. 2. In case of such donation and acceptance, said City of Milwaukee is hereby authorized and empowered to establish and maintain in said city a free Public Museum, exhibitions of objects in Natural History and Ethnology, and for that purpose to receive, hold and manage the collection so donated, and any devise, bequest or donation that may be made to said city for the increase and maintainance of such Museum under such regulations and conditions as are herein contained, or may be agreed upon by and between the donors and said city, or as may be hereafter provided in this act.

SEC. 3. The Museum established and maintained under this act shall be under the general management, control and supervision of a board of nine trustees, who shall be styled "The Board of Trustees of the Public Museum of the City of Milwaukee." Said Board of Trustees shall consist of the president of the School Board and the Superintendent of Schools of said city, ex-officio, of three members of the Common Council of said city, designated and appointed by the Mayor thereof, and of four residents and tax-payers of said city, to be appointed by the Mayor as herein provided. The first appointments of trustees by the Mayor under this act shall be made within ten days after the formal acceptance by the Common Council of said city, of a donation by said Natural History Society, as authorized in the first section of this act. Of the first three trustees appointed from the members of the Common Council of said city, one shall be appointed from the three-year class, one from the two-year class, and one from the one-year class of aldermen, and they shall serve as such trustees during their respective terms as such aldermen. And annually on the third Tuesday of April thereafter, at the expiration of the term of any such trustee, the Mayor shall appoint his successor for three years, from the aldermen then having three years to serve. In case any such trustee shall vacate the office of alderman before the expiration of his term, he shall at the same time cease to be a trustee under this act, and the Mayor shall appoint some other member of the Common Council of his class in his place for the balance of his term. In the appointment of the four remaining trustees and their successors, the Mayor shall prefer such persons as may be recommended for such appointment by said Natural History Society. Such four trustees first appointed shall, at the first meeting of the Board after their appointment, determine by lot their term of service, so that one of their number shall serve for one year, one for two years, one for three years, and one for four years from the third Tuesday of May next after the organization of such Board. And all vacancies shall be filled by like appointment of the Mayor for the remainder of the term, and annually on the third Tuesday of April a trustee shall be appointed by said Mayor in like manner for the term of four years, in place of the trustee whose term shall expire the following May. None of said trustees shall receive any compensation from the city treasury, or otherwise, for their services as such trustees. And no member of said Board of Trustees shall become, or cause himself to become interested, directly or indirectly, in any contract or job for the purchase of any matter pertaining to the Museum, or of fuel, furniture, stationery or things necessary for the increase and maintenance of the Museum. Said trustees shall take the official oath, and be subject to the restrictions, disabilities, liabilities, punishments and limitations prescribed by law as to aldermen in the said City of Milwaukee.

SEC. 4. The first meeting of said Board of Trustees for the purpose of organizing, shall be held on the third Tuesday of the month next following their appointment, and the City Clerk shall give at least one week's previous notice of the time and place of such meeting to each member of such Board in writing. At such first meeting said Board shall organize by the choice of one of their number as president to serve until the third Tuesday of May next following, and until his successor shall be chosen. The annual meeting of said Board shall be held on the third Tuesday of May in each year, and at such meeting a president shall be chosen from their number to serve for one year and until his successor shall be chosen.

SEC. 5. The Board of Trustees shall have general care, control and supervision of the Public Museum, its appurtenances, fixtures and furniture, and of the selection, arrangement and disposition of the specimens and objects appertaining to said Museum, and also of the disbursements of all the moneys appropriated for and belonging to the Museum fund, in the manner hereinafter provided. And the said Board shall adopt, and at their discretion modify, amend or repeal by-laws, rules and regulations for the management, care and use of the Public Museum, and fix and enforce penalties for their violation, and generally shall adopt such measures as shall promote the public utility of the Museum; provided, that such by-laws, rules and regulations shall not conflict with the provisions of this act.

SEC. 6. The Board of Trustees shall, at their first meeting, or thereafter, as soon as practicable and every five years thereafter, at an annual meeting, elect by ballot a person of suitable scientific attainments, ability and experience for custodian, who shall so act and be ex-officio secretary of said Board of Trustees. The custodian first appointed shall hold his office for five years from the time of the first annual meeting, unless previously removed, and thereafter the term of appointment shall be for the term of five years, and the compensation of the custodian shall be fixed by said Board of Trustees. Said Board of Trustees shall also appoint such assistants and employes for said Museum as they may deem necessary and expedient, and shall fix their compensation. All vacancies in the office of custodian, assistants and other employes, shall be filled by said Board of Trustees, and the person so elected or appointed shall hold for the unexpired term.

Sec. 7. The custodian elected under this act may be removed from office for misdemeanor, incompetency or inattention to the duties of his office, by a vote of two-thirds of the Board of Trustees; the assistants and other employes may be removed by the Board for incompetency, or for any other cause.

Sec. 8. It shall be the duty of the Board of Trustees, within ten days after the appointment of the custodian and other salaried employes, to report and file with the City Comptroller a duly certified list of the persons so appointed, with the salary allowed to each, and the time or times fixed for the payment thereof, and they shall also furnish such comptroller with a list of all accounts and bills which may be allowed by said Board of Trustees, stating the character of the materials or service for which the same were rendered, immediately after the meeting of said Board at which such allowance shall be made. And said Board of Trustees shall also, on or before the first day of October in each year, make to the Common Council a report, made up to and including the 31st day of August of the said year, containing a statement of the condition of the Museum and of the additions thereto during the year, together with such information and suggestions as they may deem important, and such report shall also contain an account of the moneys credited to the Museum fund, and expended on account of the same during the year.

SEC. 9. From and after the organization of the Board of Trustees under this act, the Common Council of said city shall levy and collect annually upon all the taxable property of the said city, at the same time and in the same manner as other city taxes are levied and collected by law, a special tax not exceeding one-tenth of a mill upon each dollar of the assessed value of said taxable property, the amount of which shall be determined by said Board of Trustees, and certified to the Common Council at the time of making their annual report to said Council, and the entire amount of said special tax shall be paid into, and held in, the city treasury, as a separate and distinct fund, to be known as the Museum fund, and shall not be used or appropriated, directly or indirectly, in any other purpose than for the maintenance and for the increase of the Public Museum, the payment of the salaries of the custodian, assistant and other employes of the Museum, the purchase of furniture, fixtures, supplies and fuel, and the incidental expenses of the Museum.

SEC. 10. The Board of Trustees shall erect, purchase, hire or lease buildings, lots, rooms and furniture, for the use and accommodation of said Public Museum, and shall improve, enlarge and repair such buildings, rooms and furniture; but no lot or building shall be purchased, erected or enlarged for the purpose herein mentioned, without an ordinance or resolution of the Common Council of said city, and deeds of conveyance and leases shall run to the city of Milwaukee.

SEC. 11. All moneys received by or raised in the city of Milwaukee for Museum purposes shall be paid over to the city treasurer, to be disbursed by him on the orders of the president and secretary of the said Board of Trustees, countersigned by the City Comptroller. Such orders shall be made payable to the order of the persons in whose favor they shall have been issued, and shall be the only voucher of the city treasurer for the payments from the Museum fund. The said Board of Trustees shall provide for the purchase of specimens, supplies, fuel and other matters necessary or useful for the maintenance of the Museum ; provided, however, that it shall not be lawful for said Board of Trustees to expend or contract a liability for any sum in excess of the amount levied in any one year for the Museum fund, on account of such fund.

SEC. 12. All moneys, books, specimens and other property received by the City of Milwaukee by device, bequest or gift, from any person or corporation, for Public Museum purposes, shall, unless otherwise directed by the donors, be under the management and control of said Board of Trustees ; and all moneys derived from fines and penalties for violations of the rules of the Museum, or from any other source in the course of the administration of the Museum, including all moneys which may be paid to the city upon any policy or policies of insurance, or other obligation or liability, or on account of loss or damage to any property pertaining to the Museum, shall belong to the Museum fund in the city treasury, to be disbursed on the orders of the said Board of Trustees, countersigned by the City Comptroller, for Museum purposes in addition to the amount levied and raised by taxation for such fund.

SEC. 13. This act shall take effect and be in force from and after its passage and publication.

Approved March 31, 1882.

(No. 895, A.) (Published April 15, 1887.)

CHAPTER 521.

AN ACT to amend Chapter 328 of the Laws of 1882, authorizing the City of Milwaukee to establish and maintain a Public Museum, and Chapter 7, of the Laws of 1878, to establish a Public Library in the City of Milwaukee.

The people of the State of Wisconsin, represented in Senate and Assembly, do enact as follows:

* * * * * * *

SECTION 2. Hereafter all appointments of members from the Common Council for the Board of Trustees of the Public Museum of the City of Milwaukee, made by the Mayor of said city on the third Tuesday in April, shall be made from aldermen having two years to serve, and in case any person so appointed shall vacate his office of alderman before the expiration of his term, he shall thereupon cease to be a member of said Board of Trustees, and the Mayor shall appoint some other alderman of his class in his place to be such trustee for the remainder of his term. Each alderman appointed shall serve as such trustee during his term as alderman. It shall be the duty of the Mayor on the third Tuesday in April in each year to appoint a sufficient number of aldermen having two years to serve to be members of such Board of Trustees of the Public Museum to keep the number of members of such Board from the Common Council, always three.

All provisions of Chapter 328, of the Laws of 1882, which in any way conflict with the provisions of this section, are hereby amended accordingly.

SEC. 3. This act shall take effect and be in force from and after its passage and publication.

Approved April 14, 1887.

(No. 614, A.)   (Published April 20, 1887.)

CHAPTER 433.

AN ACT to amend Chapter 328, of the Laws of 1882, entitled, "An act to authorize the City of Milwaukee to establish and maintain a Public Museum in said city."

The people of the State of Wisconsin, represented in Senate and Assembly, do enact as follows:

SECTION 1. The Board of Trustees of the Milwaukee Public Museum are hereby authorized to appoint an acting custodian whenever the proper service of the Museum shall require it, and for such time and on such terms as they may deem proper. Such acting custodian shall be ex-officio the acting secretary of said Board of Trustees, and his acts as such shall receive full credit. Said Board of Trustees are also authorized to appoint from time to time honorary curators, who shall perform such duties and have such special privileges as may be provided in the by-laws of the Museum, but shall receive no pecuniary compensation. Such appointments shall be made of persons who have manifested a special interest in the Museum or some particular department thereof.

SEC. 2. This act shall be in force from and after its passage and publication.

Approved April 12, 1887.

RULES GOVERNING THE MUSEUM.

I. MEETINGS.

ART. 1. The regular meetings of the Board shall be held at the Museum rooms on the third Tuesday of each month at 4:30 P. M.

ART. 2. The annual meeting of the Board shall be held on the third Tuesday of May, at 4 P. M.

ART. 3. Special meetings shall be called by the secretary upon the written request of the president, or any three members of the Board, but the object for which the special meeting is called must be stated in the notice, and no business other than the special business shall be transacted at such meeting, unless all the members of the Board are present, and unanimous consent is obtained.

ART. 4. Five members of the Board shall constitute a quorum.

II. OFFICERS AND EMPLOYES.

ART. 5. At the annual meeting in May, the Board shall elect by ballot a president, whose duty it shall be to preside at all meetings of the Board, to sign all warrants drawn on the city treasurer by order of the Board, to appoint the standing committees for the year, and prepare for the consideration and approval of the Board, the annual report of the Board of Trustees, required by Section 8 of the "Public Museum Act."

ART. 6. The duties of the custodian shall be as follows:

To take charge of and exercise control over the museum and library, and to see that the regulations relating thereto are properly carried out.

To exercise control over all employes of the Board and the work allotted to them respectively.

To receive all specimens intended for the Museum, and with the advice and assistance of specialists to classify, label, catalogue and arrange them as soon as possible.

To receive all books and other articles intended for the library, and to label and catalogue them.

To take all precautions necessary for the good preservation of the collections, according to the most approved methods within the means of the institution.

To keep running records, containing all necessary particulars, concerning articles received or disposed of.

To purchase specimens, books and other matter under the general direction of the Board.

To inaugurate a system of exchanges with other natural history museums as soon as possible.

To correspond with scientific societies and public authorities for the purpose of obtaining reports and other documents containing information relating to natural history.

To submit from time to time to the Board or to the respective committees, measures for the efficient management and increase of the Museum, and such other matters as he may deem advisable.

To prepare and submit to the Board a monthly report in writing of the work done, stating the number of visitors, and other matters of interest to the Board.

To prepare and submit at the annual meeting in September an annual report of like contents for the preceding year ending Aug. 31st, said report to accompany the annual report of the Board, required by Section 8 of the "Public Museum Act."

To discharge such other duties as usually belong to the office of the custodian and from time to time be prescribed by the Board.

But in the performance of his duties, no debt or liability of any kind shall be incurred by him without authority from the Board.

The custodian shall be required to give bonds in the sum of one thousand dollars, with two or more sureties, to be approved by the Board, for the faithful performance of his duties.

ART. 7. It shall be the duty of the custodian as secretary of the Board of Trustees to be present at all meetings of the Board and of the committee and to keep full and correct records of their proceedings, except when otherwise directed.

To keep exact and detailed accounts of all moneys received from fines and other sources, to report the same monthly to the Board at the regular meetings, and to pay over all monesy so received promptly to the city treasurer as directed by the Board.

To keep books of account in which all the money transactions of the Board shall be set forth accurately in detail, and to make out and sign all warrants drawn on the city treasurer by order of the Board.

To take care of all business papers of the Board and keep the same neatly filed for convenient reference.

To prepare and submit a monthly statement of the finances of the Museum at the regular monthly meetings.

To give notice of all meetings of the Board, and of committees, at least twenty-four hours before the time of meeting.

To receive all documents, letters and other communications addressed to the Board or Museum, and to see to their proper disposal by the proper officer or committee.

To transact all such other business as may be required of him by the Board and its committees in his capacity as secretary thereof.

ART. 8. The janitor shall, under the direction of the custodian, attend to the heating, ventilation and cleaning of the Museum in all its parts, and perform such other work as may be assigned to him at any time by the custodian. The other assistants shall also work under the direction of the custodian and perform such work as the custodian may assign to them.

ART. 9. Engagements of employes or assistants shall be made by the executive committee, subject to approval by the Board.

III. COMMITTEES.

ART. 10. The standing committees shall be:

1. The Executive Committee, consisting of the president ex-officio, and four other members of the Board.

2. The Finance Committee, consisting of three members of the Board.

3. The Committee on Exchanges, consisting of three members of the Board, to whom, with the custodian, all applications for exchanges shall be referred for recommendation to the Board.

4. The Committee on Furniture, consisting of three members of the Board.

5. The Committee on Purchase, consisting of three members of the Board, to whom, with the custodian, all matters of purchasing specimens shall be referred for recommendation to the Board. The Committee on Purchase shall have authority to expend from month to month in the interest of the Museum a sum not exceeding $50.

ART. 11. The Natural History Society of Wisconsin shall be invited to appoint five scientific persons from among their members to act in an advisory capacity as a joint counsel, in conferences with the Executive Committee; such conferences to take place at such times as the Executive Committee may desire.

ART. 12. The Executive Committee shall have supervision of all matters relating to the purchasing, construction, leasing, repairing and heating of the buildings or rooms occupied by the Museum, and of insurance, the furnishing, order and cleanliness of the rooms and collections; the selection, purchase, preparation, arrangement, exchange, sale or other disposal of specimens, books or other articles; the acceptance or rejection of donations; the preparation, printing, sale or other disposal of catalogues and guides; provided that in all such matters no action be taken involving an expenditure or liability greater than authorized by the Board. This committee shall assign a suitable room to the Natural History Society of Wisconsin for holding their meetings and receiving their library. It shall be the duty of the committee to see that all persons employed in the service of the Museum are faithful and prompt in the performance of their duties, and that the regulations of the Museum are enforced.

ART. 13. The Finance Committee shall have the supervision of all matters pertaining to the accounts and account books of the Board. It shall be their duty to prepare the annual budget of the Board, to direct the manner of keeping and to examine all the account books; to examine the monthly and other financial statements of the secretary and custodian and certify the correctness of the same to the Board; to examine and audit all vouchers and accounts against the Museum; to report to the Board upon the correctness of the same, and to make such suggestions from time to time concerning the finances of the Museum as they may deem advisable. Said committee shall also at the regular meeting in September each year, submit an estimate of the amount that will be needed for maintaining the Museum during the following year, and the action of the Board upon such estimates shall be forthwith certified by the secretary to the comptroller of the city of Milwaukee.

ART. 14. A majority of any committee shall constitute a quorum.

ART. 15. The standing committees shall prepare and submit to the Board at the annual meeting in May, a report of all matters subject to their supervision.

ART. 16. The reports of all standing committees shall be in writing.

IV. MUSEUM AND LIBRARY.

ART. 17. The Museum shall be conducted, according to the intention of the "Public Museum Act" and the conditions made by the Natural History Society of Wisconsin in donating the "Engelmann Museum" with the following aims in view.

The exhibition of natural history and ethnology, so as to provide material and help for scientific investigation and public instruction.

The collections therein contained are to represent and illustrate as far as possible the natural history and the natural resources of the city and county of Milwaukee and state of Wisconsin in the first order, and then of the United States and remainder of our planet for purposes of comparison and generalization.

The Museum shall be placed in a building reasonably fireproof, and kept insured for at least five-sixths of its value.

No objects in the collection can be loaned, and the removal of specimens from the room cannot be permitted, except if sold or for the purpose of exchange or identification and under proper authority from the Executive Committee. All matters relating to the arrangement, preservation and use of the collection are under the immediate direction of the custodian, subject to the supervision of the Executive Committee, who will give more detailed instructions if needed.

ART. 18. The library is to be considered a reference and working library. Its contents cannot be loaned, but may be used for study or reference in the rooms during museum hours under necessary restrictions.

V.   MISCELLANEOUS.

ART. 19.   It shall be the duty of every member of the Board to frequently visit the Museum and of the members of the Executive Committee to do so at least once every week, for the purpose of general superintendence and direction.

ART. 20.   The term of service of all the employes of the Museum except the custodian shall be during good behavior. They shall only be removed for cause of which the Board shall be the exclusive judge.

ART. 21.   The records of the proceedings of the Board of Trustees and its committees and the books of account shall be kept in the secretary's office and shall be open at all times to inspection and examination by any member of the Board.

ART. 22.   The order of business of the Board of Trustees, except at special meetings, shall be as follows:

1.   Calling the Roll.
2.   Reading Minutes of previous Meeting.
3.   Report of Custodian and Secretary.
4.   Report of Standing Committees.
5.   Report of Special Committees.
6.   Reading of Communications.
7.   Unfinished Business.
8.   Election of Officers.
9.   New Business.

ART. 23.   All resolutions and amendments before the Board or any committee shall be presented in writing.

ART. 24.   All persons employed at the Museum must be promptly at their posts, as directed, and must remain there during the hours of their regular duty.   They will remember that their time, while in the Museum, should constantly be occupied in its service, and it is the duty of the custodian and Executive Committee to enforce this rule.

ART. 25.   No amendments to the rules of the Board, or the regulations of the Museum shall be acted upon until the next regular meeting after the same shall have been proposed.

REGULALIONS.

The Museum will be open:

On Sundays, from 1:30 to 5 P. M.

Saturdays, from 9 to 12 A. M. and 1 to 5:30 P. M.

On all other days, from 1 to 5:30 P. M.

Visitors are admitted on condition that they observe the following regulations:

SECTION 1. Any person of good deportment can be admitted during the above named hours. Children less than fourteen years of age will be admitted only if accompanied by parents, teachers or other responsible adults. Dogs or other live animals will not be admitted.

SEC. 2. Admission is free. Employes of the Museum are forbidden under penalty of discharge, to receive fees from visitors.

SEC. 3. The removal of books, specimens or any other objects belonging to the Museum from any of its rooms, is strictly prohibited.

SEC. 4. The use of tobacco, and all other conduct not consistent with the quiet and orderly use of the Museum, are prohibited.

SEC. 5. Visitors are not allowed to touch any object.

SEC. 6. Visitors will be held responsible for any mutilation or other injury to specimens, books, furniture, or other property of the Museum caused by them.

SEC. 7. The time for closing will be announced by three bell signals ten minutes previous to the appointed hour.

OFFICE HOURS OF EMPLOYES.

Custodian, from 9 to 12 A. M. and 1 to 4 P. M.

Assistant Custodian, from 8:30 to 11:30 A. M. and 1 to 5 P. M.

Taxidermist, from 8 to 12 A. M. and 1 to 5 P. M.

First Assistant, from 8:30 to 11:30 A. M. and 1 to 5:00 P. M.

Janitor, from 7 to 11:30 A. M. and 1 to 5:30 P. M.

In the regular meeting of the Board of Trustees, held August 18th, 1893, the following resolution, introduced by Trustee Aug. Stirn, was adopted :

WHEREAS, The original address issued by a great number of our most prominent citizens to the Natural History Society of Wisconsin, requesting said society to donate their collection of specimens of Natural History and Ethnology to the city as a nucleus for a Public Museum, is missing and undoubtedly lost; and

WHEREAS, Such important document relating to the creation and establishment of the Public Museum should, if possible, be placed on our official records; and be it, therefore,

Resolved, That said address be printed from a copy still in existence and then be annexed to our next annual report; and be it further

Resolved, That two extra copies of said address be either nicely printed or illuminated and handsomely framed, and one of them assigned a proper place in the main hall of the Museum, and the other one in the office of the Museum Board.

Petition of Citizens to the Natural History Society of the City of Milwaukee to Present its Museum to the City.

———— ▬ ————

GENTLEMEN:—We are deeply interested in the very valuable collection of specimens of nature gathered in your museum, and beg to say that very great thanks are due to the disinterested labor of your members in getting it together. But it seems to us that, while the museum is fully appreciated by all who know it, it has hardly received that public recognition of its worth, nor taken that position as a disseminator of useful knowledge, to which it is fairly entitled. This is due, we think, in part to its present location and partly to the inadequate spaces allotted to it. Knowing that it is and always has been the ardent wish of your members to place the collection where it will do the largest possible good, and that enlarged quarters, a central location and freedom of access are essential for that purpose, we take the liberty to suggest the tender of the museum to the City of Milwaukee, on the condition that it be permanently maintained by the City as a Free Public Museum for the benefit of all citizens. We cannot doubt that the general attention it would receive as a public institution would lead to constant and liberal additions to its treasures, and it would become an object of interest and pride to our community at large. It would prove to our city not only a very rare attraction, but a most valuable aid in the study of natural history for both young and old.

Very respectfully yours,

(Signed:)

Jas. MacAlister.
Edward O'Neil.
West & Co.
Ch. H. Haskins.
Alex. Mitchell.
Wm. E. Cramer.
Dr. E. A. Knotser.
Wm. Rohlfing & Co.
Bosworth & Sons.
H. Sigel.
J. B. Hoeger & Son.
C. Eisfeld & Bro.
F. C. Winkler.
Inbusch Brothers.
John Plankinton.
Guido Pfister.
Emil Von Baumbach.
John R. Goodrich.
Edw. W. Hicks.
T. A. Chapman.
Ch. G. Stark.
Mathews Bros. & Co.

Wm. McLaren.
Rud. Nunnemacher.
John E Hansen.
Ramien Bros. & Co.
M. Heiman & Co.
W. W. Coleman.
Geo. Koeppen.
Ed. P. Allis.
Espenhain & Bartels.
H. M. Benjamin.
August Uihlein.
Val. Blatz.
John Rugee.
Gustav Wollaeger.
Horace Rublee.
H. Haertle.
Otto A. Thiele.
Ferd. Kuehn.
Henry M. Mendel.
Marshall & Ilsley
Singer & Benedict.
John Black.

John H. Tesch.
Wm. Frankfurth.
Isaac Ellsworth.
Thos. H. Brown.
Josuah Stark.
Meyer Friend.
David Adler & Sons.
C. A. Meissner.
Fred. Dohmen.
Ed. Schmidt.
Goll & Frank.
Adolph Meinecke.
Goldsmith & Co.
W. H. Jacobs.
Louis Auer.
Fred. Pabst.
John Pritzlaff.
William E. Smith.
Moritz v. Baumbach.
John Johnston.
Carl Doerflinger.

THIRTEENTH

ANNUAL ⊙ REPORT

————OF THE————

BOARD OF TRUSTEES

————OF THE————

PUBLIC MUSEUM

————OF THE————

CITY OF MILWAUKEE.

———————

September 1st, 1894, to August 31st, 1895.

———————

OCTOBER 1st, 1895.

———————

MILWAUKEE, WIS.

A. Wetzel & Bro., Printers, 614-616-618 East Water Street.

1895.

BOARD OF TRUSTEES.

CITIZENS APPOINTED.

AUGUST STIRN	Term expires May, 1899
JULIUS GOLDSCHMIDT	Term expires May, 1898
ADOLPH MEINECKE	Term expires May, 1897
EDWIN W. BARTLETT	Term expires May, 1896

ALDERMEN APPOINTED.

THOMAS F. RAMSEY	Term expires May, 1896
CHAS. J. KOEHLER	Term expires May, 1896
JAMES R. WILLIAMS	Term expires May, 1896

EX-OFFICIO.

GEO. W. PECKHAM, Sup't of Schools	Term expires May, 1896
JULIUS BLEYER, Pres't School Board	Term expires May, 1896

OFFICERS.

GEO. W. PECKHAM, President.
HENRY NEHRLING, Secretary, Ex-officio.

MUSEUM SERVICE.

HENRY NEHRLING	Custodian.
CARL THAL	Assistant Custodian.
GEO. B. TURNER	Taxidermist.
ALEXANDER GOETHEL	Assistant Taxidermist.
LYDIA NEHRLING	Assistant.
ALMA WALDBART	Assistant.
CARL BINDRICH	Janitor.

*To the Honorable, the Common Council of the City of Mil-
waukee:*

GENTLEMEN:—The Board of Trustees of the Public Museum, in accordance with Section 8, Chapter 328, of the laws
of 1882, presents herewith its annual report as required by
law. It respectfully refers to the annual report of Mr. H.
Nehrling, the custodian of the Museum, for such details and
information as are not contained in this report.

The Museum contains the following specimens:

118,984	Zoological specimens, valued at	$34,823 04
16,003	Botanical specimens, valued at	1,004 70
14,833	Anthropological specimens, valued at	9,760 75
11,054	Palaeontological specimens, valued at	5,191 75
4,106	Mineralogical and Lithological specimens, valued at	3,798 79
5,953	Books, Pamphlets, Catalogues, Atlases and Charts, valued at	5,707 87
3,035	Bird's Eggs and Nests, valued at	10,000 00
	Furniture, Tools, Jars, Vessels, valued at	14,175 22
	Upham collection of Indian garments, held in trust,	350 00
	Total	$84,812 12

The number of visitors during the year was 88,320, a gain
of 61,096 as compared with the attendance of last year, which
increase was due to the fact that the Industrial Exposition was
held during the year.

The insurance on the property of the Museum is now $85,-
320 against $63,000 of last year.

The financial statement of the Board is as follows :

Balance in Museum fund, Sept. 1, 1894	$3,787 73
Appropriation for 1895	13,588 45
Refunded insurance premium	48 00
Warrant No. 1277, cancelled	4 00
Total	$17,428 18
Total expenditures during last year	13,127 63
Leaving a balance on Sept. 1, 1895, of	$4,300 55

My thanks are due to the members of the Board and the officers of the Museum for their cordial assistance in furthering the best interests of the Museum.

Respectfully submitted,

GEO. W. PECKHAM,

President.

REPORT OF THE CUSTODIAN.

MILWAUKEE, WIS., Sept. 17, 1895.

*To the Board of Trustees of the Public Museum of the City
of Milwaukee:*

GENTLEMEN:—In compliance with article 6 of your Rules
and Regulations I have the honor of submitting to you my
Fifth Annual Report, being the Thirteenth in the series of reports since the foundation of the Museum.

During the last few years the Museum has entirely out-
grown its quarters in the Exposition Building. Every inch of
space has been utilized, and we are at present unable to find
room for another single case. The position of the specimens
in the cases has been frequently changed in order to find room
for new objects, and the cases themselves have been brought
together as close as possible. Most of the departments of
the Museum have accomplished an almost phenomenal growth
during the past few years, and it takes much time and work
to care for all the specimens and to keep them clean from dust
and insects. Almost daily new specimens are donated, and
much valuable material is accumulated in this way.

Since I have had an opportunity of visiting the different
museums in this country I am convinced that our own Public
Museum has attained an importance and dignity among its
contemporaries of late that other similar institutions have required many years to accomplish. There is no doubt that
this Museum is a first-class institution, comparing favorably

with similar centers of learning in the East. Few cities of the same size can boast of a Museum like ours. And all this was accomplished in a comparatively short time, with an exceedingly small appropriation and a very small force of employees. Scientific men all over the country and Europe, who have had an opportunity of examining our collections, are astonished and surprised to find a first-class Museum in Milwaukee. Tourists from all parts of the world do not fail to visit the Museum during their stay in the city, and all leave with pleasant impressions and recollections.

With the exception of the Layton Art Gallery, the Museum is the only free public place in the city where strangers and tourists, as well as our own population, can find instruction and entertainment. I am so frequently called upon by strangers, by friends of nature, by teachers, scientists, specialsists and by patrons and friends of the Museum that my daily work is necessarily interrupted to a great extent or prevented entirely. Although in a certain respect a drawback to the Museum it shows on the other hand the great popularity of the institution and the interest people take in it.

The mammal groups, formed lately and now on exhibition, are the main features in the Museum. These groups are life-like and perfect in every respect, comparing well with those in the National Museum of Washington, and the American Museum of Natural History in New York. The groups of Muskrats, Porcupines, Black Bears, Coyotes or Prairie Wolves, Buffalos, Pumas, Skunks, Orang-Outangs, Reindeers, Otters, Foxes, Badgers, etc., are admired by all visitors. The collection of North American mammals, as a whole, leaves little to desire, though not arranged systematically on account of space. Our systematic collection of North American birds meets with the approval of all those interested in the subject. The collection of Central and South American birds and mammals, though some material has been bought, leaves much room for further additions and improvement. Tropical and beautifully plumaged birds from Asia and the South Sea Islands are well represented since the Museum purchased the fine collection brought together by Mr. Charles Hose at Sarawak, and by Mr. A. Everett at Kina Balu, Borneo. Hornbills and Birds of Paradise form the main feature among our collection of tropical birds. A small collection of the very interesting Pittas or Ant Thrushes, consisting of twelve species, attract a great deal of attention. Besides the Birds of Paradise the Hummingbirds create the most sensation. Unfortunately our collection of Hummers is very small, and those on exhibition are poorly mounted, the specimens having been donated by the Natural History Society. The department of Central and South American birds and mammals needs large additions and typical material during the next few years.

A special feature of the Museum is the very complete "B. F. Goss Collection of North American Birds' Eggs." It has required many years of hard work and a considerable amount of money to bring together this collection, which is the best on exhibition in this country.

The department of Herpetology is rich in Florida forms, collected by Mr. Adolph Meinecke, at Gotha. Fla. The department of Ichthyology is just developing under the care and constant work of Dr. Sigmund Graenicher, who also determines the snakes and lizards which are added to the collection.

The Entomological Collection has been arranged and enriched by thousands of specimens by my able predecessor, Dr. Wm. M. Wheeler, a trained and painstaking entomologist, at present professor in the natural science department of the University of Chicago. Of late valuable collections of American butterflies and beetles have been donated by Mrs. B. F.

Goss of Pewaukee, by Mr. Adolph Meinecke, of this city, and by Mr. Wm. Holle of Sheboygan, whose collection also contains large numbers of tropical butterflies.

The Herbarium has grown to such an extent that the construction of a new case has become a necessity. Mr. Adolph Meinecke has collected many fine plants at Gotha, Fla., for the Museum. Mr. Reuben Strong has donated his herbarium of plants of Milwaukee county, and Mr. Charles E. Monroe also presented an entire herbarium of excellently preserved and mounted plants from all parts of the northern United States.

Special efforts have been made to enrich the department of North American Palæontology by a large number of fine and typical specimens. The late Mr. Thomas A. Greene, who was for many years trustee of the Museum, selected and purchased most of the specimens, now on exhibition. In order to show the variations Mr. Greene has selected many duplicates. The Niagara formation is particularly well represented, the specimens coming largely from the lime stone quarries near the city. The Hamilton formation was enriched by many valuable specimens collected at the cement mills near the city. The department of Mineralogy, though not very large, contains fine and well selected exhibition material. Dr. Davenport Fisher determined and labeled most of the specimens, of which many had been purchased by Mr. Thomas A. Greene.

Since the last few years the Ethnological Collection has grown extensively by valuable donations from Mr. Carl Miller, who collected his specimens on the Gold Coast of Africa, and by Mr. Rounsevelle Wildman, at present editor of the "Overland Monthly," San Francisco, Cal. Mr. Wildman in his capacity as commissioner to the World's Columbian Exposition, donated much valuable material to the Museum, from Straits Settlements and Johore.

An exceedingly valuable and unique collection of primitive Musical Instruments, obtained by Miss Elizabeth Plankinton while travelling in Korea, and donated to the Museum by her, attracts numbers of visitors at all times the Museum is open to the public.

Wisconsin Archæology is well represented in the Museum. The collection of Copper Implements is much admired by visitors, while the thousands of specimens of the Henry Haskell collection, acquired by purchase some time ago, and the large number of Stone Implements, attract much attention. Mr. Haskell's collection has been brought together in Jefferson County of this state, especially near Atztalan, a region celebrated for its mounds and the many valuable finds. I must say with regret that many small archæological collections have found their way out of the state and are now dispersed over all parts of the world. Friends and patrons of the Museum should do all they can to induce owners of small collections of Wisconsin archæology to donate them to the Museum. Everywhere in the state such collections are found which are of little use to their owners but would be of great value to all those interested in this science if exhibited in our own Museum. I have in many cases succeeded in obtaining fine donations to this department.

The donations to the various departments, of which I only mentioned a few, together with the material bought at the World's Columbian Exposition are of such magnitude that the employees of the Museum were always kept busy in identifying, preparing, recording, cataloguing, arranging and exhibiting them.

During the past year the attendance has been a large one. More than 88,000 visitors have been recorded in our books. Most of the schools made use of the Museum, and many of the teachers manifested more interest than they formerly did, especially in regard to the more familiar forms of native birds and mammals. Prof. Irving N. Mitchell, teacher of natural science in the State Normal School, urged his classes to visit the Public Museum with the special object to study special groups of animals, commencing with the lower forms. In this way the pupils of the Normal School became so much interested in the Museum that they frequently asked me to assist them in their study, and they even made use of the Museum library.

I. ZOOLOGY.

A.—MAMMALS.

The collection of mammals has increased during the past year by some very fine acquisitions. Through the kindness of Mr. John E. Hansen we had an opportunity of purchasing a very fine Musk Ox (Ovibos moschatus) which has been mounted by our taxidermist, Mr. Geo. B. Turner, and which is now on exhibition. I doubt if there is a larger and more perfect specimen in any museum.

Mr. John E. Hansen donated a young Black Bear from Oregon.

A well-mounted American Badger (Taxidea americana) was donated by Mayor John C. Koch.

Mr. Gustav Preusser presented six young and two old Coyotes or Prairie Wolves (Canis latrans). These specimens were used by our taxidermist in forming an exquisite life-like group of these animals, a group which created quite a sensation when first put on exhibition.

In addition to this Mr. Turner finished a group of Pumas (Felis concolor) consisting of two young and two old ones, and a group of four American Bisons or Buffalos (Bison bison). He also mounted a Mule Deer, or Black-tailed Deer (Cariacus macrotis), a Zebu Cow (Bos Zebu) and a large number of small mammals.

B.—BIRDS.

The department of Ornithology has also increased considerably. As in former years, Mr. Clarence J. Allen has donated some very fine specimens, among them an American Avocet (Recurvirostra americana), a Swainson's Hawk (Buteo swainsoni) and one Townsend's Solitaire (Myiadestes townsendii). The latter bird was collected by himself in North Dakota between Kenmore and Bow Bell's stations.

Mr. Herman Boppe donated five species of very beautiful Hummingbirds which he had received from a friend at Bogota, Colombia.

Mrs. Wm. Dillmann presented a Snowy Owl (Nyctea nyctea) an almost perfect white specimen, and Mrs. Geo. Dyer several tropical birds.

Charles J. Munkwitz donated a King Rail (Rallus elegans) and Alderman W. C. Okershauser three Old Squaws (Clangula hyemalis), which he collected last winter on the Lake near Bay View. This bird, also known by the names Long-tailed Duck, Old Wife and South-southerly, is a resident of Greenland, Iceland and the sea-coast of Alaska. In the United States it is only found in winter.

Mr. August Stirn donated six White Rice Birds.

These are only a few of the many donations, in addition to which the Museum purchased quite a number of Pheasants and of birds collected in different parts of Borneo.

A large and fine nest of *Ostinops decumana* (Cassique), collected by Col. N. S. Goss, the author of the "Birds of Kansas," at Chiriqui, Panama, was donated by Mrs. B. F. Goss of Pewaukee.

C.—ICHTHYOLOGY.

As indicated in last year's report, Dr. S. Graenicher has brought together a fine collection of Wisconsin fishes, about fifty species, all preserved in "formaline." When we commenced to use this liquid we were hoping that the bright colors would be preserved, but they are fading more rapidly than in alcohol. On the other hand the forms of the objects placed in formaline are well preserved.

D.—HERPETOLOGY.

During the past year the collection of Snakes has increased considerably by specimens donated by Dr. S. Graenicher.

Mr. Adolph Meinecke donated quite a number of different species collected by him at Gotha, Fla.

The whole Herpetological Collection was examined thoroughly by my friend Dr. Leonhard Stejneger, the celebrated naturalist, and at present curator of the department of herpetology in the United States National Museum. Dr. Stejneger determined most of the snakes and lizards, which renders now the collection very valuable.

E.—ENTOMOLOGY.

Mrs. B. F. Goss of Pewaukee, Wis., donated the whole collection of native butterflies and beetles, left by her husband. The collections consists of 2,388 specimens.

Our President of the Museum Board, Dr. Geo. W. Peckham, donated a case containing eggs, larvæ and full-grown specimens of the common Mud-dauber Wasp, (Pelopæus cæruleus). The peculiar mud-nests are mounted in a very natural way and with great care on rough boards. This highly interesting and instructive piece of biological work is accompanied by a full "History of the Mud-dauber Wasp."

II. BOTANY.

Prof. Emil Dapprich, director of the German-English Academy, donated a very large and fine herbarium of Colorado plants, collected among the mountains by himself during his vacation.

III.—MINERALOGY.

Mr. Herman Schlichting of Lake Linden, Mich., donated fine specimens of drift copper.

IV.—PALÆONTOLOGY.

Mr. Adolph Meinecke donated a tooth of Elephas americanus obtained by him in a phosphate bed on the Peace River, Fla.

V.—ARCHÆOLOGY.

Mr. Adolph Meinecke presented forty-seven specimens of stone-axes, spear and arrow heads, all found at Gotha, Fla.

VI.—ETHNOLOGY.

Miss Elizabeth Plankinton donated nineteen very valuable and unique musical instruments collected by herself while travelling in Korea. She also donated five mats from the same country. An extra case has been constructed for the reception of Miss Plankinton's generous gift.

VII.—LIBRARY.

Very few books have been added to our Museum Library. There is no doubt that all the great illustrated works on natural history should find a place in our library. The valuable colored plates in these works are often better than specimens.

INVENTORY.

118,984	Zoological specimens	$34,823 04
16,003	Botanical specimens.	1,004 70
14,833	Anthropological specimens	9,760 75
11,054	Palæontological specimens	5,191 75
4,106	Mineralogical and lithological specimens	3,798 79
5,953	Books, pamphlets, catalogues, atlas:s and charts	5,707 87
3,035	Birds' eggs and nests	10,000 00
	Furniture, tools, jars, vessels, conservation supplies and stationery	14,175 22
	Upham collection held in trust	350 00
	Aggregate value of the contents of the Museum	$84,812 12

FINANCIAL TRANSACTIONS OF THE MUSEUM.

Debit.

Balance in Museum fund Sept. 1st, 1894	$3,787 73
Appropriation to Museum fund January 1st, 1895	13,588 45
Refunded insurance premium	48 00
Warrant 1277, cancelled	4 00
Total	$17,428 18

Credit.

Amounts paid by warrants on the city treasurer since the last annual statement was rendered :

Fuel and light	$570 40
Repairs	4 55
Postage and freight	48 05
Stationery and printing	102 85
Furniture	538 98
Mammals	301 90
Birds	653 30
Crustaceans and insects	30 00
Fossils and casts	10 00
Insurance	2,113 02
Rent	1,350 00
Library	46 15
Pay roll	6,375 25
Conservation supplies	55 66
Wages	769 76
Miscellaneous	157 76
Total	$13,127 63
Balance in Museum fund Sept. 1st, 1895	$4,300 55

INSURANCE.

Grand Rapids Fire Insurance Co. of Grand Rapids, Mich...	$1,500 00
Rutger's Fire Insurance Co. of New York, N. Y...............	1,500 00
Palatine Insurance Co. (Limited) of Manchester, England...	1,500 00
Norwich Union Fire Insurance Society of England............	2,500 00
Palatine Insurance Co. (Limited) of Manchester, England..	2,500 00
St. Paul Fire and Marine Insurance Co. of St. Paul, Minn...	1,500 00
Hamburg-Bremen Fire Insurance Co. of Hamburg, Germany	1,500 00
Westchester Fire Insurance Co. of New York....................	1,500 00
Svea Assurance Co. of Gothenburg.................................	1,250 00
Netherlands Fire Insurance Co. of Zutphen, Holland.........	8,750 00
Commercial Lloyds, New York.....................................	2,500 00
Mutual Lloyds, New York.........	7,500 00
Tradesmens Fire Lloyds, New York.................	2,500 00
Broadway Lloyds, New York..	3,000 00
Union Lloyds, New York...	2,500 00
Assurance Lloyds, New York......:	1,500 00
Traders Fire Lloyds, New York	2,500 00
Inter-State Fire Association, New Orleans, La..	1,500 00
Keystone Fire Insurance Co. of St. John........................	2,500 00
Quebec Fire Assurance Co. of Quebec...........................	1,000 00
Quebec Fire Assurance Co. of Quebec...........................	1,500 00
Citizens Insurance Co. of Evansville, Ind......................	1,000 00
Cincinnati Insurance Co., Cincinnati, Ohio....................	1,000 00
Michigan Miller's Mutual Fire Insurance Co., of Lansing, Mich............	1,500 00
German American Fire Insurance Co. of Baltimore...........	1,000 00
Merchants Insurance Co. of New Orleans, La..................	1,500 00
Standard Fire Insurance Co. of Wheeling, W. Va.............	1,000 00
Farmers' and Mechanic's Insurance Co. of Alexandria, Va.	1,500 00
Saginaw Valley Fire and Marine Insurance Co. of Saginaw, Mich..	2,500 00
Germania Insurance Co. of New Orleans.........................	1,500 00
Peabody Insurance Co. of Wheeling, W. Va.....................	1,000 00
Manufacturers' and Merchants' Mutual Insurance Co. of Rockford, Ill.............................	2,500 00
North German Fire Insurance Co. of Hamburg, Germany...	2,500 00
Pacific Fire Insurance Co. of the City of New York...........	1,500 00
Security Insurance Co. of New Haven, Conn....................	1,500 00

Mercantile Fire and Marine Insurance Co. of Boston.....	1,000 00
Michigan Fire and Marine Insurance Co. of Detroit, Mich.	1,000 00
Rhode Island Underwriters Association, Providence, R. I.	2,000 00
Phenix Insurance Co. of Brooklyn, N. Y...........................	1,000 00
Phenix Insurance Co. of New Brooklyn, N. Y....................	1,500 00
Allemannia Fire Insurance Co. of Pittsburg, Pa..................	1,500 00
German Fire Insurance Co. of Peoria, Ill....	2,500 00
Royal Insurance Co. of Liverpool......................................	2,500 00
Queen Insurance Co. of America, N. Y.............................	1,500 00
Greenwich Insurance Co. of the City of New York.............	1,500 00
Total..	**$85,000 00**

VISITORS.

	1894 Sept.	1894 Oct.	1894 Nov.	1894 Dec.	1895 Jan.	1895 Feb.	1895 Mar.	1895 April.	1895 May.	1895 June.	1895 July.	1895 Aug.	1894-95 Whole year
Average daily attendance........	849	1468	49	57	53	59	75	78	58	58	69	79	241
Greatest daily attendance......	3485	5628	173	157	93	134	203	154	163	135	135	195	
Least daily attendance..........	6	1	18	25	25	16	30	26	25	21	32	37	
Av. attendance on Sundays.....	114	60	112	79	59	92	115	133	109	57	69	66	
Total attendance..............	25,468	43,519	1,478	1,779	1,689	1,657	2,313	2,340	1,794	1,728	2,144	2,461	88,320

CONCLUSION.

And now a few words more to the people of this city and the state. Visit the Museum and induce your friends to come. Partake in the enlargement of the institution and in its good work. If you find anything of interest, and that you know is of value, find out all about it, write a label and send it to the Museum. No man or woman who has received the benefit of education and feels a responsibility for the diffusion of knowledge can come within the influence of the Museum, without grateful emotions that amidst the hustling, hurrying, absorbing, ruthless business strife of the crowded city there is an institution whose high mission is and shall forever be to "reclaim the glory of the past civilization, promote the wonderful genius of the human mind, and discern and perpetuate the elevating truths of nature."

In the hope that the Museum may in future enjoy as in the past, the same kind consideration which has all the time characterized the actions of the Board of Trustees, the above is respectfully submitted.

H. NEHRLING,

Secretary and Custodian.

APPENDIX.

ZOOLOGY.

DONATIONS.

C. J. Allen, Milwaukee, Wis.

    1 American Avocet, North Dakota.

    1 Swainson's Hawk,   "

    1 Townsend's Solitaire,   "

Arthur F. Bishop, Milwaukee, Wis.

    1 Pine Grosbeak, Milwaukee, Wis.

C. Hermann Boppe, Milwaukee, Wis.

    5 Hummingbirds, Bogota, U. S. of Colombia.

W. M. Brigham, Milwaukee, Wis.

    1 Great Blue Heron, Milwaukee Co., Wis.

J. Bruchhaeuser, Milwaukee, Wis.

    1 Gray Parrot, Captivity, Milwankee.

C. N. Casper, Milwaukee, Wis.

    1 Siberian Wolf Hound,

Jos. Caspari, Milwaukee, Wis.

    1 Shoveller, Milwaukee, Wis.

    3 Red-winged Blackbirds, Milwaukee, Wis.

Chas. P. Clos, Milwaukee, Wis.

    1 Screech Owl, Milwaukee, Wis.

Prof. Emil Dapprich, Milwaukee, Wis.

    1 Water Thrush, Milwaukee, Wis.

Mrs. Wm. Dillmann, Milwaukee, Wis.

    1 Snowy Owl, North Dakota.

Mrs. Geo. Dyer, Milwaukee, Wis.

    1 Rhamphocælus brasilius, Brazil.

    1 Euphonia violacea,   "

    1 Hummingbird.

    1 Bluebird, Wisconsin.

    1 Parula Warbler, Wisconsin.

    1 Tachyphonus melaleucus, Costa Rica.

    1 Calliste demaresti.

Dr. J. C. Emmerling, Milwaukee, Wis.

    1 Zebra Finch, Captivity, Milwaukee.

Alexander Goethel, Milwaukee, Wis.

    1 Tumbler Pigeon, Milwaukee, Wis.

Otto Goethel, Milwaukee, Wis.

    1 Carolina Parakeet, Captivity, Milwaukee.

    1 Guinea Pig, Captivity,   "

    1 Pouter Pigeon,   "

Dr. Grant Goodrich, Elgin, Ill.

    1 Red African Owl.

    1 Jacobin Pigeon, Elgin, Ill.

Mrs. B. F. Goss, Pewaukee, Wis.

    2,388 U. S. Butterflies and Beetles.

John E. Hansen, Milwaukee, Wis.

    1 Young Black Bear, Oregon.

Dr. Theo. Hartwig, Cedarburg, Wis.

    1 Snake in Alcohol, Cedarburg, Wis.

H. Hirsch, Milwaukee, Wis.

    1 Northern Shrike, Humboldt, Milwaukee Co., Wis.

    1 Flicker, Milwaukee County, Wis.

    3 Sea Urchins, Florida coast.

Hon. John C. Koch, Milwaukee, Wis.

    1 American Badger, Wisconsin.

W. C. Koch, Milwaukee, Wis.

    1 Redhead Duck, Fox Lake.

Henry Kœrber, Milwaukee, Wis.

    1 Loon, Hales Corners, Wis.

John Maag, Milwaukee, Wis.

    1 Eel, Wisconsin.

Adolph Meinecke, Milwaukee, Wis.

    1 Spotted Sandpiper, Milwaukee, Wis.

    1 Cardium, St. Petersburg, Fla.

    1 Unio,   "   "   "

    33 Snakes, Gotha, Orange County, Fla.

    2 Lizards,   "   "   "   "

C. A. Meissner, Milwaukee, Wis.

    1 Golden Eagle, South Milwaukee, Wis.

Mrs. Zachara T. Merrill, Wis.

      1 Diamond Rattle Snake, Fla.

Carl Miller, Milwaukee, Wis.

      1 Leopard, West Africa.

Chas. J. Munkwitz, Milwaukee, Wis.

      1 King Rail, Milwaukee Market.

Albert A. Nero, Thiensville, Wis.

      1 Mud Puppy, Thiensville, Wis.

Wm. C. Okershauser, Milwaukee, Wis.

      3 Old Squaw Ducks, Bay View, Milwaukee Co., Wis.

Dr. Geo. W. Peckham, Milwaukee, Wis.

      History of a Mud-dauber Wasp, illustrated by
         a number of nests with specimens attached.

Gustav Preusser, Milwaukee, Wis.

      6 Young Coyotes.

      1 Great Horned Owl, Milwaukee County, Wis.

Christian Preusser, Milwaukee, Wis.

      1 Ruffed Grouse, Milwaukee, Wis.

      3 Porcupines,   Gogebic, Mich.

      1 Star-nosed Mole,   "   "

      1 Broad-winged Hawk   "   "

      1 Horned Grebe.   "   "

      1 American Coot,   "   "

      1 Barred Owl,   "   "

      1 White Rabbit,   "   "

      1 Marsh Hawk,   "   "

      1 Pileated Woodpecker, "   "

Stephen J. Reigh, Milwaukee, Wis.

      1 Yellow-headed Blackbird, Muskego Lake, Wis.

August Stirn, Milwaukee, Wis.

      6 White Rice-birds, Japan.

Frank Suelflow, Milwaukee, Wis.

      1 Loon, Pewaukee, Wis.

Geo. B. Turner, Milwaukee, Wis.

      1 White-throated Sparrow, Milwaukee, Wis.

C. Werckle, Ocean Springs, Miss.

      3 Young Opossums, taken from the pouch,
         Ocean Springs, Miss.

.H. V. Woodworth, Milwaukee, Wis.
    1 Common Opossum, Clarke, Miss.

ACQUIRED BY PURCHASE.

1 Cervus canadensis, Wapiti.
3 Vulpes vulpes var. fulvus, Red Fox.
9 Mephitis mephitica, Common Skunk.
1 Cariacus macrotis, Mule Deer, Montana.
2 Bison bison, American Bison, Montana.
1 Artomys monax, Woodchuck, Wisconsin.
1 Procyon lotor, Racoon, Wisconsin.
2 Lepus sylvaticus, Gray Rabbit, Wisconsin.
4 Spermophilus tridecemlineatus, Striped Gopher.
1 Felis concolor, Puma, Thompson Falls, Montana.
1 Ovibos moschatus, Musk Ox, Hudson's Bay.
2 Coccyzus minor, Big Marco and Cedar Keys, Fla
1 Scolecophagus cyanocephalus, San Pedro, Cal.
2 Sialia mexicana anabelae, San Pedro, Cal.
2 Amphispiza belli cinerea, Carriso, Lower Cal.
2 Sporophila morelleti sharpei, Cameron Co., Tex.
1 Basilinna xantusi, La Paz, Lower Cal.
1 Basilinna leucotis, Huachuca Mountainss, Arizona.
1 Melospiza fasciata rivularis, San Pedro, Lower Cal.
2 Helodytes brunneicapillus bryanti, San Fernando, Lower Cal.
2 Pitta mulleri,   Mt. Kalulong, Sarawak, Borneo.
2 Halcyon concreta, "   "   "   "
1 Pitta acuta,   "   "   "   "
1 Pitta granatina, Foot of Mt. Nolu, Borneo.
1 Pitta schwaneri, Mt. Kalulong, Sarawak, Borneo.
1 Halcyon, Sarawak, Borneo.
1 Terpsephone affinis,   Mt. Kalulong, Sarawak, Borneo.
1 Irena crinigera,   "   "   "   "
2 Calyptomena viridis,   "   '   "   "
2 Chloropsis zosterops, "   "   "   "
2 Eurystomus orientalis, "   "   "   "
2 Zanclostomus javanicus, "   "   "   "
2 Rhinocichla treacheri, Kina Balu, Borneo.
2 Pomatorhinus bornensis, Mt. Kalulong, Sarawak, Borneo.
2 Rubigula montis, Kina Balu, Borneo.

2 Euryglaemus javanicus,   Mt. Kalulong, Sarawak, Borneo.
2 Euryglaemus ochromelas,   "   "   "
2 Nyctiornis amictus,   "   "   "
1 Cymborhynchus macrorhynchus   "   "   "
1 Megalaema henrici,   "   "   "
1 Oriolus xanthonotus,   "   "   "
1 Rubigula webberi,   Penrisen Hills, Borneo.
1 Pericrocotus xanthogaster,   "   "   "
1 Dissemurus platurus, Mt. Kalulong, Sarawak, Borneo.
1 Rollulus roulroul, Baram River, Borneo.
1 Rollulus roulroul, Mt. Kalulong, Sarawak, Borneo.
1 Eulabes javanus,   "   "   "
1 Rollulus niger,   "   "   "
2 Trogon personatus,   U. S. of Colombia.
2 Pyroderos orenocensis,   "
2 Rupicola peruviana,   "
1 Xanthura yncas,   "
1 Carpophago chathamensis, Chatham Isl.
1 Carpophago aenea, Mt. Kalulong, Sarawak, Borneo.
1 Carpophago pickeringii, Mantanani Isl.
1 Carpococcyx radiatus,   Mt. Kalulong, Sarawak, Borneo.
1 Mulleripicus pulverulentus,   "   "   "
1 Thriponax javensis,   "   "   "
2 Urococcyx erythroquatus,   "   "   "
2 Chibia bornensis,   '   "   "
1 Platysmurus aterrimus,   "   "   "
1 Dendrocitta cinerascens,   Kina Balu, Borneo.
1 Artamides normani,   "
1 Oriolus vulnervatus,   "
2 Chloropis kinabaluensis,   "
2 Criniger ruficrissus,   "
2 Criniger phaeocephalus, Mt. Kalulong, Sarawak, Borneo.
2 Hernixus connecteus,   "   "   "
2 Phipidura perlate,   Penrisen Mt., Borneo.
2 Arachnothera longirostris,   "
1 Hypotaenidia striata, Sarawak, Borneo.
1 Philentoma velatum, Mt. Kalulong, Sarawak, Borneo.
1 Culicicapa ceylonensis,   Kina Balu, Borneo.
1 Cryptolopha schwaneri,   "

1 Pericrocotus montanus, Kina Balu, Borneo.
1 Muscicapula hyperythra,   "
1 Erythacus cyaneus,   "
1 Gecinus puniceus,   Mt. Kalulong, Sarawak, Borneo.
1 Chrysophlegma humei,   "   "   "
1 Cyanops monticola, Kina Balu, Borneo.
1 Corydon sumatrensis,   Mt. Kalulong, Sarawak, Borneo.
1 Cittocincla tricolor suavis,   "   "   "
1 Homaerus bornensis, Kina Bula, Borneo.
1 Hyloterpe hypoxanthe,   "
1 Motacilla melanope,   "
1 Chlorocheris aemiliae,   "
1 Aegithine viridis, Mt. Kalulong, Sarawak, Borneo.
1 Psittinus incertus,   "   "   "
1 Loriculus galgulus, Penrisen Mt., Borneo.
1 Turdinus atrigularis, Northern Borneo.
1 Lanius lucionensis, Kina Balu, Borneo.
1 Turdinus canicapillus, Borneo.
1 Turdinus tephrops,   Mt. Kalulong, Sarawak, Borneo.
1 Chrysophlagma malaccense,   "   "   "
1 Miglyptes tukki,   "   "   "
1 Miglyptes grammithorax,   "   "   "
2 Stoparola cerviniventris, Kina Balu.
1 Siphia elegans, Northern Borneo.
1 Siphia banyumas,   Labuan, Borneo.
1 Siphia philippinensis,   "   "
1 Hernipus picata,   Kina Balu, Borneo.
1 Rhipidura albicollis,   "
1 Pericrocotus cinereus, Northern Borneo ·
1 Rhynomyias ruficrissa, Penrisen Mt., Borneo.
1 Herpornis xantholeuca brunnesceus, Kina Balu, Borneo.
1 Dicaeum chrysorrhaeum,   "
1 Aethopyga temminckii, Penrisen Mt., Borneo.
1 Anthotreptes simplex,   "
1 Cyanodernia bicolor, Borneo.
1 Stachyris bornensis, Kina Balu, Borneo.
1 Orthotomus cineracens,   "
2 Alcippe cinerea, Penrisen Mt., Borneo.
2 Staphidia everetti, Mt. Kalulong, Sarawak, Borneo.

2 Munia cantans, Sarawak, Borneo.
2 Columba domestica, Milwaukee, Wis.
1 Phaelaema rubinoides, Colombia, S. A.
1 Panoplites flavescens, Ecuador.
1 Eriocnemis luciani,   "
1 Campylopterus lazulus, Colombia, S. A.
1 Polytmus thaumantias, Venezuela.
1 Acestrua heliodori, Colombia, S. A.
1 Metallura tyrianthina quitensis, Ecuador.
1 Heliotrypha exorbis,   Colombia, S. A.
1 Heliangelus clarissae,   "
1 Oxypogon guerini,   "
1 Steganurus underwoodi,   "
1 Thalurania columbica,   "
1 Saucerothia cyanifrons,   "
1 Rhamphomicus microrhynchus, "
1 Eucephala grayi, Ecuador, S. A.
1 Eucephala caerulea, Venezuela, S. A.
1 Lesbia forficatus, Colombia, S. A.
1 Lesbia amaryllis, Colombia, S. A.
1 Eriocnemis vestita, Colombia.
1 Eriocnemis alinae,   "
2 Chrysolampis moschita, Venezuela, S. A.
1 Lampornis nigricollis,   "
1 Lampornis violicauda,   "
2 Helinaia swainsonii, South Carolina.
2 Dendroica olivacea, Huachuca Mts., Arizona.
2 Helminthophila bachmani, Beaufort, S. C.
1 Columba domestica, Milwaukee, Wis.
3 Larus glaucus,   "
2 Basileuterus culicivorus, Tamaulipas, Mexico.
1 Junco caniceps, Colorado.
1 Basilinna xantusi, San Jose Del Rancho, Lower Cal.
1 Merula confinis, Sierra de la Laguna,   "
2 Junco bairdi,   "   "
2 Dendragapus franklinii, Rocky Mts., North Montana.
1 Graphophasianus soemmeringii, Japan.
2 Graphophasianus scintillans,   "
1 Phasianus versicolor,   "

1 Gallus ferrugineus, India.

1 Penelopina nigra, Honduras.

1 Euplocaenus pyronotus, Mt. Kalulong, Borneo.

1 Crax globicera, Honduras.

1 Penelope leucoptera, South America.

1 Lophophorus impeyanus, Asia.

1 Numida cristata, Madagascar.

1 Centrococcyx eurycercus, Mt. Kalulong, Borneo.

1 Manucodia chalybata, New Guinea.

1 Ptilorhynchus holosericeus, Australia.

1 Sericulus mellinus,   "

1 Cheiromeles torquatus, Borneo.

41 Tropical butterflies.

BOTANY.

DONATIONS.

Prof. Emil Dapprich, of this city, collected in Colorado the following plants for the Museum:

1 Mitella pantandra,

1 Sedum stenopetalum,

1 Rhus aromatica,

1 Saxifraga flagellaris,

1   "   chrysantha,

2 Sedum rhodanthum,

1 Saxifraga punctata,

1   "   rivularis,

1   "   integrifolia,

1 Polygonum bistorta, var.,

1 Berberis Fendleri,

1 Grundelia squarrosa,

1 Heeracium gracilis,

1   "   cynoglossoides,

1 Erigeron caespitosus,

1   "   flagellaris,

1   "   glabellus,

1   "   uniflorus,

1   "   mollis,

1   "   grandiflorus,

1 Erigeron Coulteri,

1   "   compositus,

1 Aster Parryi,

1 Thephrosia virginiana,

1 Cassia chamaecrista, Arkansas.

1 Clitoria mariana, Arkansas.

1 Alnus virescens,

1 Juniperus Virginiana,

1 Senecio amplecteus,

1   "   Fendleri,

1   "   borealis,

1 Antennaria alpina,

1   "   plantaginifolia,

1 Troximon aurantiacum,

1 Aster pulchellus,

1   "   Kinzii,

1   "   canescens,

1 Gnaphalium Sprengelii

1 Antennaria dioica,

1 Bigelovia Parryi,

1 Bigelovia depressa,
1 Chrysopsis hispida,
1 " villosa,
1 Kuhnia eupatorioides,
1 Aster ericaefolius,
1 " xylorrhiza,
1 " Fremonti,
1 Epilobium paniculatum,
1 Aster tanacetifolius,
1 " laevis,
1 Solidago rigida,
1 Epilobium coloratum,
1 Solidago nana,
1 " occidentalis,
1 " nemorales.
1 " multiradiata,
1 " humilis,
1 " procera,
1 Helianthus Maximiliani,
1 Gutierrezia Euthamiae,
1 Achillea millefolium,
1 Lepachys columnaris,
1 Astragalus hypoglottis,
1 Thermopsis rhombifolia,
1 Astragalus triflorus,
1 Trifolium nanum,
1 " longipes,
1 " eriocephalum,
1 Saxifraga nivalis,
1 Jamesia Americana,
1 Rubus strigosus,
1 Symphoricarpus pauciflorus,
1 Gaura coccinea,
1 Ribes lacustre,
1 Gaura biennis,
1 Mentzelia nuda,
1 Cleome lutea,
1 Viola Canadensis,

1 Aconitum Columbianum,
1 Caltha leptosepala,
1 Aquilegia cærulea,
1 Nuphar polysephalum,
1 Viola palustris,
1 Thalictrum Fendleri,
1 Anemone Nuttalliana,
1 " multifida,
1 Juniperus communis,
1 Senecio serra,
1 " petræus,
1 " eremophilus,
1 Peraphyllum ramosissimum,
1 Potentilla arguta,
1 " fruticosa,
1 Ribes prostratum,
1 Acer glabrum,
1 Prunus Virginiana,
2 Rosa Nutkana,
1 Rubus deliciosus,
1 Senecio triangularis,
1 " cernuus,
1 Taraxacum scopulorum,
1 Actinella grandiflora,
1 Arnica alpina,
1 " latifolia,
1 Corydalis aurea;
1 " Brandegei,
1 Delphinium scopulorum,
1 Claytonia sessifolia,
1 Calandrinia pygmaea,
1 Ranunculus Macauleyi,
1 " alismaefolius,
1 " leiocarpus,
1 " abortivus,
1 " hyperborea,
1 Helianthus petiolaris,
1 " annuus,

1 Helianthus pumilus,
1 Artemisia tridentata,
1 Madia glomerata,
1 Ambrosia artemisaefolia,
1 Riddellia sagetinia,
1 Hymenopappus filifolius,
1 Verbesina Hooperii,
1 Artemisia dranunculoides,
1   "   cana,
1 Cnicus Neo Mexicanus,
1 Arnica cordifolia,
1   "   Parryi,
1 Stephanomeria minor,
1 Prenanthes racemosa,
1 Cnicus Eatoni,
1 Ephedra Nevadensis,
1 Oxyria digyna,
1 Polygonum tenne,
1   "   minimum,
1   "   imbricatum,
1 Eriogonum tenellum,
1 Oxybaphus angustifolia,
1 Mirabilis multiflora,
1 Eriogonum caespitosum,
1 Abronia micrantha,
1 Urtica gracilis,
1 Sarcobatus vermiculatus,
1 Rumex salicifolius,
1 Phoradendron juniperus,
1 Sueda diffusa,
1 Acer glabrum,
1 Ribes lacustre,
1 Geum Rossii,
1 Potentilla gracilis,
1 Rubus strigosus,
1 Sibbaldia procumbens,
1 Cercocarpon ledifolium,
1 Geum strictum,

1 Eriogonum sphaerocephalum,
1 Grayia Brandegei,
1 Chenopodium leptophyllum,
1 Grayia polygaloides,
1 Eurotia lanata,
1 Atriplex confertifolia,
1 Eriogonum heracleoides,
1 Astragalus campestris,
1 Lathyrus palustris,
1 Vicia Americana,
1 Penstemon,
1 Chionophila Jamesii,
1 Phacelia circinnata,
1 Castilleia linariaefolia,
1 Lithospermum multiflorum,
1 Hydrophyllum Fendleri,
1 Polemonium foliosissimum,
1 Geum rivale,
1 Prunus demissa,
1 Amelanchier alnifolia,
1 Clematis ligusticifolia,
1 Astragalus argenteus,
1   "   leptaleus,
1   "   argophyllus,
1 Glycirrhiza lepidota,
1 Medicago saliva,
1 Castilleia,
1 Physalis lobata,
1 Mimulus alpina,
1 Androsace septentrionalis,
1 Cuscuta arvensis,
1 Campanula rotundifolia,
1 Phacelia sericea,
1 Phlox brevifolia,
1 Gilia aggregata,
1 Mertensia Sibirica,
1 Onosmodium Carolinianum,
1 Omphalodes nana,
1 Monarda fistulosa,

1 Veronica seregrina,
1   "   alpina,
1 Gilia pinnatifida,
1 Veronica Americana,
1 Primula Parryi.
1 Penstemon glaber,

1 Penstemon gracilis,
1 Gilia linearis,
1 Penstemon Fremontii,
1   "   Watsoni,
1 Castilleia miniata,
1   "   septentrionalis,

1 Crotolaria sagittalis, Hot Springs, Arks.
1 Apios tuberosa,   "   "

Sivyer & Betz, Milwaukee, Wis.

COLLECTION OF WOODS.

1 Melia Azederach,   Lake Charles, La.
1 Magnolia grandiflora,   "
1 Fagus ferruginea,   "
1 Carya alba,   "
1 Pinus palustris,   "
1 Quercus alba,   "
2 Taxodium distichum,   "
1 Ilex opaca,   "
1 Liriodendron tulipifera,   "
1 Nyssa multiflora,   "
1 Gleditschia triacanthos,   "
1 Plantanus occidentalis,   "
1 Nyssa uniflora,   "
1 Quercus castanea,   "

MINERALOGY.

DONATIONS.

Mrs. Geo. Dyer, Milwaukee, Wis.
1 Marcasite.
1 Calcite.
1 Pyrite.
3 Galenite.
4 Quartz.
1 Agate.

Ed. Kelley, Milwaukee, Wis.
1 Pyrite, Inlet of New Water Tunnel, about 160 ft. below the surface.

Adolph Meinecke, Milwaukee, Wis.

    1 Tin-bearing Ore, Custer City, S. D.

    2 Quartz, Tampa Bay, Fla.

Hermann Schlichting, Lake Linden, Mich.

    5 Drift Copper, Calumet and Heckla Mine, Lake Superior, Mich.

August Stirn, Milwaukee, Wis.

    1 Quartz, Pine Lake, Wis.

PALÆONTOLOGY.

DONATIONS.

C. B. Barnard, Tampa, Fla.

    1 Shark's Tooth, Tampa, Fla.

Horace Beach, Prairie du Chien, Wis.

    1 Cast of a Foot-print, found in loose rock, near Colorado
        Springs, Colo.

Mrs. Geo. Dyer, Milwaukee, Wis.

    1 Trilobite.

Chas. L. Hundley, Wauwatosa, Wis.

    3 Fossil shells, Wauwatosa Quarry.

Ed. Kelley, Milwaukee, Wis.

    3 Orthoceras, New Water Tunnell, about 160 ft. below the surface.

    3 Gomphoeeras,   "   "   "

Adolph Meinecke, Milwaukee, Wis.

    1 Tooth of Elephas americanus, Peace River, Fla.

Percy H. Myers, Wauwatosa, Wis.

    A number of inferior fossils, Wauwatosa Quarry.

August Stirn, Milwaukee, Wis.

    1 Zaphrentis, Pine Lake, Wis.

Geo. B. Turner, Milwaukee, Wis.

    1 Conglomerate of Shells, Shore of Lake Ontario, Forest Lawn,
        Monroe Co., N. Y.

William J. Uihlein, Milwaukee, Wis.

    1 Calymene niagarensis, Lemont, Ill.

ACQUIRED BY PURCHASE.

    1 Tooth of Mastodon. Digged out on a track on the Kickapoo
        Valley and Northern R. R., near Wauzeka, Wis.

ETHNOLOGY.

DONATIONS.

Julius Goldschmidt, Milwaukee, Wis.

    1 U. S. Fractional Currency Bill for 50c, issued in 1863.

    1 U. S.   "   "   " " 10c,   " " 1863.

    1 U. S. Postage   "   " " 5c,   " " 1862.

H. Hirsch, Milwaukee, Wis.

    1 One cancelled Dollar Bill of the State of Massachusetts-
                                                 Bay of 1780.

    1 Two   "   "   "

    1 Three   "   "   "

    1 Four   "   "   "

    1 Five   "   "   "

    1 Seven   "   "   "

    1 Eight   "   "   "

    1 Twenty   "   "   "

Hugo Opitz, Milwaukee, Wis.

    1 Fragment of a Pistol from a Skirmish on the Coast of McKea
        Island with the Natives in 1849.

Miss Elizabeth Plankinton, Milwaukee, Wis.

    19 very valuable musical instruments from Soeul, Korea.

    5 Mats, Soeul, Korea.

E. F. Reichmann, Fort Jones, Cal.

    1 Photograph, "First Mules over the Mountains," Fort Jones, Cal.

    4   "   "City of Fort Jones, Cal."

    1   "   "Shoveling the trail out on Summit of Sawyers
                 Bar Mt.," Fort Jones, Cal.

    2   "   "Fourth July at Fort Jones, 1893."

    1   "   "Resort Place and Fall," Fort Jones, Cal.

    1   "   "First Train going to the Mines," Fort Jones, Cal.

    1   "   "Pack Mule Train loading for the Mines," Fort
                 Jones, Cal.

    1   "   "Farming near Fort Jones," Cal.

    1   "   "Train on the Summit," Fort Jones, Cal.

    1   "   "View of Mt. Shasta," Fort Jones, Cal.

    1   "   "U. S. Stage on the evening of the 3rd of July,"
                 Fort Jones, Cal.

    1   "   "One of our Mining Claims," Fort Jones, Cal.

ACQUIRED BY PURCHASE.

48 Pistols.

21 Guns.

20 Carbines.

16 Sabres.

A number of cannon balls.

A number of cartridge balls.

1 Drum.

1 Texas Ranger cartridge box.

1 Mexican spur.

1 Original copy of "The Daily Citizen," Vicksburg, Miss., July 2, 1863.

17 Pennies, issued by private individuals and firms during the war of the rebellion.

1 Powder flask.

12 Photographs, taken during the war of the rebellion.

1 Little cannon, called the "Swamp Angel," used during the war of the rebellion.

1 Snuff box with allegoric figures engraved, about 100 years old, Germany.

1 Beer mug, made of tin, in the year 1797, Germany.

1 Copper kettle, made at the end of last century, Germany.

ARCHÆOLOGY.

DONATIONS.

Dr. Theo. Hartwig, Cedarburg, Wis.

1 Stone Axe, from Grafton, west side Milwaukee river, in a gravel pit.

Adolph Meinecke, Milwaukee, Wis.

6 Implements made of shells, taken from a mound in Monroe Co., Wis.

2 Stone Axes, Lake Butler, Gotha, Orange Co., Fla.

7 Stone Celts,   "   "   "

14 Stone Spearheads, Gotha, Orange Co., Fla.

5 Stone Arrowheads,   "   "

8 Stone Arrowheads, unfinished,   "

2 Stone Sinkers,   "

3 Pieces of Pottery, Mound at Lake Butler, Gotha, Fla.

ACQUIRED BY PURCHASE.

5 Stone Axes.

1 Stone Celt.

38 Stone Spearheads.

69 Stone Arrowheads.

3 Stone Perforators.

1 Wrought Stone Implement.

2 Copper Spearheads.

127 Pieces of Mound-builder's Pottery from Arkansas, consisting of Idols, Vases, Bowls, Dishes, etc.

LIBRARY.

DONATIONS.

Academia Nacional de Ciencias, Buenos Ayres.

Boletin, Tomo XII, 1890–1891.

" " XIII, 1893.

Academy of Science of St. Louis, St. Louis, Mo.

Transactions, Vol. VI, Nos. 9–18, 1894.

" Vol. VII, Nos. 1–3, 1895.

Accademia delle Science dell' Estitute di Bologna, Bologna.

Rendiconte delle Sessioni, 1893, 1894.

American Museum of Natural History, New York.

Bulletin, Vol. VI, 1894.

Annual Report, 1894.

Australian Museum, Sydney.

Annual Report, 1893, 1894.

Belfast Natural History and Philosophical Society, Belfast.

Report and Proceedings, 1892, 1893.

" " 1893, 1894.

Biblioteca Nazionale Centrale di Firenze.

Bollettins delle Publicazioni Italiane, 1894, No. 214.

Botanischer Verein in Landshut, Germany.

13. Bericht, 1892, 1893.

Buetzow, Robert, Chicago.

City Map of Chicago, 1895.

Buffalo Society of Natural Sciences, Buffalo.

Bulletins, Vols. I. to V., 1873–1894.

California Academy of Sciences, San Francisco.

 Proceedings, I Series, Vol. IV, Part I, II.

Canterbury College, Christchurch, N. Z.

 Report of the 21st annual meeting, 1893.

Cincinnati Society of Natural History, Cincinnati, Ohio.

 Journal, Vol. XVII, Nos. 2, 3, 4.

  "   Vol. XVI, No. 1.

Denison University, Granville, Ohio.

 Bulletin, Vol. VIII, Part 1 and 2.

Detroit Museum of Art, Detroit.

 Annual Report, 1895.

C. Dwight Marsh, Ripon, Wis.

 On two new species of Diaptomus, 1894.

Elisha Mitchell Scientific Society, Chapel Hill, N. C.

 Journal, 1893, Second Part.

 Journal, Vol. XI, Parts 1, 2.

Moritz Fischer, Philadelphia, Pa.

 Rules of Nomenclature adopted by the International Zoological Congress, Paris, 1889, and Petersburg, 1892.

Free Library of the Public Schools, Huntington, Ind.

 Finding List, 1894.

Free Public Library, Museum and Walker Art Gallery, Liverpool.

 42d Annual Report.

Geological and Natural History Survey of Minnesota, Minneapolis.

 21st Annual Report, 1892.

 22d Annual Report, 1893,

 23d Annual Report, 1894.

Geological Survey of Queensland. Brisbane.

 Annual Progress Report for 1893.

 Towalla and Mareeba Gold Fields. 1894.

 Ulam Gold Fields, 1894.

 Deep Lead, Cape River Gold Field.

 Bulletin No. 1, 1895.

Gesellchaft Naturforschender Freunde. Berlin, Germany.

 Sitzungsberichte, 1894.

Gesellchaft fuer Natur-und Heilkunde in Dresden, Germany.

 Jahresbericht, 1893, 1894.

Mrs. B. F. Goss, Pewaukee, Wis.
    Phin, John. How to use the Microscope.
    The American Monthly Microscopical Journal, Vols. XI, XII.

Government Museum, Madras.
    Administration Report, 1893, 1894.
    Bulletin No. 1, 1894.
        " No. 2, 1894.
        " No. 3, 1894.

Head, William R., Palaeozoic Sponges of North America.
Hungarian National Museum, Budapest.
    Termiszetrajzi Fuezetek, Vol. XVII, 1894.
       "   " Vol. XVIII, 1895.

Illinois State Historical Library, Springfield, Ill.
    Trustees Report, Dec. 16, 1894.

Iowa Ornithological Association, Salem, Ia.
    The Iowa Ornithologist, Vol. I, No. 2.

Robert L. Jack, Queensland, Australia.
    The Higher Utilitarianism, 1895.

John Hopkins University, Baltimore.
    Circulars, Vol. XIV, Nos. 119, 120.

Journal of Comparative Neurology, Granville, Ohio.
    Journal, Vol. IV, Pages 153-206, 1894.
       " Vol. V, Pages 1-70, 1895.

Kansas State Historical Society, Topeka.
    Ninth Biennial Report for 1892 to 1894.

Kais. Koenigl Geologische Reichsanstalt, Wien, Austria.
    Jahresbericht, 1894 XLIV Bd. 2 Heft.

K. K. Naturhistorisches Hofmuseum, Wien, Austria.
    Annalen, Bd. IX, Nos. 2, 3, 4, 1894.

Kgl. Saechsische Gesellschaft der Wissenschaften, Leipzig, Germany.
    Berichte ueber die Verhandlungen Math. Phys. Classe. I, II, III.

Kongl. Vitterhets Historic och Antiqvitets Akademien, Stockholm.
    Antiqvarisk Tidskrift for Sverige. Sjette Delen to Trettonde Delen. XIV, 2.

Liverpool Geological Association, Liverpool, England.

    Transactions, Vols. II, IV, V, VI, IX, X, XI, XII, XIII, 1881, 1893.

    Journal, Vol. XIV, 1893, 1894.

L'Institut Grand Ducal de Luxembourg, Luxembourg.

    Publications, Tome XXIII.

Magyar Nemzeti Museum, Budapest.

    Termeszetrajzi Fuezetek, Vol. XVII, 1894.

Mærkisches Provinzial Museum, Berlin, Germany.

    Verwaltungsbericht, 1893, 1894.

Meinecke, Adolph.

    Fuehrer durch das Museum fuer Vœlkerkunde zu Berlin.

Milwaukee Public Library.

    Quarterly Index of Additions, Vol. V, Nos. 34, 35, 36 and 37.
        "   "   "   Vol. IV, No. 32.

Minnesota Academy of Natural Science, Minneapolis.

    Preliminary Notes on the Birds and Mammals on the Philippine Islands, 1894.

Missouri Botanical Garden, St. Louis.

    Glatfelter, Dr. N. M.   A study of the venation of Salix.

    Sixth Annual Report.

Museo Nacional de Montevideo.

    Anales I, 1894.

Museo Nacional De Costa Rica, San Jose, Costa Rica.

    1 Pamphl. Estudios sobre las hormigas de Costa Rica.

    1 Pamphl. Informe Presentado al Senor Secretario de Estado en el despachs de Fomento por Anastasio Alfaro Administrator del Museo.

Museum Carolino Augusteum, Salzburg.

    Jahresbericht, 1893.

Museum Francisco Carolinum, Linz.

    53 Jahresbericht, 1895.

Museums and Lecture Rooms Syndicate, Cambridge.

    29th Annual Report, 1894.

Museum fuer Vœlkerkunde, Leipzig, Germany.

    21. Bericht, 1893.

Nassauischer Verein fuer Naturkunde, Wiesbaden, Germany.

    Jahresberichte, Jahrg 47, 1894.

Natural History Society of N. B., Saint John, N. B.

      Bulletins Nos. VIII, IX, X, XI, XII, 1890, 1801, 1892, 1893, 1894.

Natural History Survey of Illinois, Springfield, Ill.

      Ridgway, Rob. The Ornithology of Illinois, Vol. V, Part I.

Natural Science Association of Staten Island.

      Proceedings, Vol. IV, Nos. 9 and 10.

Naturforschende Gesellschaft in Basel, Switzerland.

      Verhandlungen, Bd. X, Heft 3.

Naturforschende Gesellschaft in Danzig, Germany.

      Schriften, VIII Bd. Heft 3 and 4, Neue Folge.

Naturforschende Gesellschaft in Emden, Germany.

      78 Jahresbericht, 1892, 1893.

Naturforschende Gesellschaft des Osterlandes, Altenburg.

      Mittheilungen, Neue Folge, VI Bd, 1894.

Naturhistorische Gesellschaft in Hannover, Germany.

      42 and 43 Jahresbericht.

Naturhistorische Gesellschaft in Nuernberg, Germany.

      Abhandlungen, X Bd. I Heft. 1894.

Naturhistorisches Landesmuseum in Kærnten, Klagenfurt.

      "Carinthia" Zeitschrift fuer Vaterlandskunde, etc., 80 Jahrg.,
          1890.

          "   Mittheilungen des Naturhistorischen Landesmu-
seums fuer Kærnten 81, 82 and 83, Jahrg. 1891, 1893.

      Jahrbuch des Naturhistorischen Landesmuseums von Kærn-
ten, 38 Jahrg. 21 Heft.

      Jahrbuch des Naturhistorischen Landes Museums von Kærn-
ten, 39 und 40 Jahrg.

      Diagramme der magnetischen und meteorologischen Beobach-
tungen zu Klagenfurt, von 1891–1893.

Naturhistorischer Verein der Preussischen Rheinlande and Westfalens, Bonn, Germany.

      Verhandlungen, 51 Jahrg., 1894.

Naturwissenschaftliche Gesellschaft in Chemnitz, Germany.

      13. Bericht, 1893.

Naturwissenschaftliche Gesellschaft "Isis" in Dresden, Germany.

      Sitzungsbericht und Abhandlungen, Jahrg. 1894, Jan-Juli.
          "   "   " " Juli-Dec.

Naturwissenschaftlich Medizinischer Verein, Innsbruck.

    Berichte, XXI, Jahrg. 1892, 1893.

Naturwissenschaftlischer Verein in Bremen, Germany.

    Abhandlungen, Bd. XIII, Heft 1.

    Beitræge zur nordwestdeutschen Volks-und Landeskunde, Bd.
      XV, Heft 1.

Naturwissenschaftlicher Verein zu Hamburg, Germany.

    Verhandlungen 1893, III Folge.

    Abhandlungen, VIII Bd.

Naturwissenschaftlicher Verein zu Magdeburg, Germany.

    Jahresbericht and Abhandlungen, 1893, 1894, I Halbjahr.

    Festschrift zum 25. jaehrigen Stiftungsfeste, 1894.

Naturwissenchaftlicher Verein fuer Neuvorpommern u. Ruegen,
    Greifswald.

    Mittheilungen, 26. Jahrg. 1894.

Naturwissenschaftlicher Verein zu Regensburg, Germany.

    Berichte, IV Heft 1892, 1893.

Naturwissenschaftlicher Verein fuer Schleswig-Holstein. Kiel.

    Schriften, Bd. X, Heft 1, 1893.

Naturwissenschaftlicher Verein fuer Steiermark, Graz.

    Mittheilungen, Jahrg. 1894.

Naturwissenschftlicher Verein fuer das Fuerstenthum, Lueneburg.

    Jahresheft III, 1893–1895.

Naturwissenschaftlicher Verein a. d. Universitæt Wien.

    Mittheilungen fuer 1893, 1894.

New York Academy of Sciences, New York.

    Transactions, Vol. XIII, 1893, 1894.

    Index to the Annals, Vol. XII.

    Annals, Vol. VIII, No. 5, 1884.

New York State Museum, Albany.

    47th Annual Report, 1893.

    Bulletins, Vol. III, Nos. 12 and 13.

Observatorio Astronomico Nacional, Tacubaya.

    Boletin, 1894. Tome I, Nos. 18, 19 and 20.

    Annalen, 1894.

Rev. D. Osborn.

    Biblical Anthropology. A discourse on Man.

Physikalischer Verein zu Frankfurt a. M., Germany.
    Jahresbericht, 1892, 1893.

Physikalisch Medicinische Societæt, Erlangen.
    Sitzungsberichte, 26. Heft, 1894.

Physikalish Oekonomische Gesellschaft zu Kœnigsberg.
    Schriften, 35. Jahrg. 1895.

Public Library, Boston, Mass.
    43d Annual Report.

G. W. and E. G. Peckham.   On the Spiders of the Family Attidæ,
    of the Island of St. Vincent.   1893.

G. W. and E. G. Peckham.   The Sense of Sight in Spiders with some
    Observations on the Color Sense.

Rochester Academy of Science, Rochester, N. Y·
    Proceedings, Vol. II, 1894.

Royal Irish Academy, Dublin.
    Transactions, Vol. XXX, Part 13 and 14, 1894.
    Proceedings, Third Series, Vol. III, No. 3, 1894.
    Cunningham Memoirs No. 10.

Sanderson Lillian (Mrs. L. Rummel), Berlin, Germany.
    Picture of Fuerst v. Bismark at his 80th birthday.

Schlesische Gesellschaft fuer vaterlændische Cultur, Breslau, Germany
    71. Jahresbericht, 1894.

Smithsonian Institution, Washington·
    Annual Report, July, 1893.
       "   "   July, 1891.

Societe des Sciences Neuchatel, Switzerland.
    Bulletins, Tomo XVIII, XIX, XX, 1890–1892.

Societe Imperiale des Naturalistes, Moscow, Russia.
    Anne 1893, No. 4.
    Anne 1894, Nos. 1, 2 and 3.

Societe De Physique et D'Histoire Naturelle, Geneve, Switzerland.
    Compte Rendu de Seances de la Societe de Physique et D'His-
    toire Naturelle de Geneve.   1894

Societe Scientifique du Chili, Santiago, Chili.
    Actes de la Societe Scientifique, Tomo II, 1892.
      "   "   "   "   " III, 1893.
      "   "   "   '·   " IV, 1894.

Stavanger Museum, Stavanger, Norway.

    Aarsberetning for 1893.

State Historical Society of Iowa, Iowa City.

    Wick, B. L. The Amish Mennonites, 1894.

    Shambaugh, B. F. Documentary material relating to the history of Iowa, 1894.

St. Gallische naturwissenschaftliche Gesellschaft, St. Gallen.

    Bericht, 1892, 1893.

Thurgauische Naturforschende Gesellschaft, Frauenfeld.

    Mittheilungen, 11. Heft, 1894.

Tufts College, Mass.

    Leighton, V. L. The Development of the Wing of Sterna wilsonii.

University of California. Berkeley, Cala.

    8 Bulletins, Pages 1 to 300, 1893.

    1 Pamphl. Critical Periods in the History of the Earth.

U. S. Bureau of Education, Washington, D. C.

    The History of Education in Connecticut, 1893.

    Higher Education in Tennessee, 1893.

    Higher Education in Iowa, 1893.

    History of Education in Maryland, No. 19, 1894.

    History of Education in Rhode Island, No. 18, 1894.

    Report on Introduction of domesticated Reindeer into Alaska.

    Education in Alaska, 1891, 1892.

    Report of the Commissioner of Education for 1891, 1892.

U. S. Bureau of Ethnology, Washington, D. C.

    Holmes, Wm. Hy. An ancient quarry in Indian Territory.

    Hodge, Fr. Webb. List of the Publications of the Bureau of Ethnology.

    Eleventh Annual Report, 1889, 1890.

    Twelfth Annual Report, 1890, 1891.

    Contributions to North American Ethnology, Vol. IX, 1893.

    Bibliography of the Chinookan Languages.

    Bibliography of the Algonquian Languages.

U. S. Civil Service Commission, Washington, D. C.

    Eleventh Report, 1893, 1894.

U. S. Coast and Geodetic Survey, Washington. D. C.

    Report for 1892, Part 1 and 2, 1893, 1894.

U. S. Department of Agriculture, Washington.
> Report of the Statistician, Sept., 1894.
> "   "   "   New Series Report Nos. 117, 120, 122,
> 123, 124, 125, 127.
> The Pocket Gophers of the U. S.
> Bulletin No. 1, 2 and 3 (Section of Foreign Markets).
> Farmers Bulletin, No. 23, 1894.
> Monographic Revision of the Pocket Gophers.

U. S. Department of the Interior, Washington.
> Eleventh Census of the U. S., 1890.

U. S. Geological Survey, Washington, D. C.
> Mineral Resources of the U. S. for 1892, 1893.
> Monograph, Vols. XIX, XXI, XXII, 1892, 1893.
> Bulletins Nos. 97–117.
> Annual Report, 1891, 1892, Parts 1 and 3, 1892, 1893.

U. S. National Museum, Washington, D. C.
> Proceedings, Vol. XVI, 1893.
> Bulletins, Nos. 45 and 46.

U. S. War Department, Washington, D. C.
> The War of the Rebellion, Series I, Vol. XLVI, Part 1.

Verein fuer Erdkunde, Darmstadt, Germany.
> Notizblatt, IV Folge, 15. Heft.

Verein fuer Erdkunde zu Leipzig, Germany.
> Mittheilungen, 1894.

Verein der Freunde der Naturgeschichte in Mecklenburg, Guestrow.
> 48. Jahrgang, 1894.

Verein Luxemburger Naturfreunde, Luxemburg.
> "Fauna" Nos. 6 and 7, 1894.

Verein fuer naturwissenschaftliche Unterhaltung, Hamburg, Germany.
> Verhandlungen, VIII Bd. 1891–1893.

Verein zur Verbreitung naturwissenschaftlicher Kenntnisse in Wien.
> Schriften, 34. Bd. 1893, 1894.

Videnskabs Selskabet, Christiana.
> Forhandlinger Nos. 1–21, 1893.
> Oversigt over Videnskabs-Selskabets Moder i. 1893.

Vorarlberger Museums Verein, Bregenz.
> 32. Jahresbericht, 1893.

Westfælischer Provinzial Verein fuer Wissenschaft und Kunst, Muen-
  ster.
  22. Jahresbericht, 1894.
Wiener Botanischer Tauschverein, Wien, Austria.
  Jahres-Katalog fuer 1895.
Zoological Society of Philadelphia, Pa.
  23d Annual Report, 1894.

PURCHASES.

Brockhaus, F. A.   Konversations Lexicon, Vols. 11 to 14.
The "Auk."   A Quarterly Journal of Ornithology,
      Vol. XI, No. 4.
      Vol. XII, Nos. 1 to 3.
Die " Natur " fuer 1894.
Chapman, F. M.   Handbook of Birds of Eastern North America.
Sievers, Prof. Dr. Wilh.   " Europa " Eine allgemeine Landeskunde.
Cabanis, Prof. D. Jean.   Journal fuer Ornithologie, Jahrgang 1894, Heft
      IV, Jahrg. 1895, Heft 1, bis 3.
The " American Naturalist," Vol. XXIX, Nos. 337 to 344.
Moorehead, W. K.   The " Archæologist," Vol. III, Nos. 1 to 8.
Engler and Prantl. Die natuerlichen Pflanzenfamilien, Liefg. 106 bis 121.

IN MEMORIAM.

Thomas A. Greene.

Died, September 7, 1894.

By H. NEHRLING.

In the course of the last year the Museum has lost one of its Trustees, who was present at the institutions small beginning and who has diligently assisted in raising it to its present high standing. A man of noble emotions, scrupulously conscientious in all his actions, modest and rather retiring, Mr. Thomas A. Greene was filled with a boundless love for Nature. Although mineralogy and palæontology were his chosen fields, he was also well at home in botany and zoology. In the performance of his duties as Trustee of the Public Museum he was very conscientious, never failing to be present at the regular meetings of the Board.

Mr. Greene's daughter, Mrs. Mary Greene Upham, has kindly sent me the following biographical sketch of her father: "Mr. Greene was born in Providence, R. I., November 2d, 1827. He was of Quaker parentage. His mother dying when he was very young he was sent, at the age of seven years, to the Friends Boarding School on the outskirts of Providence, where the teaching was thorough and painstaking and the discipline rigorous in the extreme. He was kept at this institution until he was old enough to enter a small school at Fruit Hill, R. I., which was especially adapted to the preparing of young men for college.

"His interest in Natural Science, especially Botany and Geology, dated from very early years. He could hardly remember the time when to gather and search for rare wild flowers. This was also his chief delight on his weekly half holiday. After leaving Fruit Hill he became retail drug clerk of Messrs. Chapin & Thurber of Providence. His knowledge of botany and chemistry soon won the love and respect of his employers, and they allowed him every means of gaining a complete understanding of the drug business. In those days druggists manufactured very many of their preparations from the crude drugs. For this advantage he felt always grateful to his employers. Feeling that the East was not the place for a man to start in business on his own account with but a limited capital, he turned his face westward, reaching Milwaukee, the situation of which delighted him, in the summer of 1848. Here he bought out the retail drug store of Henry Tess and afterward he induced his long time friend, Dr. H. H. Button, who had become a practicing physician in Brooklyn, N. Y., to enter into a business partnership with him under the firm name of Greene & Button, this partnership continuing until the death of Dr. Button in 1890. He brought west with him a small collection of Rhode Island minerals which he, encouraged by his father, had gathered in his boyhood. While always interested in these subjects, he never gave them any great degree of attention until his business career was somewhat assured—and he had a home of his own. His collection from a small beginning, grew gradually until it reached its present proportions. During portions of two summers, spent in the Lake Superior region, he greatly enlarged his collection of iron and copper ores. His interest in palæontology is of much more recent date, his first active interest dating from a summer in 1877 or 1878, when being somewhat broken in health, he was advised by his physicians to leave business alone for several months. Not wishing to undertake extensive travel his love of Nature took him into the country, and he soon became a well-known figure to the workmen of all the stone quarries in the vicinity of Milwaukee. This inclination while at first a means of simple recreation and enjoyment engendered in him before long a positive enthusiasm and fascination for the palæontology of the Niagara and Hamilton formations, and his collections of these fossils grew to great proportions."

Mr. Greene died September 7, 1894, in the sixty-seventh year of his age.

The very extensive collection of minerals and fossils in the Public Museum, especially those of the Niagara and Hamilton formations, were brought together by Mr. Greene, who bought most all of them for the Museum, being authorized to do so by the Board of Trustees.

Mr. Greene served as Trustee from February 20, 1883. until his death.

Let us cherish his memory!

Laws of Wisconsin Concerning the Public Museum.

(330, A.)   (Published April 13, 1882.)

CHAPTER 329.

AN ACT relating to the Natural History Society of the City of Milwaukee.

The People of the State of Wisconsin, represented in Senate and Assembly, do enact as follows:

SECTION 1. The board of directors of the Natural History Society of the city of Milwaukee is hereby authorized and empowered, in the name of said association or Society, to assign, transfer and convey to the City of Milwaukee, all and singular, the natural historical collections of every kind constituting the Museum belonging to said Natural History Society, in trust, to be kept, supported and maintained by said city, as a free Museum for the benefit and use of all citizens of said city, provided, the said city shall accept the trust and assume the care and maintenance of such Museum.

SEC. 2. This act shall take effect and be in force from and after its passage and publication.

Approved March 31, 1882.

(No. 329, A.)   (Published April 14, 1882.)

CHAPTER 328.

AN ACT to authorize the City of Milwaukee to establish and maintain a Public Museum in said city.

The people of the State of Wisconsin, represented in Senate and Assembly, do enact as follows:

SECTION 1. The City of Milwaukee is hereby authorized to receive and accept from " The Natural History Society of Wisconsin "—a corporation located in the said City of Milwaukee—a donation of its collection of objects in Natural History and Ethnology, or of the greater part thereof, upon such conditions as may be agreed upon by and between said city and said society, subject, however, to the provisions of this act.

SEC. 2. In case of such donation and acceptance, said City of Milwaukee is hereby authorized and empowered to establish and maintain in said city a free Public Museum, exhibitions of objects in Natural History and Ethnology, and for that purpose to receive, hold and manage the collection so donated, and any devise, bequest or donation that may be made to said city for the increase and maintainance of such Museum under such regulations and conditions as are herein contained, or may be agreed upon by and between the donors and said city, or as may be hereafter provided in this act.

SEC. 3. The Museum established and maintained under this act shall be under the general management, control and supervision of a board of nine trustees, who shall be styled " The Board of Trustees of the Public Museum of the City of Milwaukee." Said Board of Trustees shall consist of the president of the School Board and the Superintendent of Schools of said city, ex-officio, of three members of the Common Council of said city, designated and appointed by the Mayor thereof, and of four residents and tax-payers of said city, to be appointed by the Mayor as herein provided. The first appointments of trustees by the Mayor under this act shall be made within ten days after the formal acceptance by the Common Council of said city, of a donation by said Natural History Society, as authorized in the first section of this act. Of the first three trustees appointed from the members of the Common Council of said city, one shall be appointed from the three-year class, one from the two-year class, and one from the one-year class of aldermen, and they shall serve as such trustees during their respective terms as such aldermen. And annually on the third Tuesday of April thereafter, at the expiration of the term of any such trustee, the Mayor shall appoint his successor for three years, from the aldermen then having three years to serve. In case any such trustee shall vacate the office of alderman before the expiration of his term, he shall at the same time cease to be a trustee under this act, and the Mayor shall appoint some other member of the Common Council of his class in his place for the balance of his term. In the appointment of the four remaining trustees and their successors, the Mayor shall prefer such persons as may be recommended for such appointment by said Natural History Society. Such four trustees first appointed shall, at the first meeting of the Board after their appointment, determine by lot their term of service, so that one of their number shall serve for one year, one for two years, one for three years, and one for four years from the third Tuesday of May next after the organization of such Board. And all vacancies shall be filled by like appointment of the Mayor for the remainder of the term, and annually on the third Tuesday of April a trustee shall be appointed by said Mayor in like manner for the term of four years, in place of the trustee whose term shall expire the following May. None of said trustees shall receive any compensation from the city treasury, or otherwise, for their services as such trustees. And no member of said Board of Trustees shall become, or cause himself to become interested, directly or indirectly, in any contract or job for the purchase of any matter pertaining to the Museum, or of fuel, furniture, stationery or things necessary for the increase and maintenance of the Museum. Said trustees shall take the official oath, and be subject to the restrictions, disabilities, liabilities, punishments and limitations prescribed by law as to aldermen in the said City of Milwaukee.

Sec. 4. The first meeting of said Board of Trustees for the purpose of organizing, shall be held on the third Tuesday of the month next following their appointment, and the City Clerk shall give at least one week's previous notice of the time and place of such meeting to each member of such Board in writing. At such first meeting said Board shall organize by the choice of one of their number as president to serve until the third Tuesday of May next following, and until his successor shall be chosen. The annual meeting of said Board shall be held on the third Tuesday of May in each year, and at such meeting a president shall be chosen from their number to serve for one year and until his successor shall be chosen.

Sec. 5. The Board of Trustees shall have general care, control and supervision of the Public Museum, its appurtenances, fixtures and furniture, and of the selection, arrangement and disposition of the specimens and objects appertaining to said Museum, and also of the disbursements of all the moneys appropriated for and belonging to the Museum fund, in the manner hereinafter provided. And the said Board shall adopt, and at their discretion modify, amend or repeal by-laws, rules and regulations for the management, care and use of the Public Museum, and fix and enforce penalties for their violation, and generally shall adopt such measures as shall promote the public utility of the Museum ; provided, that such by-laws, rules and regulations shall not conflict with the provisions of this act.

SEC. 6. The Board of Trustees shall, at their first meeting, or thereafter, as soon as practicable and every five years thereafter, at an annual meeting, elect by ballot a person of suitable scientific attainments, ability and experience for custodian, who shall so act and be ex-officio secretary of said Board of Trustees. The custodian first appointed shall hold his office for five years from the time of the first annual meeting, unless previously removed, and thereafter the term of appointment shall be for the term of five years, and the compensation of the custodian shall be fixed by said Board of Trustees. Said Board of Trustees shall also appoint such assistants and employes for said Museum as they may deem necessary and expedient, and shall fix their compensation. All vacancies in the office of custodian, assistants and other employes, shall be filled by said Board of Trustees, and the person so elected or appointed shall hold for the unexpired term.

SEC. 7. The custodian elected under this act may be removed from office for misdemeanor, incompetency or inattention to the duties of his office, by a vote of two-thirds of the Board of Trustees ; the assistants and other employes may be removed by the Board for incompetency, or for any other cause.

SEC. 8. It shall be the duty of the Board of Trustees, within ten days after the appointment of the custodian and other salaried employes, to report and file with the City Comptroller a duly certified list of the persons so appointed, with the salary allowed to each, and the time or times fixed for the payment thereof, and they shall also furnish such comptroller with a list of all accounts and bills which may be allowed by said Board of Trustees, stating the character of the materials or service for which the same were rendered, immediately after the meeting of said Board at which such allowance shall be made. And said Board of Trustees shall also, on or before the first day of October in each year, make to the Common Council a report, made up to and including the 31st day of August of the said year, containing a statement of the condition of the Museum and of the additions thereto during the year, together with such information and suggestions as they may deem important, and such report shall also contain an account of the moneys credited to the Museum fund, and expended on account of the same during the year.

SEC. 9. From and after the organization of the Board of Trustees under this act, the Common Council of said city shall levy and collect annually upon all the taxable property of the said city, at the same time and in the same manner as other city taxes are levied and collected by law, a special tax not exceeding one-tenth of a mill upon each dollar of the assessed value of said taxable property, the amount of which shall be determined by said Board of Trustees, and certified to the Common Council at the time of making their annual report to said Council, and the entire amount of said special tax shall be paid into, and held in, the city treasury, as a separate and distinct fund, to be known as the Museum fund, and shall not be used or appropriated, directly or indirectly, in any other purpose than for the maintenance and for the increase of the Public Museum, the payment of the salaries of the custodian, assistant and other employes of the Museum, the purchase of furniture, fixtures, supplies and fuel, and the incidental expenses of the Museum.

SEC. 10. The Board of Trustees shall erect, purchase, hire or lease buildings, lots, rooms and furniture, for the use and accommodation of said Public Museum, and shall improve,.

enlarge and repair such buildings, rooms and furniture ; but no lot or building shall be purchased, erected or enlarged for the purpose herein mentioned, without an ordinance or resolution of the Common Council of said city, and deeds of conveyance and leases shall run to the city of Milwaukee.

Sec. 11. All moneys received by or raised in the city of Milwaukee for Museum purposes shall be paid over to the city treasurer, to be disbursed by him on the orders of the president and secretary of the said Board of Trustees, countersigned by the City Comptroller. Such orders shall be made payable to the order of the persons in whose favor they shall have been issued, and shall be the only voucher of the city treasurer for the payments from the Museum fund. The said Board of Trustees shall provide for the purchase of specimens, supplies, fuel and other matters necessary or useful for the maintenance of the Museum ; provided, however, that it shall not be lawful for said Board of Trustees to expend or contract a liability for any sum in excess of the amount levied in any one year for the Museum fund, on account of such fund.

Sec. 12. All moneys, books, specimens and other property received by the City of Milwaukee by device, bequest or gift, from any person or corporation, for Public Museum purposes, shall, unless otherwise directed by the donors, be under the management and control of said Board of Trustees ; and all moneys derived from fines and penalties for violations of the rules of the Museum, or from any other source in the course of the administration of the Museum, including all moneys which may be paid to the city upon any policy or policies of insurance, or other obligation or liability, or on account of loss or damage to any property pertaining to the Museum, shall belong to the Museum fund in the city treasury, to be disbursed on the orders of the said Board of Trustees, countersigned by the City Comptroller, for Museum purposes in addition to the amount levied and raised by taxation for such fund.

Sec. 13. This act shall take effect and be in force from and after its passage and publication.

Approved March 31, 1882.

(No. 895, A.]   (Published April 15, 1887.)

CHAPTER 521.

AN ACT to amend Chapter 328 of the Laws of 1882, authorizing the City of Milwaukee to establish and maintain a Public Museum, and Chapter 7, of the Laws of 1878, to establish a Public Library in the City of Milwaukee.

The people of the State of Wisconsin, represented in Senate and Assembly, do enact as follows:

*   *   *   *   *   *   *

Section 2. Hereafter all appointments of members from the Common Council for the Board of Trustees of the Public Museum of the City of Milwaukee, made by the Mayor of said city on the third Tuesday in April, shall be made from aldermen having two years to serve, and in case any person so appointed shall vacate his office of alderman before the expiration of his term, he shall thereupon cease to be a member of said Board of Trustees, and the Mayor shall appoint some other alderman of his class in his place to be such trustee for the remainder of his term. Each alderman appointed shall serve as such trustee during his term as alderman. It shall be the duty of the Mayor on the third Tuesday in April in each year to appoint a sufficient number of aldermen having two years to serve to be members of such Board of Trustees of the Public Museum to keep the number of members of such Board from the Common Council, always three.

All provisions of Chapter 328, of the Laws of 1882, which in any way conflict with the provisions of this section, are hereby amended accordingly.

SEC. 3. This act shall take effect and be in force from and after its passage and publication.

Approved April 14, 1887.

(No. 614, A.)   (Published April 20, 1887.)

CHAPTER 433.

AN ACT to amend Chapter 328, of the Laws of 1882, entitled, "An act to authorize the City of Milwaukee to establish and maintain a Public Museum in said city."

The People of the State of Wisconsin, represented in Senate and Assembly, do enact as follows:

SECTION 1. The Board of Trustees of the Milwaukee Public Museum are hereby authorized to appoint an acting custodian whenever the proper service of the Museum shall require it, and for such time and on such terms as they may deem proper. Such acting custodian shall be ex-officio the acting secretary of said Board of Trustees, and his acts as such shall receive full credit. Said Board of Trustees are also authorized to appoint from time to time honorary curators, who shall perform such duties and have such special privileges as may be provided in the by-laws of the Museum, but shall receive no pecuniary compensation. Such appointments shall be made of persons who have manifested a special interest in the Museum or some particular department thereof.

SEC. 2. This act shall be in force from and after its passage and publication.

Approved April 12, 1887.

RULES GOVERNING THE MUSEUM.

I. Meetings.

Art. 1. The regular meetings of the Board shall be held at the Museum rooms on the third Tuesday of each month at 4:30 P. M.

Art. 2. The annual meeting of the Board shall be held on the third Tuesday of May, at 4 P. M.

Art. 3. Special meetings shall be called by the secretary upon the written request of the president, or any three members of the Board, but the object for which the special meeting is called must be stated in the notice, and no business other than the special business shall be transacted at such meeting, unless all the members of the Board are present, and unanimous consent is obtained.

Art. 4. Five members of the Board shall constitute a quorum.

II. Officers and Employes.

Art. 5. At the annual meeting in May, the Board shall elect by ballot a president, whose duty it shall be to preside at all meetings of the Board, to sign all warrants drawn on the city treasurer by order of the Board, to appoint the standing committees for the year, and prepare for the consideration and approval of the Board, the annual report of the Board of Trustees, required by Section 8 of the "Public Museum Act."

Art. 6. The duties of the custodian shall be as follows:

To take charge of and exercise control over the Museum and Library, and to see that the regulations relating thereto are properly carried out.

To exercise control over all employes of the Board and the work allotted to them respectively.

To receive all specimens intended for the Museum, and with the advice and assistance of specialists to classify, label, catalogue and arrange them as soon as possible.

To receive all books and other articles intended for the library, and to label and catalogue them.

To take all precautions necessary for the good preservation of the collections, according to the most approved methods within the means of the institution.

To keep running records, containing all necessary particulars concerning articles received or disposed of.

To purchase specimens, books and other matter under the general direction of the Board.

To inaugurate a system of exchanges with other natural history museums as soon as possible.

To correspond with scientific societies and public authorities for the purpose of obtaining reports and other documents containing information relating to natural history.

To submit from time to time to the Board or to the respective committees, measures for the efficient management and increase of the Museum, and such other matters as he may deem advisable.

To prepare and submit to the Board a monthly report in writing of the work done, stating the number of visitors, and other matters of interest to the Board.

To prepare and submit at the annual meeting in September an annual report of like contents for the preceding year ending Aug. 31st, said report to accompany the annual report of the Board, required by Section 8 of the "Public Museum Act."

To discharge such other duties as usually belong to the office of the custodian and from time to time be prescribed by the Board.

But in the performance of his duties, no debt or liability of any kind shall be incurred by him without authority from the Board.

The custodian shall be required to give bonds in the sum of one thousand dollars, with two or more sureties, to be approved by the Board, for the faithful performance of his duties.

ART. 7. It shall be the duty of the custodian as secretary of the Board of Trustees to be present at all meetings of the Board and of the committee and to keep full and correct records of their proceedings, except when otherwise directed.

To keep exact and detailed accounts of all moneys received from fines and other sources, to report the same monthly to the Board at the regular meetings, and to pay over all moneys so received promptly to the city treasurer as directed by the Board.

To keep books of account in which all the money transactions of the Board shall be set forth accurately in detail, and to make out and sign all warrants drawn on the city treasurer by order of the Board.

To take care of all business papers of the Board and keep the same neatly filed for convenient reference.

To prepare and submit a monthly statement of the finances of the Museum at the regular monthly meetings.

To give notice of all meetings of the Board, and of committees, at least twenty-four hours before the time of meeting.

To receive all documents, letters and other communications addressed to the Board or Museum, and to see to their proper disposal by the proper officer or committee.

To transact all such other business as may be required of him by the Board and its committees in his capacity as secretary thereof.

Art. 8. The janitor shall, under the direction of the custodian, attend to the heating, ventilation and cleaning of the Museum in all its parts, and perform such other work as may be assigned to him at any time by the custodian. The other assistants shall also work under the direction of the custodian and perform such work as the custodian may assign to them.

Art. 9. Engagements of employes or assistants shall be made by the executive committee, subject to approval by the Board.

III. Committees.

Art. 10. The standing committees shall be :

1. The Executive Committee, consisting of the president ex-officio, and four other members of the Board.

2. The Finance Committee, consisting of three members of the Board.

3. The Committee on Exchanges, consisting of three members of the Board, to whom, with the custodian, all appli-

cations for exchanges shall be referred for recommendation to the Board.

4. The Committee on Furniture, consisting of three members of the Board.

5. The Committee on Purchase, consisting of three members of the Board, to whom, with the custodian, all matters of purchasing specimens shall be referred for recommendation to the Board. The Committee on Purchase shall have authority to expend from month to month in the interest of the Museum a sum not exceeding $50.

ART. 11. The Natural History Society of Wisconsin shall be invited to appoint five scientific persons from among their members to act in an advisory capacity as a joint counsel, in conferences with the Executive Committee; such conferences to take place at such times as the Executive Committee may desire.

ART. 12. The Executive Committee shall have supervision of all matters relating to the purchasing, constructing, leasing, repairing and heating of the buildings or rooms occupied by the Museum, and of insurance, the furnishing, order and cleanliness of the rooms and collections; the selection, purchase, preparation, arrangement, exchange, sale or other disposal of specimens, books or other articles; the acceptance or rejection of donations; the preparation, printing, sale or other disposal of catalogues and guides; provided that in all such matters no action be taken involving an expenditure or liability greater than authorized by the Board. This committee shall assign a suitable room to the Natural History Society of Wisconsin for holding their meetings and receiving their library. It shall be the duty of the committee to see that all persons employed in the service of the Museum are faithful and prompt in the performance of their duties, and that the regulations of the Museum are enforced.

ART. 13. The Finance Committee shall have the supervision of all matters pertaining to the accounts and account books of the Board. It shall be their duty to prepare the annual budget of the Board, to direct the manner of keeping and to examine all the account books; to examine the monthly and other financial statements of the secretary and custodian and certify the correctness of the same to the Board ; to examine and audit all vouchers and accounts against the Museum ; to report to the Board upon the correctness of the same, and to make such suggestions from time to time concerning the finances of the Museum as they may deem advisable. Said committee shall also at the regular meeting in September each year, submit an estimate of the amount that will be needed for maintaining the Museum during the following year, and the action of the Board upon such estimates shall be forthwith certified by the secretary to the comptroller of the city of Milwaukee.

Art. 14. A majority of any committee shall constitute a quorum.

Art. 15. The standing committees shall prepare and submit to the Board at the annual meeting in May, a report of all matters subject to their supervision.

Art. 16. The reports of all standing committees shall be in writing.

IV. Museum and Library.

Art. 17. The Museum shall be conducted, according to the intention of the "Public Museum Act" and the conditions made by the Natural History Society of Wisconsin in donating the "Engelmann Museum" with the following aims in view.

The exhibition of natural history and ethnology, so as to provide material and help for scientific investigation and public instruction.

The collections therein contained are to represent and illustrate as far as possible the natural history and the natural resources of the city and county of Milwaukee and state of Wisconsin in the first order, and then of the United States and remainder of our planet for purposes of comparison and generalization.

The Museum shall be placed in a building reasonably fireproof, and kept insured for at least five-sixths of its value.

No objects in the collection can be loaned, and the removal of specimens from any of the cases or the rooms cannot be permitted, except if sold or for the purpose of exchange or identification and under proper authority from the Executive Committee. All matters relating to the arrangement, preservation and use of the collection are under the immediate direction of the custodian, subject to the supervision of the Executive Committee, who will give more detailed instructions if needed.

ART. 18. The library is to be considered a reference and working library. Its contents cannot be loaned, but may be used for study or reference in the rooms during museum hours under necessary restrictions.

V. MISCELLANEOUS.

ART. 19. It shall be the duty of every member of the Board to frequently visit the Museum and of the members of the Executive Committee to do so at least once every week, for the purpose of general superintendence and direction.

ART. 20. The term of service of all the employes of the Museum except the custodian shall be during good behavior. They shall only be removed for cause of which the Board shall be the exclusive judge.

ART. 21. The records of the proceedings of the Board of Trustees and its committees and the books of account shall be kept in the secretary's office and shall be open at all times to inspection and examination by any member of the Board.

ART. 22. The order of business of the Board of Trustees, except at special meetings, shall be as follows:

1. Calling the Roll.
2. Reading Minutes of previous Meeting.
3. Report of Custodian and Secretary.
4. Report of Standing Committees.
5. Report of Special Committees.
6. Reading of Communications.
7. Unfinished Business.
8. Election of Officers.
9. New Business.

ART. 23. All resolutions and amendments before the Board or any committee shall be presented in writing.

ART. 24. All persons employed at the Museum must be promptly at their posts, as directed, and must remain there during the hours of their regular duty. They will remember that their time, while in the Museum, should constantly be occupied in its service, and it is the duty of the custodian and Executive Committee to enforce this rule.

ART. 25.   No amendments to the rules of the Board, or the regulations of the Museum shall be acted upon until the next regular meeting after the same shall have been proposed.

REGULATIONS.

The Museum will be open :

On Sundays, from 1:30 to 5 P. M.

Saturdays, from 9 to 12 A. M. and 1 to 5:30 P. M.

On all other days, from 1 to 5:30 P. M.

Visitors are admitted on condition that they observe the following regulations :

SECTION 1.   Any person of good deportment can be admitted during the above named hours.   Children less than fourteen years of age will be admitted only if accompanied by parents, teachers or other responsible adults.   Dogs or other live animals will not be admitted.

SEC. 2.   Admission is free.   Employes of the Museum are forbidden under penalty of discharge, to receive fees from visitors.

SEC. 3.   The removal of books, specimens or any other objects belonging to the Museum from any of its rooms, is strictly prohibited.

SEC. 4.   The use of tobacco, and all other conduct not consistent with the quiet and orderly use of the Museum, are prohibited.

SEC. 5.   Visitors are not allowed to touch any object.

SEC. 6.   Visitors will be held responsible for any mutilation or other injury to specimens, books, furniture, or other property of the Museum caused by them.

SEC. 7.   The time for closing will be announced by three bell signals ten minutes previous to the appointed hour.

OFFICE HOURS OF EMPLOYES.

Custodian, from 9 to 12 A. M. and 1 to 4 P. M.

Assistant Custodian, from 8:30 to 11:30 A. M. and 1 to 5 P M.

Taxidermist and Assistant, from 8 to 12 A. M. and 1 to 5 P. M.

All other Assistants, from 8:30 to 11:30 A. M and 1 to 5:30 P. M.

Janitor, from 7 to 11:30 A. M. and 1 to 5:30 P. M.

FOURTEENTH ANNUAL REPORT

OF THE

BOARD OF TRUSTEES

OF THE

Public Museum

OF THE

CITY OF MILWAUKEE

SEPTEMBER 1ST, 1895, TO AUGUST 31ST, 1896.

OCTOBER 1ST, 1896.

MILWAUKEE :
ED. KEOGH, PRINTER, 386–388 BROADWAY.
1897.

BOARD OF TRUSTEES.

STANDING COMMITTEES.

EXECUTIVE COMMITTEE.

A. J. Lindemann, Adolph Meinecke, Herman Buth, Julius Gold-schmidt, Geo. W. Peckham, *Ex-officio*.

FINANCE COMMITTEE.

Julius Goldschmidt, Thos. F. Ramsey, Herman Buth.

PURCHASING COMMITTEE.

Adolph Meinecke, August Stirn, Edwin W. Bartlett,

FURNITURE COMMITTEE.

August Stirn, Adolph Meinecke, Thos. F. Ramsey.

EXCHANGING COMMITTEE.

Edwin W. Bartlett, August Stirn, A. J. Lindemann.

BUILDING COMMITTEE.

W. H. Stevens, August Stirn, Julius Goldschmidt, Edwin W. Bartlett, Geo. W. Peckham, *Ex-officio*.

HONORARY CURATORS.

AUGUST STIRN, - - - - - - Ornithology.
F. RAUTERBERG, - - - - - Entomology.
CARL HAGENBECK, Hamburg, Germany, - - - Zoology.
DR. S. GRAENICHER, - - - - Ichthyology and Herpetology.
AD. MEINECKE, - - - - - - - At Large.

MUSEUM SERVICE.

HENRY NEHRLING, - - - - - Custodian.
CARL THAL, - - - - - - Assistant Custodian.
GEO. B. TURNER, - - - - - Taxidermist.
ALEXANDER GOETHEL, - - - - Assistant Taxidermist.
LYDIA NEHRLING, - - - - - Assistant.
ALMA WALDBART, - - - - - Assistant.
CARL BINDRICH, - - - - - Janitor.

REPORT OF THE PRESIDENT.

To the Honorable the Common Council of the City of Milwaukee.

Gentlemen: The Board of Trustees of the Public Museum, in accordance with Section 8, Chapter 328, of the Laws of 1882, presents herewith its annual report as required by law. It respectfully refers to the annual report of Mr. H. Nehrling, the custodian of the Museum, for such details and information as are not contained in this report.

The Museum contains the following specimens:

119,937 Zoological specimens, valued at	$36,461	09
17,132 Botanical specimens, valued at	1,117	45
15,151 Anthropological specimens, valued at	10,004	10
11,142 Palæontological specimens, valued at	5,228	95
4,191 Mineralogical and Lithological specimens, valued at	3,969	54
6,497 Books, Pamphlets, Catalogues, Atlases, valued at	6,119	87
3,035 Birds' Eggs and Nests, valued at	10,000	00
Furniture, Tools, Jars, Vessels, valued at	14,264	66
Upham collection of Indian Garments, held in trust	350	00
Total	$87,515	66

The number of visitors was 103,681, as compared with 88,320 of last year. The insurance on the property of the Museum is now $86,750.00.

The financial statement of the Board is as follows:

Balance in Museum fund September 1st, 1895.............	$4,300	55
Appropriation for 1896.................................	14,255	00
Refunded insurance premium...........................	92	48
Contributions of citizens for the purchase of the Hayssen collection.........	1,755	00
Total............	$20,403	03
Total expenditures during last year................	12,842	89
Leaving a balance on September 1st, 1896, of....	$7,560	14

My thanks are due to the members of the Board and the officers of the Museum for their cordial assistance in furthering the best interests of the Museum.

Respectfully submitted,
GEO. W. PECKHAM,
President.

REPORT OF THE CUSTODIAN.

Milwaukee, Wis., September 15, 1896.

To the Board of Trustees of the Public Museum of the City of Milwaukee.

Gentlemen: In accordance with Article VI of your Rules and Regulations, I have the honor of submitting to you my Sixth Annual Report, being the fourteenth in the series of reports since the foundation of the Museum.

An eventful year has passed, a year of the most remarkable progress. Not only is it remarkable because our new spacious quarters in the beautiful Library-Museum building are rapidly progressing, so that in a little over a year we will likely be able to move our collection, but we had also the good fortune to secure a very large number of specimens not before represented in the Museum.

The liberality of many of our public-spirited citizens enabled us to purchase the well-known "H. H. Hayssen Collection of Archæology, Ethnology and Anthropology." This collection has an especial value for us, as most of the specimens were obtained in Wisconsin, in the counties of Sheboygan, Manitowoc and Calumet. During the World's Columbian Exposition it formed an interesting feature in the Anthropological Building. The purchasing price was $2,500.00, of which $1,855.00 were subscribed by the following gentlemen:

George Brumder..	$125 00
Dr. Edwin W. Bartlett..................................	100 00
J. M. and T. J. Pereles.................................	100 00
Pabst Brewing Co......................................	100 00
Jos. Schlitz Brewing Co................................	100 00
The Edw. P. Allis Co..................................	100 00
Wm. Plankinton.......................................	100 00
Ferry & Clas..	50 00
E. Mariner...	50 00
Chas. F. Pfister......................................	50 00
Adolph Meinecke..............	50 00
John Pritzlaff Hardware Co..	50 00
Chr. Preusser..	50 00
Lindsay Bros...	50 00
First National Bank...................................	50 00
Kieckhefer Bros. Co...................................	50 00
Wm. Geuder..	25 00
A. Trostel & Sons....................................	25 00
G. Bossert...........................	25 00
H. W. Heinrichs......................................	25 00
Goll & Frank Co......................................	25 00
Stark Bros. Co.......................................	25 00
Wisconsin National Bank..............................	25 00
Milwaukee National Bank of Wisconsin..................	25 00
Dr. Jos. Schneider....................................	25 00
Val. Blatz Brewing Co................................	25 00
T. A. Chapman Co....................................	25 00
Gimbel Bros...	20 00
Wadhams Oil & Grease Co.............................	20 00
Landauer & Co..	20 00
J. A. Roundy...	20 00
J. P. Kissinger.......................................	10 00
C. W. Milbrath....,...................................	10 00
Brand Stove Co.......................................	10 00
F. Mayer Boot & Shoe Co.............................	10 00
Dr. F. W. Stewart....................................	10 00
Wm. Willer..	10 00
B. Leidersdorf & Co..................................	10 00
Joys Bros. Co..	10 00
Mendel, Smith & Co...........	10 00

Benjamin Young........................	$10 00
John Rauschenberger Co.................	10 00
Bunde & Upmeyer......................	10 00
H. G. Razall Manufacturing Co..........	10 00
L. Bartlett & Son.....................	10 00
Friend Bros. Co.......................	10 00
Straw & Ellsworth Co..................	10 00
H. Stern, Jr., & Bros. Co..............	10 00
George H. Heinemann & Co.............	10 00
David Adler & Sons Clothing Co........	10 00
Dewey & Davis........................	10 00
Koch & Loeber Co.....................	10 00
A. Geo. Schulz & Co..................	10 00
A. Geo. Schulz.......................	10 00
J. B. Le Saulnier.....................	10 00
Chas. L. Kiewert.....................	10 00
Quin Blank Book & Stationery Co.......	10 00
Gustav Reuss.........................	10 00
W. J. Turner.........................	10 00
S. Birkenwald & Co...................	5 00
The Gugler Lithographing Co...........	5 00
W. H. Starkweather...................	5 00
Otto Streissguth......................	5 00
Adam Gettelmann......................	5 00
Zoehrlaut Leather Co..................	5 00
E. Pommer............................	5 00
	$1,855 00

Thanks are due, in this connection, to Trustee Dr. Edwin W. Bartlett, to Alderman Chas. J. Koehler and Alderman J. R. Williams, who sacrificed much of their valuable time in securing the above subscriptions.

The acquisitions by donations are quite large, and among the donors Dr. Ernest Copeland, Dr. H. V. Ogden, Dr. S. Graenicher, Mr. Adolph Meinecke, Ex-Consul General Julius Goldschmidt, Mr. H. Denslow, of Gates, N. Y., Mr. Frank Suelflow, etc., deserve to be especially mentioned.

The acquisitions by purchase are not as large as could be desired, owing to our very insufficient appropriation. At every monthly meeting of the Board I could have presented a long list of desiderata, but I have refrained from doing so in view of the small endowment at our disposal, which forces me to use the utmost economy in all our business transactions. It is becoming self-evident that, with the completion of our new Museum building, and with the requirements of modern educational progress, more money is needed to carry out the plans which I have often referred to in my monthly and annual reports. The Museum is mainly an educational institution. Every visitor, be it child or man, rich or poor, must take with him certain ideas and thoughts.' The Museum must be placed at such a high standard that it can fulfill its mission as an educational factor. It must be equally useful to the scientist and to the layman. Not only correctly labeled systematic collections are necessary, but also well arranged groups of animals illustrating their life and habits. Quite a number of such groups have already been placed on exhibition, and noth-. ing in the Museum meets more with the approval of the visitors. These groups, however, are exceedingly expensive. I have contemplated for exhibition quite a number of additional groups, such as Elks, Moose, Buffalos, Virginia Deer, Raccoons, Woodchucks, Badgers, Squirrels, Robins, Barn Swallows, Purple Martins, Baltimore Orioles, Swifts, etc., but our means are at present too limited to carry out these plans. Our collection of foreign mammals is very incomplete. The beautiful Antelopes of Africa are fast disappearing from the face of the earth, and in order to procure the necessary material, steps should be taken immediately to secure specimens. In the next session of the legislature again attempts ought to be made to obtain more money, at least, one-fourth of a mill being required for a healthy increase of the different sections of the Museum. With the present resources we are barely keeping alive, and the future has nothing in prospect beyond the merest routine. work.

The public can hardly realize the great educational value of the institution. "The Museum," says our president, Dr. Geo. W. Peckham, the well-known scientist and teacher, "appeals to the many, since neither child nor man can fail to be both interested and instructed by the display of the wonderful animals, plants and minerals that are here gathered together from distant parts of the earth. In this respect the influence of the Museum is wider, though more superficial, than that of the Library. The one supplements the other, hence we find in the most enlightened communities the Museum and the Library keep pace with each other, each assuming its share in the new learning, and together helping to raise the standard of citizenship."

The halls of the Museum have been the gathering place for a large number of those who are interested in the study of natural history. Mrs. S. S. Merrill's and Mrs. H. F. Whitcomb's classes, all highly cultured ladies, have frequently met in the Museum for the purpose of studying the specimens displayed in our cases. Mrs. Merrill is particularly desirous of promoting the science of geology, while Mrs. Whitcomb delivered lectures in a more popular and interesting form on the birds that occur in this vicinity, her main object being the protection of our beautiful native songsters. An "Audubon Society for the Protection of Birds" like those in New York, Chicago and other cities will probably be the result of this attractive work.

Miss Margaret E. Mouat, teacher of natural history in the Milwaukee-Downer College, and Miss H. B. Merrill, teacher of natural science in the South Side High School, frequently came with their classes to the Museum. Many of the classes of the grammar schools also visited the institution, and much of my time has been spent in assisting the teachers in their work.

In the course of the year about fifty cases of the more common minerals have been bought by the Museum for the use of schools. A collection of ten familiar birds in fifty sets has been completed by our taxidermist for the same purpose. Each specimen has been placed in a case by itself, with a short description attached thereto for the convenience of the teachers.

Though the schools have made extensive use of our collections, and especially of the familiar birds we have placed at their disposal, much remains to be desired. The teachers are not expected to go into scientific details and technicalities. Most of those who study science in our public schools are doomed to lives of monotonous toil, beginning often before the years of childhood are past. In these lives of toil self-interest must be the prevailing motive. The knowledge the pupils can gain in school must necessarily be limited, and can go but a little way toward softening their hard conditions. The true teacher, then, during the years in which the child is under his or her care, will strive to implant that impersonal love of nature which lifts its possessor for the time above all sordid and material interests, and gives him that refreshment of spirit which comes only when thoughts of self have been laid aside.

The Museum library shows a great deficiency in scientific works. Monographs, published especially for the use of scientific institutions, are not represented in the Museum, owing to their very high price. The "Catalogue of the British Museum," which is indispensable for the arrangement and correct labeling of the zoölogical specimens from all parts of the world, has been only partially purchased. The remaining volumes of this monumental work should be added to our Museum library immediately.

The work in the Museum has been done as usual. Mr. Carl Thal, the assistant secretary and custodian, has been busily engaged in entering into our record books the many thousands of specimens which were bought or donated. He kept also the financial accounts, and did most of the business correspondence, etc. Miss Lydia Nehrling mounted and poisoned a large number of plants; she printed all our labels on the small hand press, and looked after visitors in the afternoon. Miss Alma Waldbart cleaned the glass cases in the morning, assisted Mr. Thal in keeping the duplicate record books, and guarded the back halls in the afternoon. Mr. Geo. B. Turner and his assistant, Mr. Alexander Goethel, mounted about five hundred birds for the school collection, a large Bengal tiger and many birds and smaller mammals, too numerous to be mentioned here. The Museum halls were kept clean under the charge of the janitor.

I.—ZOOLOGY.

A. MAMMALS.

Under these separate headings I shall only mention the rarer donations and acquisitions by purchase.

Dr. Ernest Copeland donated a fine albino of the Virginia Deer (Cervus virginianus), which he shot in Delta County, Mich., in the fall of 1895.

Mrs. Adolph Spranger presented a very fine and rare specimen of a species of South American Monkey, which I have not yet determined.

Dr. F. J. Toussaint shot a large specimen of Virginia Deer in Sawyer County, Wis., which he donated to the Museum.

Mr. G. W. Wolff of Town Rhine, Sheboygan County, Wis., donated an albino of the Gray Squirrel (Siurus carolinensis).

An American Panther or Ocelot (Felis pardalis), a Jaguarondi (Felis jaguarondi), a Lesser Anteater (Tamandua tetradactyla), two Weasels, one Opossum, all from Honduras, and one very fine Bengal Tiger (Felis tigris) from the Himalaya Mountains, were acquired by purchase.

B. BIRDS.

Mr. Henry Denslow of Gates, N. Y., the well-known modeler and artist of taxidermy, formerly engaged by the

Smithsonian Institution, presented an excellent and beautifully mounted Wild Turkey.

Mr. Adolph Meinecke donated fifty-seven tropical bird skins, several of them in very fine plumage.

Dr. E. Copeland and Dr. H. V. Ogden donated, besides a number of more common birds, one Pileated Woodpecker (Hylotomus pileatus), one Holboell's Grebe (Colymbus holbölli), and four Arctic Three-toed Woodpeckers (Picoides arcticus).

Mr. C. Bruchhäuser presented a beautiful Macaw (Sittace macao), and Mr. C. Carlin a Bald Eagle (Haliætus leucocephalus).

General Conrad Krez donated a very fine specimen of White-throated Sparrow (Zonotrichia albicollis); Mr. M. Mommsen, a specimen of White-winged Scoter (Oidemia deglandi), collected by him on Milwaukee Bay; Mr. Frank Suelflow, a Hooded Merganser (Lophodytes cucullatus); Mr. Frank Turner of Rochester, N. Y., one Brünnich's Murre (Uria lomvia); Walter Nehrling, Missouri Botanical Garden, St. Louis, Mo., a Parrot, and Mr. Aug. Stirn, four tropical bird skins.

Mrs. Sophia Zimmermann, Santa Barbara, Cal., donated a very beautiful nest of Bullock's Oriole (Icterus bullocki), built entirely of white unraveled cotton cloth.

Other donations to this department came from the following gentlemen: Mr. C. J. Allen, Herm. Hirsch, Jos. Caspari, Alex. Goethel, J. P. Kissinger, R. Kuehne (Sheboygan), Chas. L. Mann, Wm. J. Martin, H. W. Rohde, Carl Theis (Wanby, S. D.), Geo. B. Turner, etc.

Our systematic collection of North American birds was enriched by the following species: One Florida Wild Turkey (Meleagris gallopavo osceola), one pair of Mexican Turkeys (M. gallopavo mexicana), one pair of Allen's Ptarmigans (Lagopus lagopus alleni), one pair of Welch's Ptarmigans (Lagopus welchi), one pair of Richardson's Grouse (Dendrogapus obscurus richardsoni), one Pink-footed Shearwater (Puffinus creatopus), one Dark-bodied Shearwater (Puffinus griseus), one Black-vented Shearwater(Puffinus gavia), one Ashy Petrel (Oceanodrama homochroa), all acquired by purchase.

. The following five hundred birds, fifty of each species, were bought and mounted for the use of the public schools: Bobolink (male), Bobolink (female), Baltimore Oriole, Robin, Cedar Waxwing, Blue Jay, Downy Woodpecker, Night Hawk, Blue-winged Teal, English Sparrow.

One hundred and twenty-eight species of Humming Birds, in 168 specimens, a number of tropical American birds and a few species from Borneo were also bought. The Humming-birds are mostly duplicates from the celebrated collection of Count Hans von Berlepsch.

C.—HERPETOLOGY AND ICHTHYOLOGY.

We are indebted to Dr. S. Gränicher, honorary curator of Ichthyology and Herpetology, for the care he has given to the collection of fishes and reptiles under his charge. He has made excellent progress in identifying, arranging and storing our material. The herpetological collection has been enriched by many specimens collected by Mr. Adolph Meinecke in Gotha, Fla., as well as by Dr. Gränicher, who furnished excellent Wisconsin material. This holds true also of the ichthyological collection, to which Mr. Meinecke added a large number of salt water fishes from the Gulf of Mexico. A large number of fresh water fishes from Wisconsin were donated by Dr. Gränicher. Owing to our crowded halls, this material, which is preserved in a solution of formaline and water, is stored away for future exhibition in the basement of the Museum.

Mr. Julius Goldschmidt donated two jars, one showing the development of the Frog (Rana esculenta), the other that of the Brook Trout (Salmio fario). Such exhibits of biological work are exceedingly interesting and instructive.

D.—CONCHOLOGY.

A number of fine shells were also acquired by purchase, mostly from tropical waters.

E.—ENTOMOLOGY.

Mr. Julius Goldschmidt presented a very valuable collection of biological material in jars. The development of the following insects are shown: May Beetle (Melolantha vulgaris), Honey Bee (Apis mellifica), Common House Fly (Musca domestica), Red Ant (Formica rufa), Silk Worm (Bombyx mori), Phylloxera (Phylloxera vastatrix), Meal Worm (Tenebris molitor), Rose Bug (Cetonia aurata), Water Bug (Hydrophilus piceus).

Mr. Goldschmidt deserves especial thanks for his unique and valuable gift.

Mr. Adolph Meinecke donated an exquisite collection of very rare and valuable Beetles and Butterflies from all parts of the world. This collection, which consists of 222 specimens, was procured by Mr. Meinecke while traveling in Germany in 1895.

A lady who is well known all over the city for her nobility and the good she does, and who wishes her name reserved, donated an ornamental case of Butterflies and Beetles under glass, for which she paid $150.00.

II.—BOTANY.

Mr. Fred Rauterberg collected during the months of February, March and April a large number of plants for the Museum. These plants, which were collected on my account, have not yet been entered into our books.

The large collection of plants donated by Mr. Chas. E. Monroe, and mentioned in my last year's report, has been entered. This herbarium consists of 1,119 specimens.

Mr. A. Meinecke donated a collection of Arctic plants collected many years ago by the well-known scientist, Prof. Ludwig Kumlien.

III.—MINERALOGY AND LITHOLOGY.

From Mr. P. P. Peck, a well-known and painstaking collector of mineralogical specimens, a collection of 77 very beautiful pieces, mostly calcytes, for exhibition purposes, were bought. Most of these specimens come from Joplin, Mo.

IV.—PALÆONTOLOGY.

Mr. A. L. Story and Mr. W. E. Story presented some fine fossils collected in their quarry near Wauwatosa.

Mr. Adolph Meinecke donated a small collection of fossils from Germany and Switzerland.

Among the donors of palæontological specimens, the names of Mr. Aug. Stirn, Mr. Aug. Fiebelkorn, Cascade, Wis., and Mr. Herm. Hirsch must also be mentioned.

V.—ARCHÆOLOGY.

A very beautiful and characteristic chisel-shaped copper implement and a chain of copper beads were donated by Mr. A. L. Story and Mr. W. E. Story. These relics were found, together with an Indian skull and some bones, about five feet below the crest of the hill above Story Bros.' quarry, Wauwatosa, Wis.

Mr. Albert C. Krez presented an animal amulet made of stone and some other relics, all found in Sheboygan County, and Mr. M. C. Long, Chicago, Ill., donated 70 pieces of burnt clay picked up by him among the ruins of Aztalan, Jefferson County, Wis.

Mr. Adolph Meinecke donated a very old and valuable urn from Jaderberg, Germany, and quite a number of minor archælogical specimens.

Other donors to this department were: Franz Barthels, Gotha, Fla.; Fred Dufrenne, Middleton, Wis.; Lewis Erickson, Carl Meister, etc.

VI.—ETHNOLOGY AND ANTHROPOLOGY.

Rev. W. Chester donated an ancient Egyptian Canope.

Mr. Herm. Härtel presented a portrait of the son of the last Pottowattomie Chief of Milwaukee, painted about fifty years ago.

Mr. Adolph Meinecke presented an Ancient Japanese armor, a dancing mask and dancing spear from New Zealand, a model of an old-time country house of Oldenburg, Germany, and an Indian water jug from Arizona.

VII.—LIBRARY.

In addition to the usual number of scientific papers, pamphlets and books from the various American and foreign scientific societies and institutions, a large number of reports from the National Museum and Smithsonian Institution have been sent us free of charge. I have personally succeeded in obtaining many more pamphlets and books of such societies not yet exchanging with us.

Among the few purchases made during the last year, Dr. H. Burmeister's "Reise durch die La Plata Staaten" (three volumes), F. O. Morris' "A History of British Birds" (six volumes), and Dr. A. Reichenow's "Die Vögel Deutsch Ost Africas," must be mentioned.

INVENTORY.

119,715	Zoological specimens.....................	$36,367	99
17,132	Botanical specimens...........................	1,117	45
15,151	Anthropological specimens...........	10,004	10
11,142	Palæontological specimens......................	5,228	95
4,191	Mineralogical and Lithological specimens........	3,969	54
6,497	Books, Pamphlets, Catalogues, Atlases and Charts	6,119	87
3,024	Birds' Eggs and Nests..........................	10,000	00
	Furniture, Tools, Jars, Vessels, Conservation Supplies and Stationery...........................	14,225	20
	Upham Collection, held in trust.................	350	00
	Aggregate value of the Museum..............	$87,383	70

FINANCIAL TRANSACTIONS OF THE MUSEUM.

Debit.

Balance in Museum fund, Sept. 1st, 1895.................	$4,300 55
Appropriation to Museum fund, Jan. 1st, 1896...........	14,255 00
Refunded insurance premium.........................	92 48
Contributions of citizens for the Hayssen Collection......	1,755 00
Total.........	$20,403 03

Credit.

Amounts paid by, warrants on the City Treasurer since the last annual statement was rendered:

Permanent improvements........	$4 50	
Decrease in appropriation......................	47 20	
Fuel and light................................	239 41	
Repairs........	5 47	
Postage and freight...........................	95 66	
Furniture............	89 44	
Mammals..........	147 00	
Birds..........	654 79	
Fishes and reptiles............................	65	
Lower invertebrates...................... .	24 40	
Minerals and rocks............................	102 60	
Insurance.......	2,185 47	
Rent and tax.................................	1,350 00	
Library......	113 11	
Pay roll.............	6,888 29	
Conservation supplies.......	48 42	
Wages..........	405 05	
Miscellaneous........	342 86	
Stationery and printing.......................	98 57	
		$12,842 89
Balance in Museum fund Sept. 1st, 1896..		$7,560 14

INSURANCE.

Buffalo Commercial Insurance Co. of Buffalo, N. Y......	$1,000	00
Peabody Insurance Co. of Wheeling, W. Va.............	1,000	00
The Fire and Marine Insurance Co. of Wheeling, W. Va..	1,000	00
New York and Brooklyn Fire Underwriters.............	1,000	00
The Standard Fire Insurance Co. of Wheeling, W. Va....	1,000	00
German-American Fire Insurance Co. of Baltimore......	1,000	00
The Cincinnati Insurance Co., Cincinnati, O............	1,000	00
Citizens' Insurance Co. of Evansville, Ind..............	1,000	00
Indiana Underwriters' Policy of Indianapolis, Ind.......	1,500	00
Chicago Insurance Co. of Chicago, Ill..................	500	00
Michigan Fire and Marine Insurance Co., Detroit, Mich..	1,000	00
The Mercantile Fire and Marine Insurance Co. of Boston, Mass.........	1,000	00
Phenix Insurance Co. of Brooklyn, N. Y................	1,000	00
German Fire Insurance Co. of Peoria, Ill..............	1,000	00
The Allemannia Fire Insurance Co. of Pittsburg, Pa.....	1,500	00
The Grand Rapids Fire Insurance Co. of Grand Rapids, Mich.............	1,500	00
Westchester Fire Insurance Co. of New York City.......	1,500	00
The Palatine Insurance Co. of Manchester, England.....	1,500	00
Hamburg-Bremen Fire Insurance Co. of Hamburg, Germany...........	1,500	00
St. Paul Fire and Marine Insurance Co. of St. Paul, Minn.	1,500	00
Queen Insurance Co. of America, New York............	1,500	00
Capital Fire Insurance Co. of Concord, N. H............	1,500	00
The Greenwich Insurance Co. of the City of New York...	1,500	00
The Rutgers Fire Insurance Co. of New York...........	1,500	00
Assurance Lloyds of America, New York...............	1,500	00
Quebec Fire Assurance Co. of Quebec, Canada..........	1,500	00
Michigan Millers' Mutual Fire Insurance Co. of Lansing, Mich...........	1,500	00
Merchants' Insurance Co. of New Orleans, La...........	1,500	00

Germania Insurance Co. of New Orleans, La.............	$1,500 00
Philadelphia Mutual Fire Ins. Co. of Philadelphia, Pa...	1,500 00
Colonial Mutual Fire Insurance Co. of Philadelphia, Pa..	1,500 00
Underwriters at Protection Fire Lloyds, Manhattan Fire Lloyds..........	1,500 00
Svea Assurance Co. of Gothenburg....................	1,250 00
Rhode Island Underwriters' Association, Providence, R. I..........	2,000 00
The Schuylkill Fire Insurance Co. of Philadelphia.......	2,500 00
Tradesmen's Fire Lloyds of New York................	2,500 00
Keystone Fire Insurance Co. of St. John, N. B..........	2,500 00
Traders' Fire Lloyds of New York...................	2,500 00
The North German Fire Insurance Co. of Hamburg......	2,500 00
Saginaw Valley Fire and Marine Insurance Co. of Saginaw, Mich..........	2,500 00
Norwood Insurance Co. of New York..................	2,500 00
Royal Insurance Co. of Liverpool, England.............	2,500 00
Norwich Union Fire Insurance Society of England......	2,500 00
The Palatine Insurance Co. of Manchester, England.....	2,500 00
Manufacturers and Merchants' Mutual Insurance Co. of Rockford, Ill..........	2,500 00
Underwriters at Mutual Lloyds Fire Insurance Policy, New York..........	10,000 00
The Netherlands Fire Insurance Co....................	5,000 00
Total..........	$86,750 00

VISITORS.

	1895 Sept.	1895 Oct.	1895 Nov.	1895 Dec.	1896 Jan.	1896 Feb.	1896 Mar.	1896 April.	1896 May.	1896 June.	1896 July.	1896 Aug.	1895-96 Whole year.
Average daily attendance..	1,049	1,572	49	81	52	73	83	59	43	71	168	79	284
Greatest daily attendance..	2,372	5,689	155	1,215	109	204	210	134	77	162	1,216	150	
Least daily attendance.....	11	10	14	10	25	28	31	25	22	16	31	27	
Av. attendance on Sundays.	115	643	78	379	83	129	175	95	60	62	135	73	
Total attendance........	31,498	48,761	1,780	2,431	1,602	2,110	2,574	1,758	1,337	2,141	5,229	2,460	103,681

In conclusion, I sincerely thank the members of the Board of Trustees and all the employes of the Museum for the assistance they have given me in all the work pertaining to the progress of the institution.

Respectfully submitted,

H. NEHRLING,
Custodian and Secretary.

APPENDIX.

ZOOLOGY.

DONATIONS.

C. J. Allen, Milwaukee, Wis.
> 1 Cooper's Hawk, Milwaukee, Wis.

C. Bruchhaeuser, Milwaukee, Wis.
> 1 Parrot.

Hans Buschbauer (Gov. Francis A. Hoffmann), Jefferson, Wis.
> 5 Bony Fish Scales, Wallis, Austin Co., Tex.

C. Carlin, Milwaukee, Wis.
> 1 Bald Eagle, Palmyra, Wis.

Jos. Caspari, Milwaukee, Wis.
> 1 Great Horned Owl, Fox River, Wis.
> 1 American Long-eared Owl, Wisconsin.

Dr. E. Copeland and Dr. H. V. Ogden, Milwaukee, Wis.
> 1 Pileated Woodpecker,   Delta Co., Mich.
> 1 Holböll's Grebe,   "   "
> 1 Pine Warbler,   "   "
> 4 Arctic Three-toed Woodpeckers,   "   "
> 1 Red-breasted Nuthatch,   "   "
> 1 White Virginia Deer,   "   "

D. B. Danielson, Milwaukee, Wis.
> 1 Gray Squirrel, Eagle, Wis.

Henry Denslow, Gates, N. Y.
> 1 Mounted Wild Turkey, U. S.

August Fiebelkorn, Cascade, Wis.
> 1 Turtle Shell, Cascade, Town Mitchell, Wis.

Alexander Goethel, Milwaukee, Wis.
> 1 Slate-colored Junco, Milwaukee, Wis.
> 1 American Robin, Milwaukee Co., Wis.
> 1 Golden-crowned Kinglet, Milwaukee, Wis.

Julius Goldschmidt, Milwaukee, Wis.
> 11 Jars showing in alcohol the development of the following
> animals:
> 1 Cetonia aurata (Rosenkäfer).
> 1 Phylloxera vastatrix (Reblaus).
> 1 Hydrophilus piceus (Pechschwarzer Kolben Wasserkäfer).
> 1 Melolontha vulgaris (Maikäfer).
> 1 Rana esculenta (Wasserfrosch).
> 1 Astacus fluviatiles (Edelkrebs).

Julius Goldschmidt, Milwaukee, Wis.

    1 Salmo fario (Forelle).

    1 Apis mellifica (Honigbiene).

    1 Musca domestica (Fliege).

    1 Tenebris molitor (Mehlkäfer).

    1 Formica rufa (Rothe Ameise).

    1 Case showing the work of the Bee.

    1 Case showing the development of the Silk Worm

Hermann Hirsch, Milwaukee, Wis.

    1 Florida Gallinule, Milwaukee, Wis.

    1 Pileated Woodpecker, Wisconsin.

    2 Killdeers, Marshfield, Wis.

J. P. Kissinger, Milwaukee, Wis.

    1 American Osprey, Milwaukee Co., Wis.

General Conrad Krez, Milwaukee, Wis.

    1 White-throated Sparrow, Milwaukee, Wis.

R. Kuehne, Sheboygan, Wis.

    1 American Osprey, Sheboygan, Wis.

John Maag, Milwaukee, Wis.

    1 Fish, Green Bay, Wis.

Chas. L. Mann, Milwaukee, Wis.

    2 Canaday Jays, Captivity, Milwaukee, Wis.

Wm. J. Martin, Milwaukee, Wis.

    1 American Osprey, Lake Michigan, Wis.

Adolph Meinecke, Milwaukee, Wis.

    57 Tropical Bird Skins, Australia, India, Java and Africa.

    1 Life History of the Silk Worm (Bombyx mori).

    2 Spiders.

    222 Beetles and Butterflies from all parts of the globe.

Zachara T. Merrill, Milwaukee, Wis.

    1 Sponge.

M. Mommsen, Milwaukee, Wis.

    1 White-winged Scoter, Milwaukee Bay, Wis.

Henry Nehrling, Milwaukee, Wis.

    1 Yellow-bellied Sapsucker, Milwaukee, Wis.

Walter Nehrling, St. Louis, Mo.

    1 Parrot.

C. A. Rohde, Milwaukee, Wis.

    1 Nighthawk, Milwaukee, Wis.

H. W. Rohde, Milwaukee, Wis.

2 English Sparrows,	Milwaukee, Wis.
1 Philadelphia Virco,	" "
1 Vesper Sparrow,	" "
1 American Goldfinch,	" "

Mrs. Adolph Spranger, Milwaukee, Wis.

1 Monkey, Captivity, Milwaukee, Wis.

August Stirn, Milwaukee, Wis.

4 Tropical Bird Skins.

1 Barred Owl, Wisconsin.

1 Indigo Bunting, Milwaukee, Wis.

Frank W. Suelflow, Milwaukee, Wis.

1 Hooded Morganser, Mouse Lake, Wis.

Carl Theiss, Wanby, S. D.

1 Snowy Owl, Wanby, S. D.

Geo. B. Turner, Milwaukee, Wis.

2 Yellow-bellied Sapsuckers, Milwaukee, Wis.

Dr. F. J. Toussaint, Milwaukee, Wis.

1 Virginia Deer, Sawyer Co., Wis.

Frank H. Turner, Rochester, N. Y.

1 Brünnich's Murre, New York.

Mrs. Christian Wahl, Milwaukee, Wis.

1 Crab, Florida.

Mrs. ————, Milwaukee, Wis.

1 Ornamental Case of Butterflies.

Geo. W. Wolff, Rhine, Wis.

1 Gray Squirrel (Albino), Rhine, Sheboygan Co., Wis.

Mrs. Sophie Zimmermann, Santa Barbara, Cal.

1 Nest of Bullock's Oriole, Paso Robles, Cal.

ACQUIRED BY PURCHASE.

2 Wild Turkeys,	Cameron Co., Tex.
1 Florida Wild Turkey, Southern Florida.	
2 Richardson's Grouse, Deer Lodge Co., Mont.	
2 Allen's Ptarmigans,	St. George Bay, Newfoundland.
2 Welch's Ptarmigans,	" "
1 Pink-footed Shearwater,	Pacific Grove, California.
1 Dark-bodied Shearwater,	" "
1 Black-vented Shearwater, San Diego, Cal.	
1 Ashy Petrel, Point Reyes, Cal.	

2 Troupials, British Guiana.
20 Bobolinks.
14 Nighthawks.
23 Downy Woodpeckers.
49 Baltimore Orioles.
37 Cedar Wax-wings.
50 Bluejays.
50 American Robins.
6 Cinnamon Teals.
44 Blue-winged Teals.
1 Calliste cyaneicollis,   Rio Pastaza, Ecuador.
1   "   venusta,   "   "
1   "   yeni,   "   "
1 Chlorochrysa calliparia,   "   "
1 Rhamphastos brevicaranatus,   Nata, Panama.
1 Pteroglossus torquatus,   "   "
1 Selenidera spectabilis, Panama.
1 Aulocoramphus prasinus, Guatemala.
1 Selenidera maculirostris, Rio Grande do Sul, Brazil.
2 Aulacoramphus coeruleicinctus, Bolivia.
1 Rhamphastos dicolorus, Sao Paulo, Brazil.
2 Andigena cucullatus, Bolivia.
1 Ostinops decumanus, Panama.
1 Calocitta formosa, Guatemala.
1 Cyanocorax affinis,   Panama.
1 Columba nigrirostris,   "
1 Geococcyx affinis, Guatemala.
1 Aramides cayennensis, Panama.
1 Polyplectron schalerimacheri, Northern Borneo.
1 Momotus lessoni,   Guatemala.
1 Eumomota superciliaris,   "
1 Prionorhynchus carinatus, Panama.
1 Cyanocitta coronata,   Guatemala.
1 Xanthura melanocyana,   "
1 Diphyllodes chrysoptera septentrionalis, New Guinea.
1 Callipepla elegans, Mexico.
1 Semioptera wallacei halmaherae, Asia.
1 Cassiculus melanicterus, Mexico.
1 Sturnella magna mexicana,   Guatemala.
1 Icterus wagleri,   "
1 Cassicus microrhynchus, Panama.

1 Habia ludoviciana, Guatemala.

1 Trogon resplendens, Central America.

1   "   massenae, Panama.

1 Trogon puella, Guatemala.

1	"	chionurus, Panama.	
2	"	mexicanus,	Guatemala.
2	"	caligatus,	"
1	"	tenellus,	Panama.
1	"	calthratus,	"

1 Icterus pustulatus, Mexico.

1 Selenidera maculirostris, Sao Paulo, Brazil.

1 Pyranga testacca,			Panama.
1	"	aestiva,	"
1 Cotinga ridgwayi,			"
1 Rhamphocoelus icteronatus,			"
1	"	passerini,	"

1 Ampelis cedrorum, Guatemala.

1 Calliste gyroloides,	Panama.
1 Guiraca cyanoides,	"
1 Calliste larvata,	Panama.
1 Chlorophanes spiza,	"
1 Chiromachaeris vitellina,	"
1 Dacnis cayana,	"
1 Coereba cyanea,	"
1 Pipra mentalis,	"

1 Oroephasis derbianus, Guatemala.

HUMMINGBIRDS.

2 Oreotrochilus pichincha, Ecuador.

3 Basilinna eucotis, New Mexico.

2 Metallura tyrianthina quitensis,	Ecuador.
2 Phasolaema aequatorialis,	"
1 Psalidopryma gouldi gracilis,	"

1 Petasophora thalassinus, Western Mexico.

1 Schistes geoffroyi,	Ecuador.
1 Eriocnemis luciana,	"
1 Eugenes fulgens,	"
1 Pterophanes temminki,	"

2 Topaza pella, British Guiana.

2 Metallura opaca, Peru.

1 Rhamphodon naevius, Brazil.

1 Cyanolesbia smaragdina, Bolivia.

1 Phaethornis pretrei, Bahia, Brazil.

1 Pteropharies temminki, Bogota.

1 Bourcieria inca, Bolivia.

2 Psalidopryma gouldi, Bogota.

1 Petasophora cyanotis, United States of Colombia.

1 Popelairea conversi,   Bogota.

2 Phoethornis guyi emiliae,   "

1 Polytmus brevirostris, Neu Freiburg.

1 Eustephanus galeritus, Chile.

1 Cyanolesbia emmae, Bogota.

2 Steganura underwoodi, Colombia.

1 Metallura smaragdinicollis, Bolivia.

1 Polytmus thaumantias, Bahia, Brazil.

1 Oreothochilus estellae, Bolivia.

1 Phaethornis longirostris, Guatemala.

1 Cyanolesbia smaragdina, Bolivia.

1 Panychlora poortmani,   Colombia.

1 Phaeolaema rubinoides,   "

1 Petasophora thalassina, Mexico.

2 Thalurania colombica, Colombia.

1 Phemonoe luciani, Ecuador.

1 Thalurania eriphile, Brazil.

1 Popelairia conversi, Ecuador.

1   "   popelairei, Bogota.

1 Leucippus chionogaster, Bolivia.

1 Panoplites flavescens, Gould.

1 Polytmus thaumantias, Bahia.

1 Urosticte ruficrissus, Colombia.

1 Metallura trianthina quitensis, Ecuador.

1 Petasophora delphinae, Colombia.

1 Rhamphomicron microrhynchum, Bogota.

1 Uranomitra faustinae,   Colombia.

1 Phemonoe cupreiventris,   "

1 Phaethornis syrmatophora, Peru.

1 Chlorostilbon stybeli, Bolivia.

2 Bourcieria torquata, Bogota.

1 Juliamyia feliciana, Ecuador.

2 Klais guimeti, Bogota.

1 Lafresnaya flavicaudata, Colombia.

1 Eucephala caerulea, Venezuela.

1 Hemistephania johannae,   Colombia.

1 Antocephala floriceps,   "

1 Cyanophaia gandoti,   "

1 Lophornis delattrei,   Bogota.

1 " stictolophus,   "

1 Cyanophaia cyanea, Sao Paulo, Brazil.

1 Hemistephania ludoviciae,   Bogota.

2 Florisuga mellivora,   "

2 Acestrura mulsanti,   "

2 Amazalia cyaneifrons,   "

1 Chalybura buffoni,   "

1 Bellona exilis, Island of Martinique.

2 Chlorostilbon angustipennis, Colombia.

1 Heliotrypha exortis, Bogota.

1 Agyrtria niveipectus, Venezuela.

1 Chrysuronia aenone longirostris,   Bogota.

1 Oxypogon guerini,   "

2 Amazilia viridiventris,   "

1 Agyrtria nigricauda,   Bahia.

1 Erythronota antiqua,   "

1 Eriocnemis alinae,   Bogota.

1 Agyrtria milleri,   "

1 Cyanophaia cyanea, Sao Paulo, Brazil.

1 Agyrtria leucogastra, Bahia.

1 Eulampis jugularis, Island of Martinique.

1 Adelomyia melanogenys,   Colombia.

1 Chrysolampis moschitas,   "

1 Eupherusa eximia, Guatemala.

1 Bellona exilis, Island of Martinique.

1 Basilinna leucotis, Guatemala.

1 Lophornis stictolophus,   Bogota.

1 Cyanochloris caeruleiventris,   "

2 Helianthea helianthea,   "

1 Coeligena clemenciae, Mexico.

2 Campylopterus lazulus,   Bogota.

1 Chrysuronia eunonae longirostris,   "

1 Eucephala grayi, Ecuador.

2 Lampornis nigricollis, Bogota.

1 Polytmus tephrocephalus, Rio Grande do Sul, Brazil.

1 Heliodoxa leadbeateri, Colombia.

1 Leucochloris albicollis, Rio Grande do Sul, Brazil.

1 Amazilia warszewiczi bracata, Venezuela.
1 Bourcieria colombiana, Colombia.
1 Metallura tyrianthina, Ecuador.
1 Eriocnemis vestita,   Bogota.
1 Heliangelus clarissae,   "
2 Lafresnaya lafresnayei,   "
1 Eriocnemis aureliae,   "
1 Amazilia cerviniventris, Mexico.
1 Eriocnemis vestita,   Colombia.
1 Adelomyia melanogenys,   "
1 Damophila amabilis,   "
1 Oxypogon guerini,   "
2 Heliomaster longirostris,   "
1 Heliangelus clarissae,   "
1 Chrysuronia eunone, Venezuela.
1 Orthornis anthrophilus, Bogota.
1 Glaucis hirsuta, Sao Paulo, Brazil.
1 Campylopterus lazulus, Venezuela.
1 Helianthea helianthea,   Bogota.
1 " typica,   "
1 Eulampis holosericeus, Island of Martinique.
1 Psalidopryma victoriae, Ecuador.
1 Heliodoxa jacula,   Bogota.
1 Bourceiria prunellei,   "
1 Hypochrysea bonapartei,   "
1 Florisuga fusca, Bahia.
1 Campylopterus ensipennis, Trinidad.
1 Aglaeactis cupripennis, Bogota.
1 Docimastes ensifer, Colombia.
1 Thaumatias tobaci, Cayenne.
2 Clytolaema rubinea, Brazil.
1 Chalybura buffoni, Colombia.
1 Aphantochroa cirrhochloris, Sao Paulo, Brazil.
1 Rhamphomicron heteropogon, Colombia.
1 Heliotrypha exortis, Bogota.
1 Hylocharis sapphirina, Sao Paulo, Brazil.
1 Chiroxiphia lanceolata, Panama.
1 Petasophora iolata,   Ecuador.
1 Oreotrochilus chimborazo,   "
1 American Panther,   Central America.
1 Yaguarundi,   "   "

1 Little Anteater,	Central America.
2 Weasels,	" "
1 Opossum,	" "

3 Achatina variegata, Africa.
3   "   reticulata, Mozambique.
3   "   panthera, Mauritius.
5   "   zebra, Cape Colony.
4   '   marginata, South Africa.
3   "   granulata, Port Natal.
2   "   sinistrarsa, Prince's Island, Africa.
2   "   fulica, Madagascar.
1   "   purpurea, West Africa.
2 Bulimus ovatus, Brazil.
3 Vulsella spongiarum, Mauritius.
1 Pholas concamerata, Cala.

| 1   "   dactylus, | Mediterranean. |
| 1 Pinna nobilis, | " |

BOTANY.

DONATIONS.

Mrs. Simon Kander, Milwaukee, Wis.
    1 Cocoanut Blossom, Palm Beach, Lake Worth, Fla.
Adolph Meinecke, Milwaukee, Wis.
    32 Arctic Plants (Collected by Ludwig Kumlien).
Chas. E. Monroe, Milwaukee, Wis.
    1,119 Plants, all mounted on herbarium paper.

PALÆONTOLOGY.

DONATIONS.

August Fiebelkorn, Cascade, Wis.

| 1 Halysites catenulatus, | Cascade, Wis. |
| 1 Coral, | " " |

H. Hirsch, Milwaukee, Wis.
    2 Gomphoceras, Humboldt, Wis.
Adolph Meinecke, Milwaukee, Wis.

2 Neuropteris ovatus,	Piesberg, Germany.
2 " Scheuchzeri,	" "
3 " rarinervis,	" "
3 Calamites suckowii,	" "

2 Annularia stellata,   Piesberg, Germany.
2 Sphenophyllum cuneifolium,   "   "
1 Pecopteris miltoni,   "   "
1   "   subnerosa,   "   "
1 Cyclopteris,   "   "
1 Sigillaria,   "   "
1 Odontopteris,   "   "
1 Lepidodrendon,   "   "
1 Pinnularia,   "   "
1 Annularia microphylla,   "   "
2 Terebratula grandis,   "   "
2 Nautilus ahltenensis,   "   "
1   "   "   "
1 Scaphites Roemeri,   Lemförde, Germany.
1 Inoceramus Cripsi,   "   "
1   "   latus,   "   "
1 Pholadomya Puschi, Aztrup, near Osnabrück, Germany.
2   "   Esmarki, Lemförde, Germany.
1 Cyprina rotundata, Aztrup, near Osnabrück, Germany.
1 Pinna quadrangularis,   Lemförde, Germany.
1 Ananchytes ovatus,   "   "
1 Ostrea vesicularis,   "   "
1 Heteroceras polyplocum,   "   "
1 Pleurotomaria distincta,   "   "
1 Belemnitella mucronata,   "   "
3 Echinolampas Kleini, Bünde, Germany.
1 Fish remains, Kelley's Island, Ohio.
1 Plagirostoma radiata, Würtemberg.
1 Orthoceratites, Cincinnati, Ohio.
1 Spirifer, Coblenz, Germany.
1 Orthis proximus, Germany.
1 Bellerophon bilobatus, Cincinnati, Ohio.
1 Alveolites reticulata, Iberg, Harz, Germany.
1 Strigocephalus, Bensberg, Germany.
1 Mortonia, Alabama.
2 Productus semireliculatus, Crawfordsville, Ind.
1 Hysterolithus, Germany.
1 Crania on Strophomena, Germany.
1 Monticulipora, Cincinnati, Ohio.
1 Emmonsia, Louisville, Ky.
1 Dalmanites, Kelley's Island, Ohio.

August Stirn, Milwaukee, Wis.

    1 Coral, Elkhart, Wis.

A. L. Story and W. E. Story, Wauwatosa, Wis.

    5 Calymene niagarensis, Wauwatosa, Wis.

ACQUIRED BY PURCHASE.

27 Calymene niagarensis, Wauwatosa, Wis.

MINEROLOGY AND LITHOLOGY.

Carl Bindrich, Jr., Milwaukee, Wis.

    1 Muscovite, Missouri.

Adolph Meinecke, Milwaukee, Wis.

    1 Serpentine, Chester Co., Pa.

August Stirn, Milwaukee, Wis.

    1 Mineral, Wisconsin.

Herman Weisleder, Milwaukee, Wis.

    1 Large piece of lead.

A. E. Williams, Milwaukee, Wis.

    1 Pot-hole cobble, Star Lake, Vilas Co., Wis.

ACQUIRED BY PURCHASE.

1 Calcite with star crystal of Marcasite, New Cave, Leadville, Col.

1 Calcite with Lead,   Leadville, Col.

1 Calcite,   "   "

2 Calcites,   Aurora, Mo.

1 Calcite with Lead,   "   "

6 Calcites, Leadville, Col.

2 Calcites, Aurora, Mo.

4 Calcites, Joplin, Mo.

1 Calcite with Lead, Carterville, Mo.

1 Calcite with Zinc and Dolomite, Leadville, Col.

1 Calcite with Zinc, Joplin, Mo.

1   "   "   "   Leadville, Col.

1 Calcite and Galena, Leadville, Col.

1 Lead with Calcite crystal, Carterville, Mo.

1 Galena with the form of the crystals, destroyed by mineral tar, Joplin, Mo.

2 Galena,   .   Joplin, Mo.

1 Galena, Calcite and Zinc,   "   "

3 Galena Crystals with mineral tar,   "   "

10 Galena,   "   "

2 Galena, Dolomite and Zinc,   "   "

1 Galena on Zincblende,   "   "

1 Galena Crystal, Blandon Mine, Jasper Co., Mo.

3 Zinc Crystals, Joplin, Mo.

1 Zincblende with Galena, Carterville, Mo.

1 Zinc, Joplin, Mo.

1 Zinc with Greenockite, Joplin, Mo.

1 Dolomite, Lead and Zinc, Joplin, Mo.

1 Zincblende, Carterville, Mo.

1 Dolomite, Lead and Zinc, Missouri.

5 Workite,   Joplin, Mo.

1 Marcasite,   "   "

1 Chalcedony, replacing coral, Bijou Basin, Col.

1 Carbonate of Zinc, Boone Co., Ark.

1 Chalcotricite, Clifton, Arizona.

2 Peacock Galena, Joplin, Mo.

1 Silicate of Zinc, Aurora, Mo.

3 Smithsonite, Boone Co., Ark.

1 Zinc Blende, Joplin, Mo.

1 Vanadinite, Arizona.

1 Chalcotricite and hard Carbonate of Copper, Clifton, Ariz.

2 Greenockite, Joplin, Mo.

3 Selenite, Utah.

ETHNOLOGY.
DONATIONS.

Geo. Bunsen, Milwaukee, Wis.

     1 Gun, Germany.

Rev. Wm. Chester, Milwaukee, Wis.

     1 Canope with cover, representing a Hawk's head.

Hermann Härtel, Milwaukee, Wis.

     1 Portrait of the son of the last Pottawattomie Chief of Milwaukee.

Adolph Meinecke, Milwaukee, Wis.

     3 Images made of Wood,   New Ireland.

     1 Image made of Chalk,   "   "

     2 Dancing Spears,   "   "

Adolph Meinecke. Milwaukee, Wis.

    1 Ancient Japanese Armor, Japan.

    1 Dancing Mask, New Ireland.

    1 Lower Saxon Farmhouse, Saterland, Oldenburg.

    1 Indian Water Jug, Grand Canyon, Arizona.

Miss Hedwig Schlichting, Milwaukee, Wis.

    10 pieces of Paper Money from Civil War times.

August Stirn, Milwaukee, Wis.

    2 Indian Skulls, Elkhart, Wis.

A. L. Story and W. E. Story, Wauwatosa, Wis.

    1 Indian Skull with 4 other Indian Bones, found about five feet below crest of hill above Story Bros.' Quarry, Town of Wauwatosa, Wis.

ACQUIRED BY PURCHASE.

    1 Pair of Snow Shoes, used in the fall and winter of 1887 by Lou Mak Saba, side chief of the Chippewa tribe.

ARCHÆOLOGY.

DONATIONS.

Franz Barthels, Gotha, Fla.

    1 Stone arrowhead, Gotha, Orange Co., Fla.

Fred. Dufrenne, Middleton, Wis.

    5 Photographs of Indian Implements, Middleton, Wis.

Lewis Erickson, Milwaukee, Wis.

    1 Unique Spearhead, Wind Lake, Wis.

Albert C. Krez, Milwaukee, Wis.

    1 Animal amulet,   Sheboygan Co., Wis.

    1 Unfinished stone arrowhead,   "   "

M. C. Long, Chicago, Ill.

    70 Pieces of burnt clay, Aztalan, Wis.

Adolph Meinecke, Milwaukee, Wis.

    53 Flint stones, Glaner Haide, Wildeshausen, Oldenburg.

    23 Unfinished Flint arrowheads,   Wildeshausen, Oldenburg.

    2 Flint knives,   "   "

    27 Arrowhead chips,   "   "

    20 Unfinished Flint knives,   "   "

    26 Flint chips,   "   "

    1 Urn, Jaderberg, Oldenburg.

Adolph Meinecke. Milwaukee. Wis.

    1 Stone celt with deer horn handle, Robenhausen, Switzerland.

2 Bottles of charred wheat,	Robenhausen, Switzerland.	
1 Bottle of charred barley,	"	"
1 Bottle of charred wild apples,	"	"
1 Piece of woven cloth,	"	"
1 Stone Celt,	"	"
1 Stone Axe,	"	"
10 Pieces of pottery,	"	"
1 Awl of deer horn,	"	"
1 Knife of bone,	"	"
3 Awls of bone,	"	"
2 Stone knives,	"	"
1 Stone object,	"	"

    1 Machine, showing the supposed method used by the Mound Builders and Pile Dwellers of boring holes into solid rock.

Carl Meister, Milwaukee, Wis.

    1 Stone axe, Kenosha Co., Wis.

Story Bros., Wauwatosa, Wis.

1 Chisel shaped copper implement,	Wauwatosa, Wis.
1 Chain of copper beads,	" "

LIBRARY.

Academie Nationale de Sciences, Buenos Aires, S. A.
    Boletin, Tomo 14, Entegra 2.

Academy of Science of St. Louis, Mo.
    Transactions, Vol. VII., Nos. 4-9.

American Medical Association, Washington, D. C.
    Resolution on the Defense of Vivisection.

American Museum of Natural History, New York, N. Y.
    Bulletin, Vol. VII., 1895.
    Visitors' Guide, 1892.

Anthropologische Gesellschaft in Wien, Austria.
    Mittheilungen, Nos. 2, 3.
        " Bd. XXVI., Neue Folge XVI., Bd.

Australian Museum, Sydney, Australia.
    Records, Vol. II., Nos. 6, 7.

Belfast Naturalists' Field Club, Belfast, Ireland.
>   Annual Report and Proceedings, Sec. II., Part III., Vol. IV.,
>   1895-1896.

Belfast Natural History and Philosophical Society, Belfast, Ireland.
>   • Report and Proceedings for 1894 to 1895.

Bergens Museum, Bergen, Germany.
>   Aarbog for 1893.

Biblioteca Nazionale Centrale di Firenze, Italy.
>   Bollettino Nos. 238, 244.

Boston Public Library, Boston, Mass.
>   Annual Report.

Boston Society of Natural History, Boston, Mass.
>   Proceedings, Vols. XXVI., XXVII., Nos. 1-6.

Botanischer Verein zu Landshut, Bavaria.
>   14 Bericht, 1894-1895.

California Academy of Sciences, San Francisco, Cal.
>   Proceedings, Vol. V., Part I., II.

Chicago Academy of Sciences, Chicago, Ill.
>   Bulletins Nos. 1 to 10.
>   38th Annual Report.

Cincinnati Museum Association, Cincinnati, Ohio.
>   Catalogue of the Spring Exhibition in the Art Museum.
>   15th Annual Report.

Cincinnati Society of Natural History, Cincinnati, Ohio.
>   Journal, Vol. XVIII., Nos. 1-4.

Civico Museo di Storia Naturale Ferdinando Maximiliano, Trieste,
>   Illyria.
>   Atti del Museo Civico di Storia Naturale di Trieste, 1895, IX.

Commissioners of Lincoln Park, Chicago, Ill.
>   Report for 1895.

Connecticut Historical Society, Hartford, Conn.
>   Annual Reports, 1894-1895.

Detroit Museum of Art, Detroit, Mich.
>   Annual Report, 1896.

Elisha Mitchell Scientific Society, Chapel Hill, N. C.
>   Journal, II. Part, Twelfth Year.

Entomological Society of Ontario, Toronto, Canada.
>   22d and 23d Annual Report, 1891-1892.

Field Columbian Museum, Chicago, Ill.
>   Publications Nos. 1 to 7.

Hy. P. Fischer, Milwaukee, Wis.
>43 Pictures relating to the Civil War.

Free Public Library, Museum and Walker Art Gallery, Liverpool, England.
>39th and 43d Report, 1892 and 1896.

Geological Survey of Australia, Brisbane, Australia.
>- Annual Progress Report.
>Report on the Leichhardt Gold Field and other Mining Centers in the Cloucurry District.

Gesellschaft fur Natur und Heilkunde, Dresden, Germany.
>Jahresbericht, 1894-1895.

Government Museum of Madras, India.
>Administration Report for 1894-1895.

Historical Society of New Mexico, Santa Fé, N. M.
>The Stone Idols of New Mexico.

Hungarian National Museum, Budapest.
>Periodical, Vol. XVIII., 1895, Parts 3-4.
>Termeszetrajzi Füzetec, XIX., Heft, 1896.

Instituto Fisico Geographico National de Costa Rica.
>Anales, Tomo V., VI., 1892-1893.
>Cherry, Geo. K., Bird Exploration of the Valley of Rio Naranjo, 1893.

John Hopkins University, Baltimore.
>Circulars, Vol. XV., No. 121-126.

Journal of Comparative Neurology, Granville, Ohio.
>The Journal, Vol. V., Page 1-214.
>" Vol. IV., No. 1.
>" Vol. VI., No. 2.

Kansas Academy of Science, Topeka, Kansas.
>Transactions, 1893-1894.

K. K. Geologische Reichsanstalt, Wien, Austria.
>Jahrbuch, 45, Bd 1-3, Heft, 1895.
>Verhandlungen, Nos. 4, 5.

K. K. Naturhistorisches Hofmuseum, Wien, Austria.
>Annalen, Bd. XI., No. 1.

K. K. Naturhistorisches Hofmuseum, Wien, Austria.
>Annalen, Bd. X.. No. 1.
>Separatabdruck aus Bd. XI., Heft I.
>Jahresbericht, 1894.

Kais. Leopoldina Carolinischen Deutschen Akademie der Naturforscher, Halle, Germany.

"Leopoldina." 30 Heft, Jahrg. 1894.
"   31 Heft, Jahrg. 1895.

Königl Böhmische Gesellschaft der Wissenschaften, Prag, Böhmen.
Jahresbericht, 1895.

Kgl. Sammlung für Kunst und Wissenschaft, Dresden, Germany.
Bericht über die Verwaltung, 1892-1893.

Kgl. Sächsische Gesellschaft der Wissenschaften, Leipzig, Germany.
Berichte über die Verhandlungen, Math. Phys. Classe, 1895,
Heft II.-IV.

Berichte über die Verhandlungen, Math. Phys. Classe, 1896,
Heft I.

Köngl. Vitterhets Historie och Antiqvitets Akademien, Stockholm,
Sweden.
Antiqvarisk Tidskrift fôr Sverige, Vol. XVL., No. 1.

Dr. Otto Kuntze, Leipzig, Germany.
Kuntze, Dr. Otto, Geogenetische Beiträge, 1895.

Kurländische Gesellschaft für Literatur und Kunst, Mitau, Russland.
Sitzungsberichte, 1895.

L'Institut Grand Ducal de Luxembourg, Luxembourg.
Publications, Tomo XXIV.

Library Association of Portland, Oregon.
31st Annual Report, 1894.

Magyar Nemzeti Muzeum, Budapest, Hungary.
Termeszetrajzi Fuezetec, Vol. XIX., 1896.

Magyar Nemzeti Muzeum, Budapest, Hungary.
Termeszetrajzi Fuezetec, Vol. XIX., 1896.

Märkisches Provinzial Museum, Berlin, Germany.
Verwaltungsbericht, April, 1894, bis März, 1895.

Adolph Meinecke, Milwaukee, Wis.
1 Map. Die erste Hilfe beim Knochenbruch und bei Verwun-
dungen darstellend.

1 Map. Die Künstliche Atmung darstellend.

1 "   Altertümer aus unserer Heimath.

1 "   Vor- und frühgeschichtliche Denkmäler aus
Oestreich-Ungarn.

1 Pamphl. Die erste Hilfe bei Unglücksfällen.

3 Lieferungen, Heyse, A. Die exotischen Käfer in Wort
und Bild.

1 Photograph of a curious-shaped oak-tree.

Milwaukee Public Library, Milwaukee, Wis.

 Quarterly Index, Vol. V., No. 38, 39, 40.

 18th Annual Report.

Milwaukee School Board, Milwaukee, Wis.

 Pereles, James M. Address on the History of the Milwaukee Public Schools, 1895.

Missouri Botanical Garden, St. Louis, Mo.

 The Sturtevant Prelinnean Library of the Missouri Botanical Garden.

 Seventh Annual Report.

Museo Nacional de Buenos Aires, Buenos Aires, Argentine Republic.

 Anales, Tomo IV. (Ser. 2, t. I.)

Museo Nacional de Costa Rica, San José, Costa Rica.

 Informe Presentado al Senor Secretario de Estado en el Despacho de Fomento.

Museo Nacional de Montevideo, Colombia.

 Anales, 1895, III. 1896, IV.

Museu Paulista in Sao Paulo, Brazil.

 Ihering, Dr. H. v. Revista do Museu Paulista.

Museum Carolino Augusteum, Salzburg, Austria.

 Jahresbericht, 1894.

Museum of Comparative Zoology, Cambridge, Mass.

 Annual Report, 1893-1894.

Museum Francisco-Carolinum, Linz, Austria.

 54. Jahresbericht.

Museum Schlesischer Alterthümer, Breslau, Germany.

 Schlesiens Vorzeit in Bild und Schrift, Bd. VI.; Heft III.

Museum für Völkerkunde zu Leipzig, Germany.

 22. Bericht, 1894.

Naturforschende Gesellschaft in Basel, Schweiz.

 Verhandlungen, Bd. XI., Heft I., II.

Naturforschende Gesellschaft in Bern, Schweiz.

 Mittheilungen, 1894.

Naturforschende Gesellschaft in Danzig, Germany.

 Schriften, Neue Folge, Bd. IX., Heft I.

Naturforschende Gesellschaft in Emden, Germany.

 79. Jahresbericht, 1893-1894.

Naturforschende Gesellschaft in Görlitz, Germany.

 Abhandlungen, 21. Bd.

Naturhistorisches Landes Museum von Kärnten, Klagenfurth, Austria-Hungary.

    Jahrbuch, 1895.

    Mittheilungen ("Carinthia").

Naturhistorisch Medicinischer Verein, Heidelberg, Germany.

    Verhandlungen, 1895.

Natural History Society of New Brunswick, B. A.

    Bulletin No. XIII.

Natural History Society of Glasgow, Scotland.

    Transactions, Vol. IV. (New Series), Part II.

Naturhistorische Gesellschaft zu Nürnberg, Bavaria.

    Abhandlungen, Bd. X., Heft III.

Naturhistorischer Verein zu Passau, Bavaria.

    16. Bericht, 1890-1895.

Natural Science Association of Staten Island, New Brighton, N. Y.

    Proceedings, Vol. V., No. 5.

Naturwissenschaftlicher Verein zu Bremen, Germany.

    Abhandlungen, XIII. Bd., III. Heft.

        "   XIV. " I. Heft.

Naturwissenschaftlicher Verein zu Hamburg, Germany.

    Abhandlungen, XIV. Bd.

    Verhandlungen, 1895, III. Folge.

Naturwissenschaftlicher Verein zu Karlsruhe, Baden.

    Verhandlungen, 11. Bd., 1888-1895.

Naturwissenschaftlicher Verein zü Elberfeld, Germany.

    Jahresbericht, 8. Heft.

Naturwissenschaftlicher Verein zu Osnabrück, Germany.

    10. Jahresbericht, 1893-1894.

Naturwissenschaftlicher Verein "Pollichia," Dürkheim, Bavaria.

    Mittheilungen, 51. Jahrg., No. 7, 1893.

        "   52. " " 8, 1894.

Naturwissenschaftlicher Verein zu Düsseldorf, Germany.

    Mittheilungen, III. Heft.

Naturwissenschaftliche Gesellschaft "Isis," Dresden, Germany.

    Sitzungsberichte und Abhandlungen, Jan. bis Dec., 1895.

Naturhistorischer Verein der Preussischen Rheinlande und Westfalen, Bonn, Germany.

    Verhandlungen, 52. Jahrg., I. Hälfte.

Naturwissenschaftlicher Verein für Steiermark, Graz, Austria-Hungary.

    Mittheilungen, 32. Heft., Jahrg. 1895.

Naturwissenschaftliche Gesellschaft in St. Gallen, Schweiz.

Bericht, 1893-1894.

Naturwissenschaftlicher Verein für Schleswig-Holstein, Kiel, Germany.

Schriften, Bd. X., Heft II.

Naturwissenschaftlicher Verein in Troppau.

Mittheilungen No. 3. II. Vereinsjahr.

Naturwissenschaftlicher Verein für Neu Vorpommern und Rügen, Greifswald, Germany.

Mittheilungen, 27. Jahrg.

Henry Nehrling, Milwaukee, Wis.

Maynard, C. J. The Eggs of North American Birds.

The Ornithologist and Oologist, Vol. XI., 1886.

Strecker, H. Butterflies and Moths of North America.

List of Lepidoptera of Boreal America, 1891.

Moseley, E. L. Descriptions of two new species of Fly-catchers from the Island of Negros, Philippines.

Finch, Dr. O. Ethnologische Erfahrungen und Belegstücke aus der Südsee.

Zeitschrift für Ornithologie und praktische Geflügelzucht, XX. Jahrg., 1-5.

The Atlantic Monthly, July, 1893.

The Cliff Dwellers, 1893.

New York Academy of Sciences, New York City.

Transactions, Vol. XIV., 1894-1895.

Annals, Vol. VIII., Nos. 6-12, 1895.

Memoir I., Part I.

Annals, Vol. IX., Nos. 1-3, 1896.

New York State Museum, Albany, N. Y.

Bulletins, Vol. III., Nos. 14, 15.

Niederrheinische Gesellschaft für Natur- und Heilkunde, Bonn, Germany.

Sitzungsberichte, 1895, I. Hälfte.

Nova Scotian Institute of Science, Halifax, Nova Scotia.

Proceedings and Transactions, 1895.

Oberhessiche Gesellschaft für Natur- und Heilkunde, Giessen, Germany.

30. Bericht, 1895.

Observatorio Astronomico Nacional, Tacubaya, Mexico.

Boletins, Tomo I., No. 22-24.

Anuario, 1895.

Offenbacher Verein für Naturkunde, Offenbach, Germany.
33.-36. Bericht, 1891-1895.

Dr. Geo. W. Peckham, Milwaukee, Wis.
Ueber die Theridioiden der Spinnenfauna Ungarns.
Tuffts College Studies, No. IV.
Journal of the N. Y. Entomological Society, Vol. III., No. 1.
11 Pamphlets treating on Butterflies, Beetles and Spiders.

James M. Pereles, Milwaukee, Wis.
Pereles, James M. Historical Sketch of the Milwaukee School Board, 1845-1895.

Physikalischer Verein zu Frankfurt a. M., Germany.
Jahresbericht, 1893-1894.

Portland Society of Natural History, Portland, Oregon.
Proceedings, Vol. II., Part III., 1895.

Geo. Richardson, Milwaukee, Wis.
Photograph of a curious-shaped oak-tree.

Rochester Academy of Science, Rochester, N. Y.
Proceedings, Vol. II., III., 1895.

Royal Irish Academy of Dublin, Ireland.
Transactions, Vol. XXX., Parts 18-20.
List of Members of the Academy.

Schlesische Gesellschaft für vaterländische Cultur, Breslau, Germany.
72. Jahresbericht, 1895.

Schweizerische Naturforschende Gesellschaft, Schaffhausen, Schweiz.
Verhandlungen, 77. Jahresversammlung, 1893-1894.

Scientific Laboratories of Denisen University, Granville, Ohio.
Bulletin, Vol. IX., Part I.

Smithsonian Institution, Washington, D. C.
Howard, L. O. On the Bothriothoracine Insects of the U. S.
Annual Report for 1893.

H. W. Seton-Karr, London, England.
Discovery of Evidences of the Palaeolithic-Stone Age in Somaliland.

Siebenbürgischer Verein für Naturwissenschaften, Hermanstadt, Austria-Hungary.
Verhandlungen und Mittheilungen, Jahrg. 44. und 45.

Societé Entomologique de France, Paris, France.
Bulletin No. 8, 1896.

Societé Imperiale des Naturalistes de Moscow, Russia.
Bulletins Nos. 1-3, 1895.

Societé Zoologique de France, Paris, France.
Extrait des Memoires de la Societé Zoologique de France, '95.

State University of Iowa, Iowa City, Iowa.
>Bulletin, Vol. III., No. 3,

Stavanger Museum, Stavanger, Norway.
>Aarsberetning for 1894.

Tromsö Museum, Tromsö, Norway.
>Tromsö Museums Aarsberetning for 1890 and 1891.
>Aarshefter No. 15.

University of California, Berkeley, Cal.
>Bulletin of the Department of Geology, Vol. I, Nos. 12, 13, 14

University of Pennsylvania, Philadelphia, Pa.
>1 Pamphlet, Sommerville Talismans.
>1 " Annual Report of the Museum of American Archæology. Vol. I.. No. 1.
>1 Vol., Objects used in religious ceremonies and charms and implements for divination.
>1 Pamphlet, Report of the Board of Managers of the Department of Archæology and Palæontology.

University of Sydney, Australia.
>Calendar for 1896.

U. S. Coast and Geodetic Survey, Washington, D. C.
>Report for 1893, Parts I., II.
>Report for 1894, Parts I., II.

U. S. Commissioner of Education, Washington, D. C.
>Report, 1892-1893, Vol. I., Parts 1, 2.
>Report, 1892.

U. S. Bureau of Ethnology, Washington, D. C.
>13th Annual Report, 1891-1892.

U. S. Department of Agriculture, Washington, D. C.
>Bulletins Nos. 4-7.
>Bulletin No. 1 (Supplement).
>Farmers' Bulletin, No. 31, 29.
>Year Book for 1894.
>Report No. 126 of the Statistician.
>Report 131 and 133, New Series.
>Circulars Nos. 4 and 5, 1895.
>Monthly Crop Report, November, 1895.
>Report of the Secretary, 1895.
>North Am. Farms, No. 10, 1895.
>Report of Statistics of Agriculture at the 11th Census, 1890.
>Vivisection in the District of Columbia.

U. S. Department of the Interior, Washington, D. C.
>Report on Transportation Business in the United States at the 11th Census, Part I., II.

U. S. Department of the Interior, Washington, D. C.

> Report on Manufacturing Industries in the United States at the 11th Census, Part I., II., III.
>
> Report on Population of the United States, Part I.
> " " Wealth, Debt and Taxation, Part II.
> " " Crime, Pauperism and Benevolence, Part II.
> " " Vital and Social Statistics, Part III.

U. S. Geological Survey, Washington, D. C.

> Annual Reports, 13th, 14th, 15th, 16th, 1891-1895.
>
> Monographs, Vol. XXIII., XXIV.
>
> Bulletins, Nos. 118-134.

U. S. National Museum, Washington, D. C.

> Proceedings, Vol. XVII., 1894.
>
> Directions for collecting rocks and for the preparation of their sections.
>
> Directions for collecting minerals.
>
> Directions for collecting and preparing fossils.
>
> Bulletin No. 48.

U. S. War Department, Washington, D. C.

> The War of the Rebellion, Vol. 46, Parts II.-III.
> " " " " " Vol. 47, Parts I.-III.
> " " " " ' " Vol. 48, Part I.

Verein für Erdkunde zu Darmstadt, Germany.

> Notizblatt, IV. Folge, 16. Heft.

Verein für Erdkunde zu Leipzig, Germany.

> Wissenschaftliche Veröffentlichungen, II. Bd.

Verein der Freunde der Naturgeschichte in Mecklenburg, Güstrow, Germany.

> Archiv, 49. Jahrg,, I. and II. Abthlg.

Verein Luxemburger Naturfreunde, Luxemburg.

> "Fauna," 5. Jahrg.

Verein für die Geschichte der Stadt Nürnberg, Bavaria.

> 16. und 17. Jahresbericht, 1894-1895.
>
> Mittheilungen, Heft 11., 1895.

Verein für Naturkunde zu Kassel, Germany.

> Abhandlungen u. Bericht XXXX., 1894-1895.

Verein für Naturwissenschaftliche Unterhaltung zu Hamburg, Germany.

> Verhandlungen, IX. Bd.

Verein zur Verbreitung Naturwiss Kenntnisse, Wien, Austria.

> Schriften, 35. Bd., 1894-1895.

Videnskabs-Selskabet, Christiania, Norway.

    Oversigt, 1891-1894.

    Forhandlinger No. 1 to 11, 1891.

        "   No. 1 to 18, 1892.

        "   No. 1 to 11, 1894.

    Skrifter, I. Mathematisk naturvidenskabelig Klasse 1894, Nos. 1 to 6.

    Skrifter, II. Historisk-filosofiske Klass 1894, Nos. 1 to 6.

Westfälischer Provinzial Verein für Wissenschaft und Kunst, Münster, Germany.

    23. Jahresbericht, 1894-1895.

Wetterauische Gesellschaft, Hanau, Bavaria.

    Bericht, 1892-1895.

Wilson Ornithological Club of the Agassiz Association, Oberlin, O.

    Bulletins No. 7, 8.

Wisconsin Academy of Sciences, Arts and Letters, Madison, Wis.

    Transactions, Vol. X., 1894-1895.

Zoologische Sammlung zu Berlin, Germany.

    Lucas, Dr. Robert. Die Pompiliden Gattung Pepsis.

    Beiträge zur Fauna der südöstlichen und östlichen Nordsee, 1889-1890.

Zoological Society of Philadelphia, Penn.

    24th Annual Report.

ACQUIRED BY PURCHASE.

Edwards, W. H. The Butterflies of North America, Third Series, Part XVI.

"The Auk." A Quarterly Journal of Ornithology, Vol. XII.

Sievers, Prof. Dr. Wilh. "Europa," Eine allgemeine Landeskunde.

Brockhaus' Konversations Lexicon, Bd. 14-16.

Burmeister, Dr. H. Reise durch die La Plata Staaten, 1857-1860. II. Bände.

Finsch und Hartlaub. Beitrag zur Fauna Centralpolynesiens.

Morris, F. O. A History of British Birds. Vol. I. to VI.

Reichenow, Dr. A. Die Vögel Deutsch Ost-Afrika's.

Dörfler's Botaniker Addressbuch.

Heyne, Alexander. Die exotischen Käfer in Wort und Bild. 5. u. 6. Lieferung.

Laws of Wisconsin Concerning the Public Museum.

(330, A.)   (Published April 13, 1882.)

CHAPTER 329.

AN ACT relating to the Natural History Society of the City of Milwaukee.

The People of the State of Wisconsin, represented in Senate and Assembly, do enact as follows:

Section 1. The board of directors of the Natural History Society of the City of Milwaukee is hereby authorized and empowered, in the name of said association or society, to assign, transfer and convey to the City of Milwaukee, all and singular, the natural historical collections of every kind constituting the Museum belonging to said Natural History Society, in trust, to be kept, supported and maintained by said city, as a free Museum for the benefit and use of all citizens of said city; provided, the said city shall accept the trust and assume the care and maintenance of such Museum.

Sec. 2. This act shall take effect and be in force from and after its passage and publication.

Approved March 31, 1882.

(No. 329, A.)   (Published April 14, 1882.)

CHAPTER 328.

AN ACT to authorize the City of Milwaukee to establish and maintain a Public Museum in said city.

The People of the State of Wisconsin, represented in Senate and Assembly, do enact as follows: .

Section 1.   The City of Milwaukee is hereby authorized to receive and accept from "The Natural History Society of Wisconsin"—a corporation located in the said.City of Milwaukee—a donation of its collection of objects in Natural History and Ethnology, or of the greater part thereof, upon such conditions as may be agreed upon by and between said city and said society, subject, however, to the provisions of this act.

Sec. 2.   In case of such donation and acceptance, said City of Milwaukee is hereby authorized and empowered to establish and maintain in said city a free Public Museum, exhibitions of objects in Natural History and Ethnology, and for that purpose to receive, hold and manage the collection so donated, and any devise, bequest or donation that may be made to said city for the increase and maintenance of such Museum under such regulations and conditions as are herein contained, or may be agreed upon by and between the donors and said city, or as may be hereafter provided in this act.

Sec. 3.   The Museum established and maintained under this act shall be under the general management, control and supervision of a board of nine trustees, who shall be styled "The Board of Trustees of the Public Museum of the City of Milwaukee."   Said Board of Trustees shall consist of the president of the School Board and the Superintendent of Schools of said city, *ex-officio*, of three members of the Common Council of said city, designated and appointed by the Mayor thereof, and of four residents and tax-payers of said city, to be appointed by the Mayor as herein provided. The first appointments of trustees by the Mayor under this act shall be made within ten days after the formal acceptance by the Common Council of said city of a donation by said Natural History Society, as authorized in the first section of this act. Of the first three trustees appointed from the members of the Common Council of said city, one shall be appointed from the three-year class, one from the two-year class, and one from the one-year class of aldermen, and they shall serve as such trustees during their respective terms as such aldermen. And annually on the third Tuesday of April thereafter, at the expiration of the term of any such trustee, the Mayor shall appoint his successor for three years, from the aldermen then having three years to serve. In case any such trustee shall vacate the office of alderman before the expiration of his term, he shall at the same time cease to be a trustee under this act, and the Mayor shall appoint some other member of the Common Council of his class in his place for the balance of his term. In the appointment of the four remaining trustees and their successors, the Mayor shall prefer such persons as may be recommended for such appointment by said Natural History Society. Such four trustees first appointed shall, at the first meeting of the Board after their appointment, determine by lot their term of service, so that one of their number shall serve for one year, one for two years, one for three years, and one for four years from the third Tuesday of May next after the organization of such Board. And all vacancies shall be filled by like appointment of the Mayor for the remainder of the term, and annually on the third Tuesday of April a trustee shall be appointed by said Mayor in like manner for the term of four years, in place of the trustee whose term shall expire the following May. None of said trustees shall receive any compensation from the city treasury, or otherwise, for their services as such trustees. And no member of said Board of Trustees shall become, or cause himself to become interested, directly or indirectly, in any contract or job for the purchase of any matter pertaining to the Museum, or of fuel, furniture, stationery or things necessary for the increase and maintenance of the Museum. Said trustees shall take the official oath, and be subject to the restrictions, disabilities, liabilities, punishments and limitations prescribed by laws as to aldermen in the said City of Milwaukee.

Sec. 4. The first meeting of said Board of Trustees for the purpose of organizing, shall be held on the third Tuesday of the month next following their appointment, and the City Clerk shall give at least one week's previous notice of the time and place of such meeting to each member of such Board in writing. At such first meeting said Board shall organize by the choice of one of their number as president to serve until the third Tuesday of May next following, and until his successor shall be chosen. The annual meeting of said Board shall be held on the third Tuesday of May in each year, and at such meeting a president shall be chosen from their number to serve for one year and until his successor shall be chosen.

Sec. 5. The Board of Trustees shall have general care, control and supervision of the Public Museum, its appurtenances, fixtures and furniture, and of the selection, arrangement and disposition of the specimens and objects appertaining to said Museum, and also of the disbursements of all the moneys appropriated for and belonging to the Museum fund, in the manner hereinafter provided. And the said Board shall adopt, and at their discretion modify, amend or repeal by-laws, rules and regulations for the management, care and use of the Public Museum, and fix and enforce penalties for their violation, and generally shall adopt such measures as shall promote the public utility of the Museum; provided, that such by-laws, rules and regulations shall not conflict with the provisions of this act.

Sec. 6. The Board of Trustees shall, at their first meeting, or thereafter as soon as practicable, and every five years thereafter, at an annual meeting, elect by ballot a person of suitable scientific attainments, ability and experience for custodian, who shall so act and be *ex-officio* secretary of said Board of Trustees. The custodian first appointed shall hold his office for five years from the time of the first annual meeting, unless previously removed, and thereafter the term of appointment shall be for the term of five years, and the compensation of the custodian shal' be fixed by said Board of Trustees. Said Board of Trustees shall also appoint such assistants and employes for said Museum as they may deem necessary and expedient, and shall fix their compensation. All vacancies in the office of custodian, assistants and other employes, shall be filled by said Board of Trustees, and the person so elected or appointed shall hold for the unexpired term.

Sec. 7. The custodian elected under this act may be removed from office for misdemeanor, incompetency or inattention to the duties of his office, by a vote of two-thirds of the Board of Trustees; the assistants and other employes may be removed by the Board for incompetency, or for any other cause.

Sec. 8. It shall be the duty of the Board of Trustees, within ten days after the appointment of the custodian and other salaried employes, to report and file with the City Comptroller a duly certified list of the persons so appointed, with the salary allowed to each, and the time or times fixed for the payment thereof, and they shall also furnish such comptroller with a list of all accounts and bills which may be allowed by said Board of Trustees, stating the character of the materials or service for which the same were rendered, immediately after the meeting of said Board at which such allowance shall be made. And said Board of Trustees shall also, on or before the first day of October in each year, make to the Common Council a report, made up to and including the 31st day of August of the said year, containing a statement of the condition of the Museum and of the additions thereto during the year, together with such information and suggestions as they may deem important, and such report shall also contain an account of the moneys credited to the Museum fund, and expended on account of the same during the year.

Sec. 9. From and after the organization of the Board of Trustees under this act, the Common Council of said city shall levy and collect annually upon all the taxable property of the said city, at the same time and in the same manner as other city taxes are levied and collected by law, a special tax not exceeding one-tenth of a mill upon each dollar of the assessed value of said taxable property, the amount of which shall be determined by said Board of Trustees, and certified to the Common Council at the time of making their annual report to said Council, and the entire amount of said special tax shall be paid into, and held in, the city treasury, as a separate and distinct fund, to be known as the Museum fund, and shall not be used or appropriated, directly or indirectly, in any other purpose than for the maintenance and for the increase of the Public Museum, the payment of the salaries of the custodian, assistant and other employes of the Museum, the purchase of furniture, fixtures, supplies and fuel, and the incidental expenses of the Museum.

Sec. 10. The Board of Trustees shall erect, purchase, hire or lease buildings, lots, rooms and furniture, for the use and accommodation of said Public Museum, and shall improve, enlarge and repair such buildings, rooms and furniture; but no lot or building shall be purchased, erected or enlarged for the purpose herein mentioned, without an ordinance or resolution of the Common Council of said city, and deeds of conveyance and leases shall run to the City of Milwaukee.

Sec. 11. All moneys received by or raised in the City of Milwaukee for Museum purposes shall be paid over to the City Treasurer, to be disbursed by him on the orders of the president and secretary of the said Board of Trustees, countersigned by the City Comptroller. Such orders shall be made payable to the order of the persons in whose favor they shall have been issued, and shall be the only voucher of the City Treasurer for the payments from the Museum fund. The said Board of Trustees shall provide for the purchase of specimens, supplies, fuel and other matters necessary or useful for the maintenance of the Museum; provided, however, that it shall not be lawful for said Board of Trustees to expend or contract a liability for any sum in excess of the amount levied in any one year for the Museum fund, on account of such fund.

Sec. 12. All moneys, books, specimens and other property received by the City of Milwaukee by device, bequest or gift, from any person or corporation, for Public Museum purposes, shall, unless otherwise directed by the donors, be under the management and control of said Board of Trustees; and all moneys derived from fines and penalties for violations of the rules of the Museum, or from any other source in the course of the administration of the Museum, including all moneys which may be paid to the city upon any policy or policies of insurance, or other obligation or liability, or on account of loss or damage to any property pertaining to the Museum, shall belong to the Museum fund in the city treasury, to be disbursed on the orders of the said Board of Trustees, countersigned by the City Comptroller, for Museum purposes in addition to the amount levied and raised by taxation for such fund.

Sec. 13. This act shall take effect and be in force from and after its passage and publication.

Approved March 31, 1882.

(No. 895, A.)   (Published April 15, 1887.)

CHAPTER 521.

AN ACT to amend Chapter 328 of the Laws of 1882, authorizing the City of Milwaukee to establish and maintain a Public Museum, and Chapter 7 of the Laws of 1878, to establish a Public Library in the City of Milwaukee.

The People of the State of Wisconsin, represented in Senate and Assembly, do enact as follows:

    *   *   *   *   *   *

Section 2. Hereafter all appointments of members from the Common Council for the Board of Trustees of the Public Museum of the City of Milwaukee, made by the Mayor of said city on the third Tuesday in April, shall be made from aldermen having two years to serve, and in case any person so appointed shall vacate his office of alderman before the expiration of his term, he shall thereupon cease to be a member of said Board of Trustees, and the Mayor shall appoint some other alderman of his class in his place to be such trustee for the remainder of his term. Each alderman appointed shall serve as such trustee during his term as alderman. It shall be the duty of the Mayor on the third Tuesday in April in each year to appoint a sufficient number of aldermen having two years to serve to be members of such Board of Trustees of the Public Museum, to keep the number of members of such Board from the Common Council always three.

All provisions of Chapter 328, of the Laws of 1882, which in any way conflict with the provisions of this section, are hereby amended accordingly.

Sec. 3. This act shall take effect and be in force from and after its passage and publication.

Approved April 14, 1887.

(No. 614, A.)   (Published April 20, 1887.)

CHAPTER 433.

AN ACT to amend Chapter 328, of the Laws of 1882, entitled "An act to authorize the City of Miiwaukee to establish and maintain a Public Museum in said city."

The People of the State of Wisconsin, represented in Senate and Assembly, do enact as follows:

Section 1. The Board of Trustees of the Milwaukee Public Museum are hereby authorized to appoint an acting custodian whenever the proper service of the Museum shall require it, and for such time and on such terms as they may deem proper. Such acting custodian shall be *ex-officio* the acting secretary of said Board of Trustees, and his acts as such shall receive full credit. Said Board of Trustees are also authorized to appoint from time to time honorary curators, who shall perform such duties and have such special privileges as may be provided in the by-laws of the Museum, but shall receive no pecuniary compensation. Such appointments shall be made of persons who have manifested a special interest in the Museum or some particular department thereof.

Sec. 2. This act shall be in force from and after its passage and publication.

Approved April 12, 1887.

RULES GOVERNING THE MUSEUM.

I. Meetings.

Art. 1. The regular meetings of the Board shall be held at the Museum rooms on the third Tuesday of each month at 4 P. M.

Art. 2. The annual meeting of the Board shall be held on the third Tuesday of May, at 4 P. M.

Art. 3. Special meetings shall be called by the secretary upon the written request of the president, or any three members of the Board, but the object for which the special meeting is called must be stated in the notice, and no business other than the special business shall be transacted at such meeting, unless all the members of the Board are present, and unanimous consent is obtained.

Art. 4. Five members of the Board shall constitute a quorum.

II. Officers and Employes.

Art. 5. At the annual meeting in May the Board shall elect by ballot a president, whose duty it shall be to preside at all meetings of the Board, to sign all warrants drawn on the city treasurer by order of the Board, to appoint the standing committees for the year, and prepare for the consideration and approval of the Board, the annual report of the Board of Trustees, required by Section 8 of the "Public Museum Act."

Art. 6. The duties of the custodian shall be as follows:

To take charge of and exercise control over the Museum and Library, and to see that the regulations relating thereto are properly carried out.

To exercise control over all employes of the Board and the work allotted to them respectively.

To receive all specimens intended for the Museum, and with the advice and assistance of specialists to classify, label, catalogue and arrange them as soon as possible.

To receive all books and other articles intended for the Library, and to label and catalogue them.

To take all precautions necessary for the good preservation of the collections, according to the most approved methods within the means of the institution

To keep running records, containing all necessary particulars, concerning articles received or disposed of.

To purchase specimens, books and other matter under the general direction of the Board.

To inaugurate a system of exchanges with other natural history museums as soon as possible.

To correspond with scientific societies and public authorities for the purpose of obtaining reports and other documents containing information relating to natural history.

To submit from time to time to the Board or to the respective committees, measures for the efficient management and increase of the Museum, and such other matters as he may deem advisable.

To prepare and submit to the Board a monthly report in writing of the work done, stating the number of visitors, and other matters of interest to the Board.

To prepare and submit at the annual meeting in September an annual report of like contents for the preceding year ending August 31st, said report to accompany the annual report of the Board, required by Section 8 of the "Public Museum Act."

To discharge such other duties as usually belong to the office of the custodian and from time to time be prescribed by the Board:

But in the performance of his duties no debt or liability of any kind shall be incurred by him without authority from the Board.

The custodian shall be required to give bonds in the sum of one thousand dollars, with two or more sureties, to be approved by the Board, for the faithful performance of his duties.

Art. 7.   It shall be the duty of the custodian as secretary of the Board of Trustees to be present at all meetings of the Board and of the committee, and to keep full and correct records of their proceedings, except when otherwise directed.

To keep exact and detailed accounts of all moneys received from fines and other sources, to report the same monthly to the Board at the regular meetings, and to pay over all moneys so received promptly to the city treasurer as directed by the Board.

To keep books of account in which all the money transactions of the Board shall be set forth accurately in detail, and to make out and sign all warrants drawn on the city treasurer by order of the Board.

To take care of all business papers of the Board and keep the same neatly filed for convenient reference.

To prepare and submit a monthly statement of the finances of the Museum at the regular monthly meetings.

To give notice of all meetings of the Board, and of committees, at least twenty-four hours before the time of meeting.

To receive all documents, letters and other communications addressed to the Board or Museum, and to see to their proper disposal by the proper officer or committee.

To transact all such other business as may be required of him by the Board and its committees in his capacity as secretary thereof.

Art. 8. The janitor shall, under the direction of the custodian, attend to the heating, ventilation and cleaning of the Museum in all its parts, and perform such other work as may be assigned to him at any time by the custodian. The other assistants shall also work under the direction of the custodian and perform such work as the custodian may assign to them.

Art. 9. Engagements of employes or assistants shall be made by the executive committee, subject to approval by the Board.

III. Committees.

Art. 10. The standing committees shall be:

1. The Executive Committee, consisting of the president *ex-officio*, and four other members of the Board.

2. The Finance Committee, consisting of three members of the Board.

3. The Committee on Exchanges, consisting of three members of the Board, to whom, with the custodian, all applications for exchanges shall be referred for recommendation to the Board.

4. The Committee on Furniture, consisting of three members of the Board.

5. The Committee on Purchase, consisting of three members of the Board, to whom, with the custodian, all matters of purchasing specimens shall be referred for recommendation to the Board. The Committee on Purchase shall have authority to expend from month to month in the interest of the Museum a sum not exceeding $50.

Art. 11. The Natural History Society of Wisconsin shall be invited to appoint five scientific persons from among their members to act in an advisory capacity as a joint counsel, in conferences with the Executive Committee; such conferences to take place at such times as the Executive Committee may desire.

Art. 12. The Executive Committee shall have supervision of all matters relating to the purchasing, construction, leasing, repairing and heating of the buildings or rooms occupied by the Museum, and of insurance, the furnishing, order and cleanliness of the rooms and collections; the selection, purchase, preparation, arrangement, exchange, sale or other disposal of catalogues and guides; provided, that in all such matters no action be taken involving an expenditure or liability greater than authorized by the Board. This committee shall assign a suitable room to the Natural History Society of Wisconsin for holding their meetings and receiving their library. It shall be the duty of the committee to see that all persons employed in the service of the Museum are faithful and prompt in the performance of their duties, and that the regulations of the Museum are enforced.

Art. 13. The Finance Committee shall have the supervision of all matters pertaining to the accounts and account books of the Board. It shall be their duty to prepare the annual budget of the Board, to direct the manner of keeping and to examine all the account books; to examine the monthly and other financial statements of the secretary and custodian and certify the correctness of the same to the Board; to examine and audit all vouchers and accounts against the Museum; to report to the Board upon the correctness of the same, and to make such suggestions from time to time concerning the finances of the Museum as they may deem advisable. Said committee shall also, at the regular meeting in September each year, submit an estimate of the amount that will be needed for maintaining the Museum during the following year, and the action of the Board upon such estimates shall be forthwith certified by the secretary to the comptroller of the city of Milwaukee.

Art. 14. A majority of any committee shall constitute a quorum.

Art. 15. The standing committees shall prepare and submit to the Board at the annual meeting in May a report of all matters, subject to their supervision.

Art. 16. The reports of all standing committees shall be in writing.

IV. MUSEUM AND LIBRARY.

Art. 17. The Museum shall be conducted according to the intention of the "Public Museum Act" and the conditions made by the Natural History Society of Wisconsin in donating the "Engelmann Museum," with the following aims in view:

The exhibition of natural history and ethnology, so as to provide material and help for scientific investigation and public instruction.

The collections therein contained are to represent and illustrate as far as possible the natural history and the natural resources of the city and county of Milwaukee and state of Wisconsin in the first order, and then of the United States and remainder of our planet for purposes of comparison and generalization.

The Museum shall be placed in a building reasonably fire-proof, and kept insured for at least five-sixths of its value.

No objects in the collection can be loaned, and the removal of specimens from the room can not be permitted, except if sold or for the purpose of exchange or identification, and under proper authority from the Executive Committee. All matters relating to the arrangement, preservation and use of the collection are under the immediate direction of the custodian, subject to the supervision of the Executive Committee, who will give more detailed instructions if needed.

Art. 18. The library is to be considered a reference and working library. Its contents can not be loaned, but may be used for study or reference in the rooms during Museum hours under necessary restrictions.

V MISCELLANEOUS.

Art. 19. It shall be the duty of every member of the Board to frequently visit the Museum, and of the members of the Executive Committee to do so at least once every week, for the purpose of general superintendence and direction.

Art. 20. The term of service of all the employes of the Museum except the custodian shall be during good behavior. They shall only be removed for cause, of which the Board shall be the exclusive judge.

Art. 21. The records of the proceedings of the Board of Trustees and its committees and the books of account shall be kept in the secretary's office, and shall be open at all times to inspection and examination by any member of the Board.

Art. 22. The order of business of the Board of Trustees, except at special meetings, shall be as follows:

1. Calling the Roll.
2. Reading Minutes of Previous Meeting.
3. Report of Custodian and Secretary.
4. Report of Standing Committees.
5. Report of Special Committees.
6. Reading of Communications.
7. Unfinished Business.
8. Election of Officers.
9. New Business.

Art. 23. All resolutions and amendments before the Board or any committee shall be presented in writing.

Art. 24. All persons employed at the Museum must be promptly at their posts, as directed, and must remain there during the hours of their regular duty. They will remember that their time, while in the Museum, should constantly be occupied in its service, and it is the duty of the custodian and Executive Committee to enforce this rule.

Art. 25. No amendments to the rules of the Board, or the regulations of the Museum shall be acted upon until the next regular meeting after the same shall have been proposed.

REGULATIONS.

The Museum will be open—

On Sundays, from 1:30 to 5 P. M.

Saturdays, from 9 to 12 A. M. and 1 to 5:30 P. M.

On all other days, from 1 to 5:30 P. M.

Visitors are admitted on condition that they observe the following regulations:

Section 1. Any person of good deportment can be admitted during the above named hours. Children less than fourteen years of age will be admitted only if accompanied by parents, teachers or other responsible adults. Dogs or other live animals will not be admitted.

Sec. 2. Admission is free. Employes of the Museum are forbidden, under penalty of discharge, to receive fees from visitors.

Sec. 3. The removal of books, specimens or any other objects belonging to the Museum from any of its rooms, is strictly prohibited.

Sec. 4. The use of tobacco, and all other conduct not consistent with the quiet and orderly use of the Museum, are prohibited.

Sec. 5. Visitors are not allowed to touch any object.

Sec. 6. Visitors will be held responsible for any mutilation or other injury to specimens, books, furniture or other property of the Museum caused by them.

Sec. 7. The time for closing will be announced by three bell signals ten minutes previous to the appointed hour.

OFFICE HOURS OF EMPLOYES.

Custodian, from 9 to 12 A. M. and 1 to 4 P. M.

Assistant Custodian, from 8:30 to 11:30 A. M. and 1 to 5 P. M.

Taxidermist, from 8 to 12 A. M. and 1 to 5 P. M.

First Assistant, from 8:30 to 11:30 A. M. and 1 to 5 P. M.

Janitor, from 7 to 11:30 A. M. and 1 to 5:30 P. M.

FIFTEENTH ANNUAL REPORT

————OF THE————

BOARD OF TRUSTEES

————OF THE————

PUBLIC MUSEUM

————OF THE————

CITY OF MILWAUKEE.

SEPTEMBER 1ST, 1896, TO AUGUST 31ST, 1897.

OCTOBER 1ST, 1897.

MILWAUKEE:
ED. KEOGH, PRINTER, 386-388 BROADWAY.
1898.

FIFTEENTH ANNUAL REPORT

————OF THE————

BOARD OF TRUSTEES

————OF THE————

PUBLIC MUSEUM

————OF THE————

CITY OF MILWAUKEE.

————

SEPTEMBER 1ST, 1896, TO AUGUST 31ST, 1897.

————

OCTOBER 1ST, 1897.

————

MILWAUKEE:
ED. KEOGH, PRINTER, 386-388 BROADWAY.
1898.

BOARD OF TRUSTEES.

CITIZENS APPOINTED.

ADOLPH MEINECKE, - - - - - Term expires May, 1901.

DR. EDWIN W. BARTLETT - - - - Term expires May, 1900.

AUGUST STIRN, - - - - - Term expires May, 1899.

CHAS. L. KIEWERT, - - - - - Term expires May, 1898.

ALDERMEN APPOINTED.

THOMAS F. RAMSEY, - - - - Term expires May, 1898.

WILLIAM H. STEVENS, - - - - - Term expires May, 1898.

HERMAN BUTH, - - - - - Term expires May, 1898.

EX-OFFICIO.

H. O. R. SIEFERT, Sup't of Schools, - Term expires May, 1898.

CHARLES QUARLES, Pres't School Board, Term expires May, 1898.

OFFICERS.

EDWIN W. BARTLETT, President.

H. NEHRLING, Secretary, *Ex-Officio*.

COMMITTEES.

EXECUTIVE COMMITTEE.

. CHAS. QUARLES, ADOLPH MEINECKE, HERM. BUTH, AUG. STIRN,
DR. EDWIN. W. BARTLETT, *Ex-Officio.*

FINANCE COMMITTEE.

CHARLES L. KIEWERT, THOS. F. RAMSEY, HERM. BUTH.

PURCHASING COMMITTEE.

ADOLPH MEINECKE, AUG. STIRN, DR. EDWIN. W. BARTLETT,
H. NEHRLING, *Ex-Officio.*

FURNITURE COMMITTEE.

THOS. F. RAMSEY, CHARLES L. KIEWERT, H. O. R. SIEFERT.

EXCHANGING COMMITTEE.

H. O. R. SIEFERT, AUG. STIRN, DR. EDWIN W. BARTLETT.

BUILDING COMMITTEE.

WM. H. STEVENS, AUG. STIRN, ADOLPH MEINECKE, CHARLES
L. KIEWERT, DR. EDWIN W. BARTLETT, *Ex-Officio.*

HONORARY CURATORS.

AUGUST STIRN, - - - - - - Ornithology.

CARL HAGENBECK, Hamburg, Germany, - - - Zoology.

DR. S. GRAENICHER, - - - Ichthyology and Herpetology.

AD. MEINECKE, - - - - - - - At Large.

CHAS. E. MONROE, - - - - - - Palæontology.

MUSEUM SERVICE.

HENRY NEHRLING, - - - - - Custodian and Secretary.

CARL THAL, - - - - - - Assistant Custodian.

GEO. B. TURNER, - - - - - Taxidermist.

ALEXANDER GOETHEL, - - - - Assistant Taxidermist.

FRED. RAUTERBERG, - - - - Entomologist.

LYDIA NEHRLING, - - - - - Assistant.

ALMA WALDBART, - - - - Assistant.

CARL BINDRICH, - - - - - Janitor.

REPORT OF THE PRESIDENT.

To the Honorable the Common Council of the City of Milwaukee:

GENTLEMEN—The Board of Trustees of the Public Museum, in accordance with Section 8, Chapter 328 of the Laws of 1882, presents herewith its annual report, as required by law.

The Museum contains the following specimens:

120,844	Zoölogical specimens, valued at..................	$38,475 59
17,133	Botanical specimens, valued at...................	1,117 60
18,678	Anthropological specimens, valued at...........	13,299 55
11,558	Palæontological specimens, valued at............	5,299 55
4,747	Mineralogical and Lithological specimens, valued at...............	4,789 94
7,193	Books, Pamphlets, Catalogues, Atlases and Charts, valued at...........................	6,664 52
3,025	Birds' Eggs and Nests, valued at................	10,000 00
	Furniture, Tools, Jars, Vessels, Conservation Supplies and Stationery..........................	14,292 20
	Upham Collection, held in trust................	350 00
		$94,288 95

The number of visitors during the year was 89,698.

The insurance on the property of the Museum is now $99,550.00.

The financial statement of the Board is as follows:

Balance in Museum fund September 1, 1896..............	$7,560 14
Refunded insurance premium...........................	2 71
Appropriation to Museum fund, January 1, 1897........	14,377 16
Total...	$21,940 01
Total expenditures during last year....................	16,343 01
Leaving a balance on September 1, 1897, of........	$5,597 00

Your attention is directed to the annual report of Mr. H. Nehrling, the custodian of the Museum, for further particulars in regard to the additions to the Museum and to the work that has been done during the last year. The members of the Board of Trustees have all been unusually faithful in attending meetings and laboring for the interest of the Museum. The completion of the new building on Grand Avenue has required a large amount of care and attention, and the magnificent result is entirely appropriate to the work intended.

Thanks are due to the officers of the Museum for their faithful services, and also to the assistants for the care given to the collections and uniform courtesy to the public.

Respectfully submitted,

EDWIN W. BARTLETT.

REPORT OF THE CUSTODIAN.

MILWAUKEE, September 30, 1898.

To the Board of Trustees of the Public Museum of the City of
Milwaukee:

GENTLEMEN.—In compliance with Article VI of your
Rules and Regulations, I have the honor of presenting to you
my Seventh Annual Report, being the fifteenth in the series
of reports since the foundation of the Public Museum.

During the past few years our Museum has become a very
large and important institution. Including the various extensive collections of beetles, butterflies, etc., not yet placed
on record, the Museum consists of over 200,000 specimens.
The accessions of material during the year just ended have
been so gratifying that almost nothing beyond the mere
routine work could be done by me and my assistant. We
were only able to classify the specimens, to label them, to enter
them into the proper record books, and to store them away for
future use. The mounted specimens in the cases are crowded
in such a way that all new additions had to be packed into the
drawers underneath the cases, and into packing boxes in the
basement of the building. Our taxidermist, Mr. Geo. B.
Turner, has finished several fine groups, but no room any-
where in the Museum could be found to place them on
exhibition. In order to make room for a number of birds
mounted by Mr. Henry Denslow, of Rochester, N. Y., I had
to rearrange the general bird and mammal collection several
times, placing the specimens just where I could find a small
space without regard to their systematical sequence. Of late

all the collections have been changed around and divided up in such a way that it is sometimes very difficult to find a certain object about which one or the other visitor inquires for information. In the new building, where about 36,000 square feet of exhibition room is at our disposal—against 12,000 square feet in our present quarters—all the specimens can be exhibited to their best advantage, and no crowding will be necessary. Several of our present exhibition cases—I refer especially to the coral case—contain such an amount of valuable material that at least ten ordinary cases are necessary to receive these objects.

The lower floor in the new building will be set aside for a general Museum collection. Here the megatherium, the skeleton of the whale, the casts of most of the extinct animals, the mammal and bird groups, as well as interesting ethnological and archæological specimens will be exhibited. The second floor will contain the systematical zoölogical collections. One of the special rooms on this floor will be used as a laboratory for scientific research, and the other one for the entomological and botanical collections. The third floor will contain the mineralogical, palæontological, archæological and ethnological collections. The two special rooms on this floor will be used by the schools as lecture halls.

I.—ACCESSIONS.

Zoology.—The most important and valuable gift to the Zoölogical Department came from Dr. S. Graenicher, honorary curator of ichthyology and herpetology, who collected for the Museum a large number of fishes inhabiting the lakes, rivers and creeks near Milwaukee and Lake Michigan. The collection consists of thirty-eight species. The same gentleman, whose special study is at present the pollination of flowers by insects, donated 111 specimens of hymenoptera. All these objects are determined and nicely prepared and labeled, which materially increases their value. Several new

species of hymenoptera have been discovered by Dr. Graenicher, which were named in honor of their discoverer by Prof.
Wm. Ashmead, of the United States National Museum.

Dr. Graenicher also determined and labeled most of the
fishes collected by Mr. Adolph Meinecke, Sen., in the Gulf of
Mexico, near Tampa, Fla.

During the last few years the love of nature and of nature
study has made great progress. Not only do many of our
educated men and women go out in the woods and fields as
often as possible, but they frequently come to the Museum to
identify birds and plants they have seen and to make com-
parisons. Scarcely a day passes without visitors calling
at my office in order to obtain information about what they
have seen in their rambles. Though most bird lovers study
their favorites in the freedom of nature, there are quite a number who keep their pets in cages. Most of the birds kept in
confinement are the more common exotic species, such as
Canaries, white Japanese rice-birds, common rice-birds (Munia
orizivora), zebra finches (Tænopygia castanotis), cut-throat
finches (Amadina fasciata), magpie finches (Spermestes
cucullata), undulated parakeets (Melopsittacus undulatus),
Chinese sun-birds (Liothrix lutea), European goldfinches
(Carduelis carduelis), and many others. Of native birds only
cardinals (Cardinalis cardinalis), mocking birds (Mimus poly-
glottus), and painted buntings (Spiza ciris), are usually kept
in confinement here. These bird lovers are always looking for
information in the Museum, and for this reason I have started
a collection of the more popular and easily kept foreign cage
birds. Mr. August Stirn has contributed largely to this
collection in former years, and recently he again donated
eleven fine specimens of white rice-birds, which were mounted
by our taxidermist on two branches, making a very impressive and beautiful group.

Mrs. Olive D. Barker donated a fine male zebra-finch from
Australia, one of the most popular and beautiful of all exotic
cage-birds, and a very highly colored specimen of the

Dominican cardinal (Paroaria cucullata) from Southern Brazil, which she kept in confinement for a period of nine years.

The collection of fancy pigeons was enriched by Mr. F. Gallun, Jr., who donated three fine specimens of pouters.

Prof. Adolph Hempel, at present one of the curators of the Museum at Sao Paulo, Brazil, presented twenty-three specimens of fresh water shells, which he collected near Gotha, Fla.

Mr. Herm. Hirsch, who has always been a warm friend of the Museum, has again donated quite a number of objects, among them a fine specimen of the American rough-legged hawk (Archibuteo lagopus sancti-johannis).

Dr. Chas. J. Lange, another ardent friend of the institution, donated eight species of the more common birds in their breeding plumage. In May he collected at West Baden, Indiana, one old and two young turkey buzzards (Cathartes aura), the latter in downy plumage. In the same locality he collected a family of five woodchucks (Arctomys monax), one common mole (Scalops aquaticus), one prairie mole (Scalops argentatus), and a species of lizard, not yet determined.

Mr. Adolph Meinecke has not only brought together large collections of fishes, snakes, turtles, etc., which he donated to the Museum, but he also obtained for the institution a collection of very unique beetles from all parts of the world. For a full list of Mr. Meinecke's donations I refer to the appendix.

Mr. A. H. Meinecke donated a very fine pair of white-winged scoters (Oidemia deglandi), which were shot on Lake Michigan, near the harbor.

Mr. Fred. Rauterberg, heretofore honorary curator of entomology and at present one of the regular staff of the Museum, donated his entire collection of North American beetles, consisting of over 7,000 specimens, and also a very fine representative collection of butterflies.

Mr. August Stirn, who in former years donated almost all the specimens of birds of paradise now on exhibition, made another addition to this wonderful group of birds. He also presented ten tropical birds, which I had not yet time to determine.

Mr. Geo. B. Turner, together with Dr. H. V. Ogden, collected a family of woodchucks. They carefully dug out three young and captured two old ones, made sketches of the burrow and of the nest, and gathered material for a group of these mammals. They also obtained a family of flying squirrels (Sciuropterus volans).

The institution acquired by purchase 288 exotic birds not yet represented in our collection, and a number of rare North American forms, collected during the past few years by Mr. A. W. Anthony. Through the kindness of Prof. Robert Ridgway, of the Smithsonian Institution, Washington, D. C., I was able to select twenty-three specimens from a large collection of Patagonian birds, among them four condors (Sarcorhamphus gryphus).

The Department of Zoölogy has grown steadily and many donations worthy of special mention have been added, but lack of space prevents my going more into detail. For the names of the donors, etc., I refer to the list of accessions.

Botany.—To the herbarium only few additions were made during the year. Mr. Ernest Bruncken donated a small collection of rare plants obtained by him at Fish Creek, Wis.

Dr. Edwin W. Bartlett presented a piece of wood which shows clearly the letters J. W.

In the new building the botanical collections will occupy a separate room together with the entomological collections.

Mineralogy.—Mr. Chas. L. Kiewert presented eight fine specimens of amber with insects enclosed, which he obtained in Germany, while traveling along the Baltic Sea.

The most valuable donation during the year was added to this department. A number of public-spirited citizens purchased a large collection of beautiful exhibition specimens, consisting of 452 pieces, brought together by Mr. P. P. Peck in different parts of the country. Mr. John E. Burton, being well aware of the importance and value of this collection, spent much of his time in obtaining the subscriptions. He then packed the specimens and sent them over to the Museum. The following names are those to whom we are indebted for the splendid gift. The subscriptions follow in the order in which they were received:

Mrs. S. S. Merrill	$100 00
Wm. Plankinton	50 00
Chas. F. Pfister	50 00
Dr. Edwin W. Bartlett	50 00
F. G. Bigelow	50 00
Frederick Pabst	100 00
Rudolph Nunnemacher Estate	25 00
Ernest G. Miller	25 00
H. C. Payne	50 00
J. H. Van Dyke	50 00
D. E. Murphy	25 00
Charles Ray	50 00
H. F. Whitcomb	25 00
Fred Vogel, Jr	25 00
John Pritzlaff Hardware Co	25 00
Uihlein Bros	100 00
	$800 00

Palæontology.—Mr. Chas. E. Monroe, appointed honorary curator of palæontology by the Board of Trustees, August 24. 1897, has charge of this department, and he will, whenever his time permits, arrange the collections in systematical order.

Though no purchases have been made this department has largely increased by donations.

Mr. Samuel J. Brockman, member of the Board of Public Works, donated a fossil coral, beautifully polished on one side, showing plainly the peculiar construction and form of the species. It comes from Iowa.

Mr. Adam Weber, Fond du Lac, Wis., presented to the institution two large pieces of rock showing a large number ot perfect specimens of Pentamerus oblongus. It is a peculiar fact that most people, not acquainted with palæontological study, call these fossils invariably "petrified hickory nuts."

Ethnology.—Mr. Chas. L. Kiewert presented a prayer book of a Hindoo priest, which he had obtained while traveling in India. The book is made of palm leaves and the writing seems to be in India ink. Altogether this is a very unique gift and of great value. The same gentleman donated a Chinese pepper mill and a stiletto from Morocco.

The most valuable gift to this department comes from Mr. Walter Lacy, of this city. It consists of 128 mostly very old Chinese coins.

By mail I received a very interesting small Chinese idol made of ivory. The name of the donor, who simply signed his letter "A Museum Friend," could not be ascertained.

Archæology.—This department grows more rapidly than any other in the Museum. Flint arrow and spear heads, tomahawks, pipes of peace, copper implements, etc., are constantly added to our archæological collection. The Haskell collection of Jefferson, Wis., and the Hayssen collection of New Holstein, Wis., have only recently been acquired by purchase, while a few small collections have been donated by their owners.

Miss Mary E. Stuart donated a copper implement, and Mr. F. J. Toussaint presented an interesting copper hatchet and two idols which he obtained in the State of Guerrero, Mexico. Mr. Toussaint promised me to collect other archæological specimens of value during his present trip through Mexico.

Although this institution is entirely maintained by the city it is free to all, thus becoming an educational factor of high rank for the city as well as for the entire State. During the annual State fairs and congresses held in Milwaukee the halls of the Museum are crowded with visitors from all parts of the State and the country. Old and young, residents and strangers are equally benefitted by the Museum. Therefore, it ought to be the aim of everybody to enrich the institution by donations. This can best be accomplished when its friends call the attention of their acquaintances to the good work we are doing. There are hundreds of small collections of prehistoric relics in the hands of Wisconsin people that ought to be preserved forever, together with the name of the donor, in this Museum.

Library.—A natural history Museum should contain in its library all the valuable monographs published of late in the interest of just such institutions. I refer especially to the set of valuable monographs written by Mr. D. G. Elliot, and of the surpassingly beautiful works of J. Gould. So far our insufficient appropriation has not allowed us to purchase more books than a few offered for an exceptionally low price. During the past year we added the following important works to our reference library:

1. Proceedings of the Zoölogical Society of London, complete from the beginning in 1830 to 1894, with indexes from 1848 to 1890, illustrated with many hundreds of fine chromo-lithographic plates of mammals, birds, fishes, shells, etc., besides numerous plain plates and wood-cuts, all drawn from nature and executed by eminent artists. Sixty-four volumes, bound in 55.

2. Transactions of the Zoölogical Society of London, complete set from the beginning in 1833 to 1890, illustrated with about 800 finely engraved plates, mostly colored, 12 vols., royal. These extremely scarce sets were bought of H. Sotheran & Co., London, England, for the low price of $549.26.

3. W. Hamilton Gibson, Our Edible Toadstools and Mushrooms and How to Distinguish Them, with thirty colored plates. Harper & Bros., 1895.

4. British and European Butterflies and Moths. By Kappel & Kirby.

5. Royal Natural History. By Richard Lydekker. Six volumes.

6. Ornithologie Nord-Ost Africas. Von Theodor von Heuglin. 2 vols.

7. Australien und Oceanien. Von Prof. Dr. Wilh. Sievers.

8. Pflanzenleben. Von Kerner von Marilaun. 2 vols.

9. Illustrated Flora of the Northern United States and Canada. By N. L. Britton and H. A. Brown. 2 vols.

Quite a number of smaller works and second-hand books have been also added by purchase, while many hundreds of exceedingly valuable government publications and proceedings of scientific societies have been donated.

II.—WORK DONE.

Special care has been taken by me and the taxidermist to keep the collections clean from dust and insect pests. In our present quarters the dust accumulates in such a way, even in the exhibition cases, that a constant vigilance is necessary in order to keep the specimens clean and in good condition.

Though the exterior aspect of the Museum has not changed in the eyes of the laymen, nevertheless a great amount of work has been accomplished. My correspondence with scientific men, with scientific institutions and societies, and with individuals, asking for information on special subjects, has been exceedingly large. From all parts of the State, and even from Illinois, Texas, Florida, etc., specimens have been sent to me for identification, especially plants, birds, fishes, snakes, shells and insects. Thousands of labels had to be prepared so that they could be printed on our small hand press.

Indeed, the classifying, labeling and arranging of whole collections has taken up much of my time. This kind of work, which is exceedingly tedious and tiresome, does not appeal to those not entirely familiar with Museum work, though it is the most important of all the duties of the custodian. My assistant and myself had to attend not only to the necessary routine work, but we had to perform a good deal of special work, particulary regarding the new building and its furnishing. As we not yet have a scientific staff (except the honorary curators, Dr. S. Graenicher and Mr. Chas. E. Monroe), I had to take care of all the specimens that were received by donations and by purchase, and had also to inspect all the work done by the taxidermist and his assistant. I had to control the work pertaining to the cleaning of the glass cases and floors and to attend to such visitors who particularly needed my assistance. To those who are accustomed to visit our collections frequently it is a matter of surprise that so much work has been accomplished with so limited an appropriation and with so small a force of workers. Indeed, the steadiness and uniformity of progress in all departments presents a most gratifying retrospect. When everything is properly and systematically arranged in new and suitable cases on the spacious floors of the new building, the public will be astonished about the beauty and magnitude of our collections.

During the last session of the Legislature we succeeded in obtaining a larger appropriation for the maintainance of the Museum, although not enough to carry out the plans which I so often have laid before you in my monthly reports. Instead of one-quarter of a mill of all the taxable property of the City of Milwaukee, the amount asked for, we were allowed only one-seventh of a mill—against one-tenth of a mill, our present appropriation. This will give us for the coming year about $20,500—against $14,377.16 for the year 1897. In order to make the different branches of science useful to the people several scientific men, specialists in their chosen fields, must be employed. It is an utter impossibility for me to take care of all the various departments besides the managing and superintending of the institution and the work in the division of mammals and birds. In other Museums of equal size five or six scientists are constantly employed in addition to the custodian and his assistant. However it may be we are thankful for what the Legislature has given us. Thanks are due in this connection to the President of our Board, Dr. Edwin W. Bartlett, Trustees Chas. L. Kiewert and A. J. Lindemann, who several times appeared before the Legislature in Madison to urge an increase of our appropriation. Senator Wm. H. Devos and Assemblyman F. A. Anson deserve our special thanks for their efforts to make known the importance and educational value of the Museum to their colleagues in the Legislature.

On June 1 a special meeting was called by President Bartlett to consider the furnishing of the new Museum building. Trustee Thos. F. Ramsey reported that the Common Council had allowed the Museum an amount of $36,400 for this purpose and that immediate steps should be taken to have the cases made. In order to obtain the very best furniture, the board instructed me to visit the Eastern Museums, with the following objects in view:

1. To study the different exhibition cases and their construction and to obtain sketches and specifications of the most practical ones in use.

2. To learn what has been done of late years to make the Museums most useful and attractive to the people.

3. To make as thorough a study as possible of the different scientific collections and their arrangement.

4. To find out the best method how skins and skeletons for the use of scientific study are preserved and arranged.

5. To investigate how such specimens as are liable to be easily injured by the light, as for instance, birds of paradise and other highly colored birds, are best protected and preserved.

6. To make notes how our Museum can be improved by additional material in the different branches.

7. To obtain information what has been done in the leading Museums of the East to make the collections most useful to the schools.

I left Milwaukee June 5, and returned July 3. The following Museums were visited:

Chicago Academy of Science, Field Columbian Museum, Chicago, Ill.

Smithsonian Institution, U. S. National Museum, Department of Agriculture, New Congressional Library, Army Medical Museum, all in Washington, D. C.

Academy of Science, Commercial Museum, Pennsylvania University, Memorial Hall, Independence Hall, all in Philadelphia, Pa.

American Museum of Natural History, New York.

Museum Boston Natural History Society, Boston, Mass.

Museum of Comparative Zoölogy, Peabody Archæological Museum, both in Cambridge, Mass.

Bussey Institute, Herbarium of the Arnold Arboretum Jamaica Plain, Mass.

A detailed report of this trip has been submitted to your honorable body in the regular July meeting.

The most practical as well as the most beautiful exhibition cases are those in the U. S. National Museum. Through the kindness of Prof. Fred. True, I obtained blue prints, photographs and specifications of all those cases which I thought would be suitable for our new building. These plans, etc., are very valuable, as they will give the architect as well as contractor an idea how good exhibition cases should be made.

There is scarcely a Museum in the country that can compete with the American Museum of Natural History of New York in regard to fine groups in the mammal and bird departments. The exhibition material in the departments of Palæontology, Mineralogy and Ethnology is almost overwhelming.

The exquisite groups of birds with their nests, often amidst beautifully flowering and foliaged shrubs, the immense groups of buffalos, etc., in cases made of the best French plate glass and mahogony wood, are without a rival. There is, perhaps, no Museum in the world which has been so generously supported by wealthy citizens of New York than this institution. An immense hall containing in fine glass cases all the woods of North America, has been furnished and supplied with specimens by Mr. Morris K. Jesup. The celebrated dendrologist, Prof. C. S. Sargent, of Harvard University, is the curator of this department.

A large and really wonderful collection of Peruvian antiquities, collected by the famous A. F. Bandelier, has been donated by Mr. Henry Villard. Then there are the Emmon's collection of the tribes of the North Pacific; the very large and complete collections of the Haida and other Indians, the gift of Mr. Herbert Bishop; the immense Tiffany collection of gems and gem material, the gift of Mr. D. Jackson Stewart. These are only a few of the many grand donations which were received by this Museum.

Some time ago Dr. Otto Finsch, the celebrated naturalist and traveler, offered us his large and unique collection of ethnological material which he personally brought together in several of the remote and little known South Sea Islands. This very large and valuable collection, systematically arranged and catalogued and accompanied by maps, charts and many water-color paintings and drawings, made by Dr. Finsch himself, was offered to our Museum for $4,000. The whole collection consists of about 6,500 specimens. As the aborigines of the South Sea Islands rapidly pass away from the face of the earth, little or nothing can be obtained from them in a few years hence that will illustrate their mode of living, their conduct in joyful and sad events, etc. A small collection exhibited by Dr. Finsch at the World's Columbian Exposition in the Anthropological Building was purchased by the Field Columbian Museum. I think it my duty to call the attention of all Museum friends and our wealthy and public-spirited citizens to this exquisite collection, hoping that perhaps some one may be found who is willing to secure it for the Museum.

Mr. Geo. B. Turner, the taxidermist of the Museum, and his assistant, have completed a few very fine mammal groups, among them a skunk group, representing seven young ones, the old male and female, together with their nest under a tree. The species represented is our common Mephitis mephitica. Every specimen in the group, the burrow, the tree, the ground on which some of the young ones play, is perfect, and as a whole the group is very striking. Another group, scarcely less impressive, is a family of three young and two old wood-chucks (Arctomys monax). Mr. Turner also finished a group of one old and two young turkey buzzards (Cathartes aura), the latter in their nest and the old female near them on a bough. A group of three young red-shouldered hawks (Buteo lineatus) and a red fox (Vulpes vulpes) is nearly ready for exhibition, as is also a group of flying squirrels (Sciuropterus volans). A very striking and life-like group, mostly in different positions, has been formed of eleven white rice-birds (Munia oryzivora). About five hundred specimens of birds, consisting of robins, Baltimore orioles, blue jays, English sparrows, blue-winged teal, night hawks, downy woodpeckers, bobolinks, have been mounted for the school collection. As our taxidermist and his assistant are not able to attend to all the material on hand, about three hundred bird skins have been sent to Mr. Henry Denslow, of Gates, N. Y., for mounting. About one-third of these have been returned. They are all beautifully mounted and will make our collection of exotic birds a grand feature in the new building.

SCHOOLS AND THE PUBLIC MUSEUM.

Most of our public as well as private schools have made good use of the Museum during the past year. Not only have the collections made up especially for the use of the schools *i. e.*, the collections of minerals, pre-historic relics and familiar birds, been in constant demand, but the Superintendent of our schools, Prof. H. O. R. Siefert, has inaugurated a system which enables all the different grades to visit the Museum several times during the year under the guidance of their teachers. I have been constantly requested by the teachers to assist them in their nature study, which I have done as far as my time permitted. Many of the teachers have followed my advice to join Mrs. A. B. Whitcomb's nature study class, and they all have become enthusiastic students. But there is much left yet to be done. It is a peculiar fact that the word "science" and even the expression "nature study" has a formidable sound to many teachers, though it really means nothing but systematic knowledge. Every child during the earlier years of his life is engaged almost continually in what is practically called scientific study. He is examining every phenomenon that presents itself to his senses; he observes things, compares them, and naturally forms some idea of their alliances and classifies them by their prominent characters. The best thing a teacher can do is to encourage him in just this kind of work, instead of giving him a dry text-book. Natural science is the most convenient for training the eye and the mind to note relations with alertness. Material for this study is found everywhere. Every bird, every plant, every butterfly and beetle, etc., invites investigation—all open wide fields for delightful study as the student's mind improves and he becomes more able to draw conclusions from what he sees. It is true, in order to acquire science we must study, but study, so far as from drudgery, is delightful occupation. Studious habits are easily acquired by the young if properly directed by their teachers. Besides this natural history is a study which brings one in close contact with nature, and stimulates a love for her beauties which will increase with years and prove a life-long joy and solace.

It would be of great value and a blessing to all our schools if every teacher would join the Audubon Society and the classes of Mrs. A. B. Whitcomb and Mrs. S. S. Merrill. This would give them also an opportunity to visit the Museum frequently.

Four books for beginners, beautifully written, and quite inexpensive, ought to be not only in the library of every teacher, but in the hand of every lover of nature. They are the following:

1. John Henry Comstock's "Insect-Life." 2. F. Schuyler Mathews' "Familiar Flowers of Field and Garden." 3. The same author's "Familiar Trees and Their Leaves," and 4. Florence A. Merriam's "Birds of Village and Field."

The last named volume is the ideal bird book for the teacher and for beginners, especially for the school children. It is written in such a plain, fascinating and beautiful style and is so tastefully illustrated and is so accurate in every respect that no other work can compete with it. No school library in city or country can be without this small volume, which really fills a long felt want. With this book in hand almost every bird can easily be determined.

INVENTORY.

120,844	Zoölogical specimens..............................	$38,475 59
17,133	Botanical specimens..............................	1,117 60
18,678	Anthropological specimens........................	13,299 55
11,558	Palæontological specimens........................	5,299 55
4,747	Mineralogical and Lithological specimens.........	4,789 94
7,193	Books, Pamphlets, Catalogues, Atlases and Charts.	6,664 52
3,025	Birds' Eggs and Nests............................	10,000 00
	Furniture, Tools, Jars, Vessels, Conservation Supplies and Stationery...........................	14,292 20
	Upham Collection, held in trust..................	350 00
	Aggregate value of the Museum................	$94,288 95

FINANCIAL TRANSACTIONS OF THE MUSEUM.

Debit.

Balance in Museum fund, Sept. 1, 1896.................... $7,560 14
Refunded insurance premium........................... 2 71
Appropriations to Museum fund, Jan. 1, 1897............. 14,377 16

      Total...$21,940 00

Credit.

Amounts paid by warrants on the City Treasurer since the last
    annual statement was rendered:
Permanent improvements....................... $1 75
Fuel and light.................................. 325 58
Repairs......... .... 127 98
Furniture 236 27
Mammals........ .... 407 25
Birds 752 84
Insurance 2,423 02
Rent and tax................................... 1,350 00
Library 170 81
Payroll... 7,049 96
Conservation supplies.......................... 33 22
Wages 490 86
Miscellanies 407 99
Stationery and printing........................ 100 83
Archæology 2,400 00
Postage and freight............................ 64 65
                     ————— $16,343 01

    Balance in Museum fund, Sept. 1, 1897...... $5,597 00

INSURANCE.

Dubuque Fire and Marine Insurance Company of Dubuque, Ia..	$1,000 00
The Fire and Marine Insurance Co. of Wheeling, W. Va..	1,000 00
Indiana Underwriters' Policy of Indianapolis, Ind.......	1,500 00
Chicago Insurance Company of Chicago, Ill.............	500 00
Citizens' Insurance Co. of Evansville, Ind..............	1,000 00
Cincinnati Insurance Company of Cincinnati, O.........	1,000 00
German-American Fire Insurance Company of Baltimore	1,000 00
The Netherlands Fire Insurance Company, Department, N. Y....................	5,000 00
Quebec Fire Assurance Company of Quebec............	1,500 00
Keystone Fire Insurance Company of Saint John, N. B..	2,500 00
The Baloise Fire Insurance Company of Basle, Switzerland	2,500 00
The National Hellenic Assurance Company of Athens, Greece...........	1,500 00
Eastern Counties Insurance Company, Ltd., New York..	1,500 00
The Aachen and Munich Fire Insurance Company of Aix La Chapelle, Germany.............................	1,500 00
Kent Fire Insurance Company, Department, N. Y.......	1,500 00
The Thuringia Insurance Co. of Erfurt, Germany........	1,000 00
Green Insurance Co. of America, New York.............	1,500 00
Royal Insurance Co. of Liverpool, England.............	2,500 00
London and Lancashire Fire Insuance Company, Liverpool, England....................................	1,500 00
United States Fire Insurance Company, New York......	1,500 00
Capital Fire Insuurance Co. of Concord, New Hampshire.	2,500 00
New Hampshire Fire Insurance Company of Manchester	2,500 00
Agricultural Insurance Co. of Watertown, N. Y.........	2,500 00
Norwood Insurance Company of New York.............	4,000 00
Associated Underwriters of Rockford, Ill...............	2,000 00
United Firemen's Insurance Company of Philadelphia, Pa..	1,000 00
Allemannia Fire Insurance Company of Pittsburgh, Pa..	1,500 00
Insurance Company of the State of Illinois, Rockford, Ill.	1,000 00
German Fire Insurance Co. of Peoria, Ill...............	1,000 00

The Lancashire Insurance Company of Manchester, England	1,500	00
The Schuylkill Fire Insurance Company of Philadelphia, Pa..	2,500	00
Saginaw Valley Fire and Marine Insurance Co. of Saginaw, Mich.......................................	2,500	00
Hamburg Bremen Fire Insurance Company of Hamburg, Germany	2,000	00
Saint Paul Fire and Marine Insurance Co. of St. Paul, Minn..............	2,000	00
Norwich Union Fire Insurance Society of England......	2,500	00
The Palatine Insurance Company, Limited, of Manchester, England....................................	4,00	00
Firemen's Insurance Company of Newark, N. J..........	1,000	00
The Hartford Fire Insurance Company of Hartford, Conn..............	1,000	00
The Phoenix Insurance Company of Hartford, Conn.....	2,500	00
Rhode Island Underwriters Association, Providence, R. I..	2,000	00
The North German Fire Insurance Company of Hamburg, Germany......................................	2,500	00
Buffalo Commercial Insurance Co. of Buffalo, N. Y......	1,000	00
German Fire Insurance Co. of Peoria, Ill.................	1,000	00
Insurance Company of North America, Philadelphia, Pa.	2,000	00
Philadelphia Underwriters of Philadelphia, Pa..........	2,000	00
The Manchester Fire Assurance Company of Manchester, England.........	2,500	00
The Mutual Fire Insurance Co. of New York.............	2,500	00
The Liverpool and London and Globe Insurance Co., Liverpool, England.................................	2,500	00
Michigan Fire and Marine Insurance Co. of Detroit......	1,000	00
The Mercantile and Marine Insurance Co. of Boston, Mass........	1,000	00
The Greenwich Insurance Company of New York........	1,500	00
Manufacturers and Merchants' Mutual Insurance Company of Rockford, Ill..............................	2,500	00
The Grand Rapids Fire Insurance Co. of Grand Rapids, Mich.............	1,500	00
Phenix Insurance Company of Brooklyn, N. Y...........	1,000	00
The Boston Marine Insurance Co. of Boston, Mass.......	1,000	00
Total...	$99,500	00

VISITORS.

	1896 Sept.	1896 Oct.	1896 Nov.	1896 Dec.	1897 Jan.	1897 Feb.	1897 Mar.	1897 Apr.	1897 May.	1897 June.	1897 July.	1897 Aug.	1896-97 Whole year.
Average daily attendance	829	1,321	48	61	60	69	111	68	80	61	146	78	246
Greatest daily attendance	2,312	3,857	133	112	139	175	207	142	665	113	1,502	143	....
Least daily attendance..	10	10	19	20	19	24	28	23	24	15	16	41	....
Av· attend'ce on Sundays	113	113	93	115	63	122	153	109	225	80	59	84	....
Total attendance.....	14,889	40,960	1,428	1,894	1,863	1,935	3,442	2,054	2,476	1,825	4,519	2,413	89,698

CONCLUSION.

During the past year the Museum has been visited by 89,698 people from all parts of the state and country. Among the visitors were many teachers and scientific men who expressed their surprise of finding an institution of such magnitude in this western city, the metropolis of Wisconsin. There can be no doubt that the Public Museum, more than any other public institution, helps to make our city famous at home and abroad. All over the country the city is praised for establishing and maintaining a natural history museum free of admission to all and open throughout the year. Educators especially saw at once its value as an excellent means of instruction. When our collections have been transferred to the new cases in the new building, the people will see what a grand institution the Museum really is. They then will be aware of the fact that it is something the city can well be proud of.

In conclusion, I have to thank your honorable Board for the great interest you have shown in the institution, for the kind relations that have always existed during the year between the Board and its Secretary, and for the assistance offered me in building up and improving the Museum, in order to make it more useful to the people. The large attendance and the long list of accessions show that the efforts of the Board to increase the usefulness and beauty of the Museum are well appreciated. Thanks are due also to Mr. Carl Thal, my able and conscientious assistant, to Mr. Geo. B. Turner, our taxidermist, and, in fact, to all the other employes. Every one of them has been attentive to my every wish and instruction. All have worked with the sincere desire to help the Museum improve and to do their full duty as servants of the people, for whom the Museum was established.

Respectfully submitted,

H. NEHRLING,

Custodian and Secretary.

APPENDIX.

ZOOLOGY.

DONATIONS.

John Ahlhauser, Milwaukee, Wis.
    1 Alligator, Captivity, Milwaukee, Wis.
Mrs. O. D. Barker, Milwaukee, Wis.
    1 Taeniopygia castanotis, Captivity, Milwaukee, Wis.
Carl Bindrich, Milwaukee, Wis.
    1 Sora,   Milwaukee, Wis.
    1 Cerulean Warbler,   "   "
John A. Brandon, Milwaukee, Wis.
    1 Philadelphia Vireo,   Milwaukee Co., Wis.
    1 Ruby-crowned Kinglet,   "   "
Geo. Brumder, Milwaukee, Wis.
    1 Cooper's Hawk, Pine Lake, Wis.
Fred. Brune, Milwaukee, Wis.
    1 Red Bat, Milwaukee, Wis.
F. Gallun, Jr., Milwaukee, Wis.
    3 Domesticated Pigeons, Captivity, Milwaukee.
Edmund Goes, P. O. Williamsburg, Wis.
    1 Great Blue Heron, Fox River, Wis.
Alexander Goethel, Milwaukee, Wis.
    1 Great Blue Heron,   Saukville, Wis.
    1 Horned Grebe,   "   "
    4 English Sparrows,   "   "
    2 Muskrats,   "   "
    1 Fox Squirrel,   "   "
Alfred and Alexander Goethel, Milwaukee, Wis.
    3 Young Hawks, Saukville, Wis.
Dr. Sigmund Graenicher, Milwaukee, Wis.
    1 Bullhead,   Lake Tichigan, Wis.
    1 War-mouth,   "   "
    2 Blue Sun Fishes, Pewaukee Lake, Wis.
    1 Black Bass, Milwaukee River, Wis.
    1 White Bass,   Milwaukee Fish Market.
    1 Sucker-mouthed Buffalo,   "

Dr. Sigmund Graenicher, Milwaukee, Wis.

1 Common Sucker,	Milwaukee River, Wis.	
1 Grass Bass,	"	"
1 Stone Cat,	"	"
1 Brook Trout,	"	"
1 Horny Head,	"	"
1 Rock Bass, Pewaukee, Wis.		
1 Little Pickerel,	Milwaukee River, Wis.	
1 Bullhead,	"	"
1 Perch, Lake Michigan, Wis.		
1 Wall-eyed Pike, Milwaukee Fish Market.		
1 Golden Shiner,	Milwaukee River, Wis.	
1 Hog Sucker,	"	"
1 Lake Red Horse,	"	"
1 Chub Sucker, Tichigan Lake, Wis.		
1 Mud Minnow,	Milwaukee River, Wis.	
1 Common Shiner,	"	"
1 Horned Dace,	"	"
1 Stone Lugger,	"	"
1 "Johnny,"	"	"
3 Minnows,	"	"
1 Long-nosed Dace,	"	"
1 Brook Stickleback,	"	"
1 Trout Perch,	"	"
1 Nine-spined Stickleback,	"	"
1 Red-bellied Minnow, Honey Creek, near Wauwatosa, Wis.		
1 Black-sided Darter,	Milwaukee River, Wis.	
1 Lawyer,	"	"
1 Miller's Thumb,	"	"
1 Fan-tailed Darter,	"	"
1 Log Perch,	"	"
1 Snowflake,	Milwaukee Co., Wis.	
28 Syrphidae,	"	"
111 Hymenoptera,	"	"

John F. Heim, Milwaukee, Wis.

1 Parrot, Captivity, Milwaukee.

Adolph Hempel.

8 Helix, Lake Hatchincha, Fla.

13 Planorbis, Johnson Island, Osceola Co., Fla.

1 Unio, Lake Tohopekaliga, Osceola Co., Fla.

1 Cerithium, Bird Island, Fla.

Robert Herdegen, Milwaukee, Wis.

    1 Oven-bird,   ·   Milwaukee, Wis.

    1 Red Bat,   "   "

Gardiner Hibbard, Milwaukee, Wis.

    1 Flicker, Milwaukee, Wis.

Hermann Hirsch, Milwaukee, Wis.

    1 Sora, Wauwatosa, Wis.

    1 American Rough-legged Hawk, Pewaukee, Wis.

Chas. L. Kiewert, Milwaukee, Wis.

    1 Antelope's Horn, Africa.

    1 Glass-rope Sponge, Japan.

Wm. Koehne, Gotha, Fla.

    1 Alligator, Florida.

Conrad Krez, Milwaukee, Wis.

    1 Olive-backed Thrush, Milwaukee, Wis.

William Lahmann, Milwaukee, Wis.

    1 Blue Fin,   Lake Michigan, Wis.

    1 Great Lake Trout,   "   "

    1 Lawyer,   "   "

    2 Lake Herring,   "   · "

Dr. Chas. J. Lange, Milwaukee, Wis.

    3 American Mergansers, Pewaukee Lake, Wis.

    1 American Golden-eye, Green Bay, Wis.

    1 American Long-eared Owl,   Milwaukee Co., Wis.

    1 Western Fox Squirrel,   "   "

    2 Loons, North Lake, Wis.

    1 Horned Grebe, Pewaukee, Wis.

    1 Horned Grebe, Milwaukee Co., Wis.

    1 Great Blue Heron, Green Bay, Wis.

    1 Common Mole,   West Baden, Ind.

    1 Prairie Mole,   "   "

    5 Woodchucks,   "   "

    3 Turkey Buzzards,   "   "

Adolph Meinecke, Milwaukee, Wis.

    1 Jaw of Shark,   St. Petersburg, Fla.

    1 Backbone of Shark,   "   "

    1 Tooth of Shark,   "   "

    1 Lower Jaw of Wild Boar.

    1 Glass-snake in alcohol, Gotha, Fla.

    96 Beetles, Europe.

H. A. Meinecke, Milwaukee, Wis.

    2 White-winged Scoters, Wisconsin.

William P. Merrill, Milwaukee, Wis.

    1 Horse-shoe Crab, Florida.

Emil Müller, Milwaukee, Wis.

    1 American Osprey, Cement Mills, Wis.

Bruno Nehrling, Milwaukee, Wis.

    1 Slate-colored Junco, Milwaukee, Wis.

Dr. H. V. Ogden, Milwaukee, Wis.

    1 Woodchuck, Delafield, Wis.

C. Pfeifer, Plymouth, Wis.

    1 Barred Owl, Plymouth, Wis.

F. Rauterberg, Milwaukee, Wis.

    1 Spreading Adder,   Gotha, Fla.

    1 Ground Rattlesnake,   "   "

    1 Blue-tailed Lizard,   "   "

    1 Parrot, Captivity, Milwaukee.

Mrs. Frieda Rieck, Milwaukee, Wis.

    1 Centipede,   South America.

    2 Scorpio sp.,   "

August Stirn, Milwaukee, Wis.

    1 Diphyllodes magnifica, Malayan Archipelago.

    10 Tropical Bird Skins.

    1 Canary Bird Skin.

H. F. Strong, North Greenfield, Wis.

    1 Great-horned Owl, North Greenfield, Wis.

Frank Suelflow, Milwaukee, Wis.

    1 Flicker, Milwaukee, Wis.

Rev. Judson Titsworth, Milwaukee, Wis.

    1 Water Thrush, Milwaukee, Wis.

Geo. B. Turner, Milwaukee, Wis.

    1 English Sparrow, Milwaukee, Wis.

ACQUIRED BY PURCHASE.

1 Bubo maximus, Japan.

2 Cuncuma leucogaster, New South Wales.

1 Falco tinnunculus, France.

1   "   biarmicus, South Africa.

1 Ibycter americanus, South America.

1 Hierocoglaux strenua, Victoria, Australia.

1 Spilornis cheela, Himalaya, India.
1 Strix tenebricosa, New South Wales, Australia.
1 Melierax polyzonus, Abyssinia, Africa.
1 Ketupa javanensis, Malay Peninsula, Asia.
1 Leptodon cayanensis, Venezuela, S. A.
1 Elanus scriptus, Australia.
1 Gymnocephalus calvus, Cayenne, S. A.
1 Gymnostinops bifasciatus, Lower Amazon, S. A.
1 Tinnunculus cenchroides, Australia.
2 Xanthura beechi, Mexico.
1 Cassiculus melanicterus, Mexico.
1 Cassicus haemorrhous, Rio Janeiro, Brazil.
1 " microrhynchus, Panama.
1 Icterus cucullatus nelsoni, Mexico.
1 " pectoralis,   Guatemala.
1 " giraudii, .   "
1 Pitylus celæno, Mexico.
1 Leistes superciliaris, South America.
1 " guianensis, Panama.
1 Pyrocephalus rubineus, Colombia, S. A.
2 Pica colleri, Mexico.
1 Ceryle torquata, Cayenne, French Guinea.
1 Pyroderos granadensis, Colombia, S. A.
1 Ostinops atrocastaneus, South America.
1 Cassicus uropygialis, Ecuador, S. A.
1 Dacelo gaudichaudi, New Guinea.
1 Ceryle amazona, Colombia, S. A.
1 Eumomota superciliaris, Guatemala.
1 Icterus wagleri, Guatemala.
1 Paroaria gularis, South America.
1 Rhodinocichla rosea, Colombia, S. A.
1 Trupialis militaris, Chili.
1 Cassiculus melanicterus, Mexico.
1 Pheuticus chrysoseptus, Mexico.
1 Lurocalis semitorquatus, South America.
1 Bucco radiatus, Panama.
1 Ampelion arouta, Ecuador, S. A.
1 Gymnocorvus senex, New Guinea.
1 Corvultor albicollis, South Africa.
1 Corone cornix, Asia Minor.
1 Gymnorhina leuconota, New South Wales.

1 Gracalus cassius, Cape Colony.

1 Tropidorhynchus corniculatus, New So. Wales, Australia.

1 Anlacops calvus, Kina Balu, India.

1 Pycnonotus capensis, Cape Colony, Africa.

1 Collurio nigriceps, India.

1 Miro albifrons, New Zealand.

1 Copsychus saularis, Malacca, Asia.

1 Eopsaltria australis, New South Wales, Australia.

1 Malurus splendens, Australia.

1 Calamanthus fuliginosus, Australia.

1 Campephaga humeralis, Australia.

1 Eucometes cassini, Panama.

1 Niltava grandis,   Sikkim, India.

1 Hemixus flavata,   "   "

1 Hemicurus guttatus,   "   "

1 Trochalopteron squamatum,   "   "

1 Alcurus striatus, Darjeeling, India.

2 Petrophila erythrogastor, Sikkim, India.

2 Acridotheres tristis,   Sandwich Islands.

1 Psittirostra psittacea,   "   "

2 Drepanis sanguinea,   "   "

2 Turtur chinensis,   "   "

1 Dacelo gouldii, New Guinea.

1 Megaceryle guttata, Yokohama, Japan.

1 Pelargopsis amauroptera burmanica, Malacca, Asia.

1 Entomobia pileata, Malacca, Asia.

1   "   smyrnensis, Ceylon, India.

2 Ceryle rudis, Congo, Africa.

1 Halcyon malimbica cinerifrons,   Congo, Africa.

1   "   cyanoleuca,   "   "

1   "   semicaerulea,   "   "

2 Alcedo pulchella, Malacca, Asia.

1   "   cristata, Congo, Africa.

1   "   bengalensis, Japan.

1 Todirhamphus sancta, Australia.

1 Alcyone azurea, New South Wales, Australia.

1 Hirundo rusticola, Europe.

1 Myiomoria macrocephala, New Zealand.

1 Pratincola rubicola, Gloucester, England.

1 Mohna ochrocephala, Dunedin, New Zealand.

1 Pomatostomus superciliosus, New South Wales, Australia.

2 Cypselus melba, Europe.

1 Merops viridis, India.

1 " ornatus, Australia.

1 " swinhoii, Mergui, B. Burma.

1 Mycantha garrula, New South Wales, Australia.

1 Prosthemadera Nova-zealandiae, New Zealand.

1 Anthochaera inauris, New South Wales, Australia.

1 Seleucides niger, New Guinea.

1 Ptilorhis paradiseus,   Queensland, Australia.

1 Coracias affinis,   "   "

1 Eurystomus pacificus, Philippine Islands.

1 Urospatha martii, Panama.

1 Pteroglossus phoenicinctus,   Brazil.

1 " castonatis,   "

1 Rhamphastos ambiguus, Colombia, S. A.

1 Ara militaris, Mexico.

1 Opisthocomus cristatus, British Guiana, S. A.

1 Rhamphastos toco, Brazil.

1 Coronideus hyacinthus, Brazil.

1 Momotus subrufescens, South America.

1 Chasmonhynchus variegatus, Guiana, S. A.

2 Merula flavirostris, Mexico.

1 Gymnomystax melanicterus, Guiana, S. A.

1 Pheuticus chrysopeplus, Mexico.

1 Icterus jamaicai, Brazil.

1 " sclateri,   Mexico.

1 " gularis,   "

2 Platypsaris aglajæ,   ·   "

1 Rhampocœlus jacapa, Brazil.

2 Phoenicocercus carnifex, Demerara, S. A.

1 Thamnophilus melanocrissus, Panama.

1 Phoenicothraupis salvinii, Panama.

1 Tanagra abbas, Guatemala.

1 Eucometes cristata, Panama.

1 Tanagra cana, Colombia, S. A.

1 Calliste ruficervix, South America.

1 Melanotis hypoleucus, Guatemala.

1 Tityra fraserii, Panama.

1 Taemoptera pyrope, Chili.

1 Cyanothrus sericeus,   South America.

1 Phoenicothraupis lunulata,   "

1 Tachyphonus malaleucus, Colombia.
1   "   coronatus, Brazil.
1 Chlorophona callophrys, Panama.
1 Chiroxiphia pareola,   Colombia, S. A.
1 Lessonia nigra,   "   "
1 Chiromachaeris manacus,   South America.
1 Calliste vitriolina,   "
1   "   aurulenta,   "
1   "   yeni,   "
1   "   cyaneicollis,   "
1   "   inornata, Panama.
1 Pipra leucocilla, Ecuador, S. A.
1   "   chrysoptera, Colombia.
1   "   vitellina, Panama.
1 Euphonia trinitatis, Colombia.
1   "   hirundinacea, Mexico.
1   "   violacea lichtensteini, Brazil, S. A.
1   "   xanthogaster, Colombia, S. A.
1 Piaya cayana, Mexico.
1 Strepera graculina,   New South Wales.
1   "   anaphonensis,   "
1 Heteralocha gouldii, New Zealand.
1 Anthochæra carunculata,   New South Wales.
1 Calluricincla harmonica,   "
1 Artamus superciliosus,   "
1 Creadion carunculatus, New Zealand.
1 Monticola solitarius, Japan.
1 Campephago hartlaubi, South Africa.
1 Colornis metallicus, Duke of York Island.
1 Collurio vittatus, India.
1 Juida melanogaster, Natal.
1 Collurio schach, China.
1 Ampelis phoenicoptera, Yokohama, Japan.
1 Loniarius cubla, Natal, Africa.
1 Pycnonotus atricapillus, China.
1 Sauloprocta motacilloides, Victoria.
1 Seisura inquieta, New South Wales, Australia.
1 Parus varius, Japan.
1 Myiagra nitida, New South Wales.
1 Monticola rupestris, Cape Colony, Africa.
1 Bessonornis verticalis, West Africa.

1 Psophodes crepitans,   Victoria, Australia.

1 Anallobia lunulata,   "   "

1 Phyllornis cyanopogon, Malacca.

1   "   icterocephala, Malayan Peninsula.

1 Grallina pictata, New South Wales, Australia.

1 Garrulus japonicus, Yokohama, Japan.

1 Garrulus japonicus, Yokohama.

1 Mino dumonti,   New Guinea.

1 Ptilorhis intermedia,   "

1 Amydrus morio, Cape Colony, Africa.

1 Acridotheres cristatellus, China.

1 Cracticus nigrogularis, New South Wales, Australia.

1 Mainatus javanus, India.

1 Manucodia atra, New Guinea.

1 Amydrus morio, Cape Colony, Africa.

1 Gallirex porphyrocephala, East Africa.

1 Manucodia comrii, New Guinea.

1 Temnurus leucopterus, Malacca.

1 Paradisea setacea, New Guinea.

1 Rhamphococcyx colorhynchus, Celebes.

1 Oreocincla lunulata, New South Wales, Australia.

1 Monticola solitarius, Japan.

1 Pitynasis gymnocephala, Borneo.

1 Mino kreffti, New Britain.

1 Lamprocolius amethistinus, Niam Niam, Africa.

1   "   phoenicopterus, Southeast Africa.

1 Sphecotheres maxillaris, New South Wales, Australia.

1 Atelornis pittoides, Madagascar.

1 Hypsipetes McLallandii, Sikkim, India.

1 Bessonornis melanotis, Africa.

1 Schlegelia wilsoni,   New Guinea.

1 Pitta strepitans,   "

1 Laniarius sulphureipictus, Natal, Africa.

1 Pachycephalia gutturalis, Australia.

1 Fiscus collaris,   Natal, Africa.

1 Vidua axillaris,   "   "

1 Phyllornis chorocephalus, Amherst.

1 Petroica phoenicosa, Tasmania.

1 Pardalotus striatus,   Australia.

1   "   punctatus,   "

1 Ruticilla hodgsoni, Sikkim, India.
1   "   aurorea, China.
1 Oriolus galbula, Asia Minor.
1   "   larvatus,   Natal, Africa.
1 Dicrurus assimilis,   "   "
1   "   laemostichus, New Britain.
1 Euphonia personata, Yokohama, Japan.
1 Artamus sordidus, New South Wales, Australia.
1 Meristes chloris, Congo, Africa.
1 Monarcha carinata, New South Wales, Australia.
1 Tschitrea cristata, Natal.
1 Pyrrhula orientalis, Japan.
1 Melithreptus chloropsis, New South Wales, Australia.
1 Petroica multicolor, Tasmania, Australia.
1 Ptilorhis auricomis, Australia.
1 Ephtianura albifrons, New South Wales, Australia.
1 Myiagra nitida,   Tasmania, Australia.
1 Malurus cyaneus,   "   "
1 Cercotrichas macrura, Malacca.
1 Climacteris scandens, New South Wales, Australia.
1 Acanthorhynchus superciliosus, Australia.
1 Zanthopigia narcissina, Japan.
1 Falcunculus frontalis, New South Wales, Australia.
1 Euplectes flammiceps, Africa.
1 Manorhina melanophrys, New South Wales, Australia.
1 Saxicola bifasciata, Cape Colony.
1 Cittocincla suavis, Borneo.
1 Meliphaga phrygia, New South Wales.
1 Bessonornis melanotis, Africa.
1 Lichmera australianus, Tasmania, Australia.
1 Pochycephala falcata, Australia.
1 Oxylabes madagascarensis, Madagascar.
1 Ixos sinensis, China.
1 Macronyx capensis,   Africa.
1 Pomatorhinus temporalis,   "
1 Dryoscopus major,   "
1 Hypsipetes amaurotis, Yokohama, Japan.
1 Graucalus melanops, Australia.
1 Cyanopelius cyana, Japan.
1 Chibia hottentotta, India.
1 Oreocincla varia, Yokohama, Japan.

1 Gymnorhina tibicen, New South Wales, Australia.

1 Callaenas cinerea, New Zealand, Australia.

1 Meliphaga novae-hollandiae, Australia.

2 Guara rubra, Orinoco River, Venezuela, S. A.

1 Corvus caurinus, British Columbia.

1 Meleagris gallopavo osceola, Florida.

[*]

26 Dryobates pubescens, New York and Massachusetts.

2 Chordeiles virginianus, Massachusetts.

13 Ampelis cedrorum, Burlington, Ia.

27 Dilichonyx oryzivorus, Wisconsin.

1 Rhynchophanes maccownii, Huachuca Mountains.

2 Conurus carolinensis, Osceola Co., Fla.

1 Phoebetria fuliginosa, South Pacific, off Mexico.

1 Diomedea nigripes, off Ensenada, Lower California.

1 Haematopus frazeri, San Geronimo Island.

1 Puffinus puffinus, England.

1 Fulmarus glacialis columba,   10 miles off San Diego, Cal.

1   "   "   glupischa,   "   "

1 Oceanodroma furcata, Alaska.

1 Bulweria bulweri, Sta. Ursula.

1 Oceanodroma melania,   San Benito Island.

1   "   socorroensis,   "

1 Halscyptena microsoma,   "

2 Carpodacus amplus,   Guadaloupe Island, Cal.

2 Salpinctes guadaloupensis,   "   "

2 Junco insularis,   "   "

1 Clytolaema aurescens, Ecuador.

1 Lamprolaema rhami, Mexico.

[*]

1 Eriocnemis luciani,   Ecuador.

1 Lafresnaya gayi,   "

1 Bourcieria fulgidigula,   "

1 Aithurus polytmus, Jamaica.

1 Oreotrochilus pipinchae, Ecuador.

1 Thalurania glaucopis, Bahia.

1 Heliangelus strophianus,   Ecuador, S. A.

1 Helianthea lutetiae,   "   "

1 Urosticte benjamini,   "   "

1 Cephalolepis delalandi, Rio.

1 Lophornis magnifica, Rio de Janeiro.
1   "   ornata, Trinidad.
1   "   helenae, Guatemala.
1 Phaethornis guyi,   Bogota, S. A.
1 Chlorostilbon prasinus,   "   "
1 Selasphorus scintilla, Costa Rica.
1 Spathura melanothera, Ecuador, S. A.
1 Acestrura heliodori, Colombia, S. A.
1 Alces malchis, female,   Eagle River, Ontario, Canada.
1   "   ".   young,   "   "   "
1   "   "   calf,   "   "   "
1 Ovibos moschatus, female,   Arctic America.
1   "   "   calf,   "   "
1 Felis tigris, Northern Asia.
1 Vulpes vulpes, var. fulvus, Wisconsin.
2 Tusks of Walrus.
1 Bird's Nest, British Guiana.
1 Euplectella aspergillum, Philippines.
1 Meoma ventricosa, Bahamas.
32 Corals, Key West, Fla.
58 Shells, Sugar River, Brodhead, Wis.
5 Starfishes, Pacific Ocean.

Geo. B. Turner, Taxidermist of Museum, collected the following specimens:

2 Green Herons,   Delafield, Wis.
1 Rose-breasted Grosbeak,   "   "
2 American Redstarts,   "   "
1 Magnolia Warbler,   "   "
1 Chestnut-sided Warbler,   "   "
1 Blackburnian Warbler,   "   "
4 Woodchucks,   "   "
4 Common Flying Squirrels,   "   "

---

* Scientific names of exotic birds are taken from the labels of the skins.

BOTANY.

DONATIONS.

Dr. Edwin W. Bartlett.

1 Piece of wood with the letters J. W. grown in, Brillion, Wis.

The letters were grown to the depth of 1½ feet along the grain of the wood.

PALÆONTOLOGY.

DONATIONS.

Samuel J. Brockman, Milwaukee, Wis.

    1 Coral, cut and beautifully polished, Iowa.

Adolph Meinecke, Milwaukee, Wis.

    1 Asaphus gigas, Oxford, Ohio.

6 Orthis simeata,	Richmond, Ind.	
11 " biforata acutilirata,	"	"
11 Streptorhynchus sulcata,	"	"
10 " subtentus,	"	"
7 Monticulipora quadrata,	"	"
3 " manulata,	"	"
8 Rhynchonella capax,	"	"
2 Orthoceras expositum,	"	"
13 Monticulipora ramosa,	"	"
3 Bellerophon bilobatus,	"	"
8 Tropidoleptus carinatus,	"	"
6 Streptorhynchus filitextus,	"	"
4 Crania scabiosa,	"	"
6 Orthis biforata laticosta,	"	"
5 " occidentalis,	"	"
4 Pleuroton subcorica,	"	"
11 Ortenela honesi,	"	"
2 Scheydonta trumeata,	"	"
2 Sphenolium Richmondense,	"	"
3 Pschyrodorota decificos,	"	"
1 Trenatis nillepunctata,	"	"
1 Zygospira modesta,	"	"
1 Modeolodon oreformis,	"	"
6 Ryssonychia alveolata,	"	"
3 Streptelasma corniculum,	"	"

Adam Weber, Fond du Lac, Wis.

    2 Pentamerus oblongus, Fond du Lac Co., Wis.

ACQUIRED BY PURCHASE.

    3 Pentamerus oblongus, Laramie City, Wyo.

    66 " " Wisconsin.

    29 Fossils, Fairmount, Cincinnati, Ohio.

    5 Corals, " " "

    1 Turtle, Yellowstone Park.

44 Shells,   Michigan and Wisconsin.
80 Corals,   "   "
3 Calcareous Rock with Crinoid Stems, Michigan.
4 Baculites,   Bad Lands, S. D.
1 Mastodon Tooth,   "   "
1 Belemnites,   Hamilton, Ill.
1 Halonia pulchella,   "   "
2 Orthoceras,   Wisconsin.
2 Crinoids,   "
10 Leaves.
1 Petrified Wood, forming into Coal.
3 Blastoids,   Bowling Green, Ky.
3 Pentromites florialis,   "   "
2 Sea Urchins.
1 Calymene niagarensis,   Calumet Co., Wisconsin.
2 Archimedes Wortheni,   Hancock Co., Ill.
2 Bactocrinus Chrystyi,   "   "
1 Strombodis gracilis, Calumet Co., Wis.
1 Syringopora verticillata, Wisconsin.

MINERALOGY.

DONATIONS.

Dr. Edwin W. Bartlett, Milwaukee, Wis.
    2 Quartz, Keokuk, Ia.
Chas. L. Kiewert, Milwaukee, Wis.
    8 Amber, with insects enclosed.
H. Nehrling, Milwaukee, Wis.
    1 Amber, with insect enclosed.
August Stirn, Milwaukee, Wis.
    1 Calcite, Joplin, Mo.
Mrs. S. S. Merrill, William Plankinton, Chas. F. Pfister, Dr. Edwin
    W. Bartlett, Frank G. Bigelow, Capt. Fred. Pabst, Ernst G.
    Miller, Rud. Nunnemacher estate, Hy. C. Payne, J. H. Van Dyke,
    D. E. Murphy, Chas. Ray, H. F. Whitcomb, Fred Vogel, Jr., John
    Pritzlaff Hardware Co., Uihlein Bros.:
    49 Calcites.
        2   "   and Zinc.
        1   "   and Milorite.
        1   "   and Greenockite.
        3   "   and Galena.

3 Calcites and Marcasite.
2 " and Iron.
2 " and Pyrites.
1 " and Flint.
2 " and Chalcopyrite.
58 Galena.
2 " and Silicate of Zinc.
6 " and Zinc.
4 " and Dolomite and Ruby Zinc.
5 " and Marcasite.
2 " and Flint.
1 " and Greenockite.
1 " and Calcite.
1 " and Iron.
2 Greenochite on Zinc.
1 Native Silver.
1 " " and Copper.
1 " Copper.
1 " Silver and Silver Glance.
1 " Copper and Calcite.
10 Zinc.
4 " and Galena.
1 " and Smithsonite.
2 " Ore.
2 " Crystals.
1 " Lead and Dolomite.
1 " and Dolomite.
145 undetermined specimens.
1 Aragonite.
4 Spars.
1 Agate.
3 Beryl.
5 Silicates of Zinc.
1 Smithsonite.
1 Lava Rock.
14 Dolomite.
4 " and Galena.
1 " and Galena and Calcite
1 " and Zinc.
8 " and Pyrite.
1 " and Garnets.

16 Marcasite.

1 Midorite on Flint.

1 Cidarite on Quartz.

1 Zinc Concretion.

2 Twined Crystal of Calcite on Zinc.

2 Calcopyrite on Dolomite.

2 Amethyst.

1 Amethyst, Calcite and Marcasite.

1 Amethyst, Quartz and Calcite.

10 Iron Ores.

4 Quartz Crystals.

1 Quartz and Chalcopyrite.

1 Flint.

1 Siderite.

1 Cerusite.

1 Garnet.

1 Pyrite on Galena.

2 Petrified Wood.

1 Albite var. Peristerite.

2 Sphalarite.

2 Pyrite.

1 Chalcopyrite on Dolomite.

23 Hematite.

ACQUIRED BY PURCHASE.

6 Mica, Diamond Mica Mine, Black Hills, S. D.

2 Barite.

2 Calcites.

4 Malachite.

6 Calcites, Linden Mine, Wis.

2   "   Dodgeville, Wis.

2   "   Wisconsin.

1   "   Mineral Point, Wis.

1 Black Tourmaline, St. Lawrence Co., N. Y.

1   "   "   Calumet Co., Wis.

1 Iron Pyrites, Gogebic, Mich.

1   "   "   Linden Mine, Wis.

2 Barite, Wisconsin.

1 Hematite.

1 Azurite, Mineral Point, Wis.

1 Beryl, Chester Co., Pa.

1 Gold Ore, India.

1 Silver Ore, Nevada.

3 Copper, Michigan.

2 Copper sp., containing silver.

ETHNOLOGY.

DONATIONS.

A Museum Friend, Milwaukee, Wis.

1 Ancient Chinese Idol, China.

Joseph Friedrich, Milwaukee, Wis.

22 Calico and Wall Paper Hand-printing Forms and Types, Germany.

Geo. W. Goetz, Milwaukee, Wis.

1 Piece of Iron taken from Marble Column of the Temple of Artemis, which was built by Hermogenes 200 B. C., Magnesia, Asia Minor.

Chas. L. Kiewert, Milwaukee, Wis.

1 Prayer Book of a Hindoo Priest on Palm Leaf in Sanscrit, Ceylon, India.

1 Chinese Coffee Mill from the 17th Century, China.

1 Stiletto, Morocco.

Albert H. Krell, Milwaukee, Wis.

1 Map of the Free City of Lindau from the 30 years' war.

Walter Lacy, Milwaukee, Wis.

6 Plates containing 128 old Chinese Coins, China.

Adolph Meinecke, Milwaukee, Wis.

1 Ancient Norwegian Beer or Meth Mug, Norway.

ACQUIRED BY PURCHASE.

1 French Helmet, France.

1 Gun, Germany.

1 Old Dutch Coffee Pot and Stand, made of Copper, Holland.

1 Pewter Coffee or Tea Can, Germany.

1 Pewter Milk Pot	Germany.
1 Pewter Lamp,	"
1 Pewter Plate,	"
1 Tin Lamp,	"
1 Brass Candlestick,	"
2 Pair of Scissors.	"
1 Pewter Salt Box,	"
1 " Candlestick,	"
1 Silver Candlestick,	"

1 Samovar, Russia.

1 Wooden Lance,   South Sea Islands.

3 Spears,   "

1 Club.

1 Indian Pipe, United States.

1 Part of Indian Pipe, United States.

1 Old Scale, Saxony.

1 Chain, made out of one Piece of Wood.

1 Figure, made out of Deer Horn.

1 Miniature War Club.

1 Miniature Gun.

2 Relics, Fort Mackinaw, Mich.

1 Swiss Money Belt, Switzerland.

1 Pair of Indian Leggings, used in War Dances.

1 Small Bag, used for carrying Trinkets, Mackinaw Island, Mich.

1 Dance Belt, Chippewa Indians, Northern Wisconsin.

1 Pair of Indian Leggings,   Chippewa Indians, Michigan.

1 Indian Head Dress,   "   "

1 Pair of Indian Leggings, Sioux Indians.

1 Bag of Cedar Bark, Chippewa Indians, Michigan.

2 Indian Garnishes.

1 Knitting Needle Holder,   Germany.

1 Antique Saxon Padlock,   "

1 Iron Implement, used for sharpening scythes, Schleswig-Holstein.

3 Old Iron Axes, Germany.

2 Iron Hatchets,   Green Bay, Wis.

1 " Hoe,   "   "

3 Old Broad Iron Axes, New Holstein, Calumet Co., Wis.

2 Old Iron Halberts, Germany.

2 Iron Tools for working Slate, Ireland.

1 Ancient Pipe, Fort Mackinaw, Mich.

1 Iron Lance Head.

1 Bowie Knife, formerly owned by "Ne-gwa-gan," Indian Chief.

1 Old Iron Knife, from the great Indian War at Michillimackina, now Mackinaw.

1 Old Horse Bit.

2 Cowboy's Spur and Ring Bit.

1 Bowie Knife, formerly owned by old Chippewa Chief, "She-boy-way," Michigan.

1 Bowie Knife, Japan.

1 Bowie Knife with Scabbard.

1 Old Iron Knife.

2 Table Knives and Knife Holder.

2 Stems of Indian Pipes.

3 Iron Implements.

1 Autograph of August, Elector of Saxony, Anno 1567.

1 Old Parchment Document from Frederick William Markgraf zu Brandenburg, etc., with Seal attached, April 4, 1668.

1 Old Parchment Document from the year 1688.

1 Ghost Shirt, taken from dead Indian on "Wounded Knee Battle Field."

1 Esquimaux Coat.

1 Book from "Wounded Knee Battle Field," painted and written by "Red Hawk," captured by Capt. R. Miller, Rapid City, S. D.

34 Old Books.

1 Old German Butcher Belt with Brass Buckle, Germany.

2 Old Locks,   Germany.

7 Old Flat Irons,   "

6 Guns.

4 Pistols.

1 Sabre with Belt.

3 Modern Indian Pipestone Carvings.

ARCHÆOLOGY.

DONATIONS.

Adolph Meinecke, Milwaukee, Wis.

1 Fibula, Pile Dwellings, Switzerland.

H. Nehrling, Milwaukee, Wis.

1 Stone Arrowhead, Gotha, Orange Co., Fla.

Miss Mary E. Stewart, Milwaukee, Wis.

1 Copper Implement, Pierre, S. D., Island in the Missouri River.

F. J. Toussaint, Milwaukee, Wis.

1 Copper Hatchet, dug out of a Mound near Rio del Oro, District of Mina, State of Guerrero, Mexico.

1 Idol, found in Ruins of an old City, which has been discovered recently in site of the City of Telolopan, Guerrero, Mexico.

1 Idol, found near Cutzamala, Guerrero, Mexico.

ACQUIRED BY PURCHASE.

62	Copper	Spearheads,	Wisconsin.
19	"	Knives,	"
10	"	Lances,	"
9	"	Arrowheads,	"
7	"	Chisels,	"
5	"	Scrapers,	"
5	"	Awls,	"
4	"	Spades,	"
1	"	Punch,	"
1	"	Axe,	"
1	"	Point,	"
1	"	Sinker,	"

189 Tomahawks,   "
149 Stone Celts,   "
76 Oval, round and flat stones,   "
16 Slate Ornaments,   "
23 Stone Ornaments,   "
  1 Double-bitted miniature Tomahawk,   "
  1 Ornamental Hatchet,   "
  4 Fragments of ornamental Hatchets,   "
  1 Peculiar formed Stone Celt or Skinner,   "
  6 Pipes of Stone and Pottery,   "
  1 Stone Vessel,   "
  1 Tanning Tool,   "
  2 Ornaments, made of Pipestone,   "
  1 Part of Pipe Bowl,   "
  2 Fragments of Pottery Pipes,   "
  1 Pipe Bowl,   "
  1 Stone Wedge,   "
  2 Flat Drilled Stone Implements,   "
  1 Sandstone Implement,   "
  1 Pipe of Lead, Michigan.
  1 Stone Axe, Bavaria.
  1 Large Stone Pestle, Charleston, R. I.
  6 Stone Beads, made by the Apache Indians, New Mexico.
32 Rare Agricultural Stone Implements, Illinois.

From the Indian Grave on the farm of J. Berg, Rantoul, Calumet Co., Wis.

  4 Beads.
23 Thimbles.

1 Ring.

96 Ear-rings.

41 Parts of Ear-rings.

2 Shell Pendants.

1 Silver Teaspoon, marked G. S. B.

1 Pocket Mirror.

1 Mirror.

2 Boxes Wampum Beads.

1 Toy Saucer.

1 " China Tea-pot, encased in Toy Iron Kettle.

1 " Pitcher.

1 Indian Woman's Hand with Ring.

1 " " Arm with 14 Bracelets.

1 " " " " 12 "

8 Corroded Iron Trinkets.

2 Indian Ears with Ear-rings and Coins.

1 Bunch of matches, tied together with hair.

2 Clay Pipes.

Hairs of Skull, with Wampum Beads, Ear-rings, etc.

1 Cluster of 30 Chains, each 1 foot long, with Rings, Beads and Ribbons.

8 Various fancy-beaded Pouches, each being attached to a Chain.

1 Remainder of Petticoat Trimming, made of Silk.

1 Petticoat Trimming with 13 Ornaments.

1 Indian Skull.

3 Mortars and Pestles, Santa Barbara, Cal.

4 Modern Pueblo Pottery, Belen, New Mexico.

10 Antique Cliff Dwellers Pottery, Joseph, New Mexico.

17 Pieces of Mound-builders Pottery, Arkansas.

1 Indian Idol, Arizona.

19 Pieces of Pueblo Indian Pottery, Belen, N. M.

19 Pieces of Pueblo Indian Pottery, Belen, N. M.

2 Pieces of Aztec Stone Work, " "

48 " " Mound-builders Pottery. Wisconsin.

112 Flint and Quartz Skinners, "

722 Stone Spearheads, "

1,407 Stone Arrowheads, "

26 Leaf-shaped Flint Implements. "

35 Stone Lanceheads, "

13 Flint Drills,   Wisconsin.
5 " Knives,   "
2 Quartz Knives,   "

LIBRARY.

DONATIONS.

Academia Nacional de Ciencias en Cordoba, Buenos Aires.
  Boletin, Tomo XIV., Entregas 3 and 4.
   " Tomo XV., Entregas 1a.
Academy of Science of St. Louis.
  Transactions, Vol. VII., No. 10-16.
Aceademia Dell' Scienze dell' Istituto di Bologna.
  Rendiconto, 1894-1895.
American Institute of Mining Engineers, Philadelphia, Pa.
  Frazer, P. Notes on the Northern Black Hills of South
   Dakota.
American Museum of Natural History, New York.
  Bulletin, Vol. VIII., 1896.
  Annual Report, 1896.
Australian Museum, Sydney.
  Report of the Trustees, 1895.
Belfast Natural History and Philosophical Society, Belfast.
  Report and Proceedings, 1895-1896.
Biblioteca Nazionale Centrale di Firenze.
  Bolletino, No. 256, 258, 265.
Boston Society of Natural History, Boston.
  Proceedings, Vol. 27.
   " Vol. 28, Nos. 1-5.
Botanischer Verein der Provinz Brandenburg, Berlin.
  Verhandlungen, 37. Jahrg. 1895.
   " 38. " 1896.
Botanical Society of America, Buffalo.
  Address of the retiring president, Wm. Trelease, 1896.
California Academy of Sciences, San Francisco.
  Proceedings, II. Serie, Vol. VI., 1896.
   " III. Serie, Vol. I., No. 2, 1897.
  Announcement concerning the publications of the Academy.
Chicago Academy of Sciences, Chicago.
  Bulletin No. 1. 2. Geol. and Nat. History Survey.
  39th Annual Report.

Cincinnati Museum Association, Cincinnati.
> 16th Annual Report for 1896.

Cincinnati Society of Natural History, Cincinnati.
> Journal, Vol. XIX., No. 1, 2.

City Comptroller, Milwaukee, Wis.
> Annual Report for 1896.

Colorado College Scientific Society, Colorado Springs.
> Collorado College Studies, Vol. VI.

Henry W. Dunlop, Milwaukee, Wis.
> Ulster County, N. Y., Gazette of Jan. 4th, 1800, containing the obituary address on the death of Genl. Washington.
>
> Call to the loyal Democrats of Wisconsin to assemble, dated August 20th, 1861.

Elisha Mitchell Scientific Society, Chapel Hill, N. C.
> Journal, January-June, 1896.
>
> " Vol. XIII., Part II., 1896.

Entomologiske Föreningen i Stockholm.
> Entomologiske Tidskrift, Arg. 17, Heft 1-4.

Erben von Fritz Ruehl, Zürich-Hottingen.
> Societas entomologica, No. 1-24, Jahrgang XI.
>
> " " No. 1-9, Jahrgang XII.

Essex Institute, Salem.
> Bulletin, Vol. 26, Nó. 7-12.
>
> " Vol. 27, No. 1-12.

Field Columbian Museum, Chicago.
> Publication No. 11, Zoölogical Ser., Vol. I., No. 3.
>
> " " 12 " Vol. I., No. 4.
>
> " " 14, Annual Report, 1895-1896.
>
> " " 15, Botanical Ser., Vol. I., No. 3.
>
> " " 16, Ornitholog. Ser., Vol. I., No. 2.
>
> Annual Exchange Catalogue, 1896-1897.
>
> Publication No. 18, Geolog. Ser., Vol. I., No. 2.
>
> " 19 and 20, Zoölog. Ser., Vol. 1, Nos. 6 and 7.

Free Museum of Science and Art, Philadelphia.
> Bulletin, Vol. I., No. 1.

Gesellschaft zur Beförderung der gesammten Naturwissenschaften zu Marburg.
> Sitzungsberichte, 1894-1895.

Gesellschaft Naturforschender Freunde zu Berlin.
> Sitzungsberichte, 1895.

Gesellschaft für Natur- und Heilkunde, Dresden.
    Jahresbericht, 1895-1896.

Geological Survey of Queensland, Brisbane.
    Bulletin No. 4-5.

Government Museum of Madras.
    Administration Report, 1895-1896.
    Bulletins, Vol. II., No. 1.

Hayssen, H. H.
    Riggs, C. W. How We Find Relics.

Historical and Philosophical Society of Ohio, Cincinnati.
    Annual Report, 1896.

Historical and Scientific Society of Manitoba, Winnipeg.
    Annual Reports for 1894 and 1895.
    Transactions No. 48, 1896.

Historischer Verein zu Brandenburg a. d. Havel.
    26-28. Jahresbericht.

Illinois State Laboratory of Natural History, Springfield.
    Bulletin, Vol. IV., Art. X.

Interstate Commerce Commission, Washington.
    Tenth Annual Report, 1896.

Iowa Geological Survey, Des Moines, Ia.
    Iowa Geolog. Survey, Vols. I. to V.

Johns Hopkins University, Baltimore.
    Circulars, 1896.

Journal of Comparative Neurology, Granville, Ohio.
    Journal, Vol. VI., No. 3, pages 133-344.
        "   Vol. VII., No. 1.

K. K. Naturhistorisches Hofmuseum, Wien.
    Annalen, Bd. X., Nos. 3, 4.
        "   Bd. XI., Nos. 2, 3, 4.

K. Sächsische Gesellschaft der Wissenschaften, Leipzig.
    Berichte über die Verhandlungen, Mathemat., Physische,
        Classe, II., III., V., VI.
    Zur 50 jahrigen Jubelfeier der K. Sächs. Ges. der Wiss., 1896.

Kongl. Vitterhets Historie och Antiqvitets Akademien, Stockholm.
    Antiqvarisk Tidskrift för Sverige XV., 1.
    Manadsblad, 1893.

Kais. Leopoldino-Carolinischen Deutschen Akademie der Natur-
    forscher, Halle.
    "Leopoldina," Organ der Akademie, 1896.

K. K. Geologische Reichsanstalt, Wien.
Jahrbuch, 1895, Bd. XLV., Heft 4.
"   1896, Bd. XLVI., Heft 1-8.
"   1897, Bd. XLVII., Heft 1.
Verhandlungen, Nos. 5-13, 1894.
"   Nos. 4-18, 1895.
"   Nos. 1-15, 1896.
"   Nos. 1-8, 1897.
Lackawanna Institute of History and Science, Lackawanna.
Scientific Series, Nos. 2, 4, 5.
Liverpool Geological Association, Liverpool.
Journal, Vol. XV., 1894-1895.
Magyar Nemzeti Muzeum, Budapest.
Természetrajzi Füzetek, Vol. XIX., 1896, Parts 3 and 4.
"   "   Vol. XX., 1897, Parts 1 and 3.
Märkisches Provinzial Museum, Berlin.
Verwaltungsbericht, April, 1895-März, 1896.
Adolph Meinecke, Milwaukee.
"Unsere Vorzeit." Ein Beitrag zur Urgeschichte und Alter-
tumskunde Niedersachsens.
Milwaukee City Service Commission, Milwaukee, Wis.
Civil Service Act and Revised Rules for the Civil Service of
Milwaukee.
Second Annual Report of the Commissioners.
Milwaukee Public Library, Milwaukee, Wis.
Quarterly Index of Additions, Vol. 5, 1894-1895.
"   "   "   Vol. 6, Nos. 1-4, 1895-1896.
Fiction Title Index, 1896.
Minnesota Academy of Natural Science, Minneapolis, Minn.
Bulletin, Vol. IV., No. 1.
Minnesota Historical Society, St. Paul.
9th Biennial Report. 1896.
Missouri Historical Society, St. Louis.
Publication No. 12 for 1896.
Museum für Naturkunde zu Berlin.
16 Pamphlets on Natural History.
Museum für Völkerkunde zu Leipzig.
22. und 23. Bericht, 1894-1895.

Museo Nacional de Costa Rica, San José.
>   Moluscos Terrestres Y Fluviatiles De La meseta central de Costa Rica.
>   Insectos de Costa Rica.
>   Antîquedades de Costa Rica, 1896.

Museo Nacional de Montevideo.
>   Anales, V. to VII., 1896.

Museum of Comparative Zoölogy, Cambridge.
>   Annual Report, 1895-1896.

Museums and Lecture Rooms Syndicate, Cambridge.
>   31st Annual Report, 1896.

Nassauischer Verein für Naturkunde, Wiesbaden.
>   Jahrbuch, Jahrg. 49. and 50.

Natural History Society of Glasgow, Glasgow.
>   Transactions, Vol. IV., Part III., 1895-1896.

Natural History Society of New Brunswick.
>   Bulletins Nos. 14 and 15.

Natural Science Association of Staten Island, New Brighton.
>   Proceedings, Vol. VI., Nos. 2-8.

Naturforschende Gesellschaft zu Emden.
>   80. Jahresbericht, 1894-1895.

Naturforschende Gesellschaft des Osterlandes, Altenburg.
>   Mittheilungen, Neue Folge, IV. Bd., 1896.

Naturwissenschaftliche Gesellschaft zu St. Gallen.
>   Bericht, 1894-1895.

Naturhistorische Gesellschaft zu Nürnberg.
>   Abhandlungen, X. Bd., IV. Heft.

Naturhistorischer Verein der preussischen Rheinlande und Westfalens, Bonn.
>   52. Jahrgang, II. Hälfte.
>   53.   "   I. Hälfte.

Naturwissenschaftlicher Verein zu Osnabrück.
>   11. Jahresbericht, 1895-1896.

Naturwissenschaftliche Gesellschaft "Isis" Dresden.
>   Sitzungsberichte, 1896.

Naturwissenschaftlicher Verein für Neu Voerpommern und Rügen, Greifswald.
>   Mittheilungen, 1896.

Naturwissenschaftlicher Verein zu Magdeburg.
>   Jahresbericht und Abhandlungen, 1894.

Naturwissenschaftlicher Verein zu Regensburg.
>Berichte, Heft 5, 1894-1895.

Naturwissenschaftlicher Verein des Reg. Bez. Frankfurt, Berlin.
>14. Bd., "Helios" Abhandlungen und Mittheilungen.

Naturwissenschaftlicher Verein zu Hamburg.
>Verhandlungen, Dritte Folge, IV., 1896.
>Abhandlungen, XV. Bd.

Naturwissenschaftlicher Verein für Steiermark, Graz.
>Mittheilungen, Jahrg. 1896, 33. Heft.

Naturwissenschaftlicher Verein der Universität Wien.
>Mittheilungen, 1896.

Naturwissenschaftlicher Verein für Schwaben und Neuburg, Augsburg.
>XXXII. Bericht.

Naturkundig Genootschap, Groningen.
>Vijfennegentigste Verslag, 1895.

H. Nehrling, Milwaukee, Wis.
>Bulletin 9-15 of the Wilson Ornitholog. Chapter of the Agassiz Association.
>Krider, John. Forty years notes of a Field Ornithologist.

New York Academy of Sciences, New York.
>Transactions, Vol. XV., 1895-1896.
>Annals, Vol. IX., Nos. 4-12.

New York State Museum, Albany, N. Y.
>48th Annual Report.
>43 Plates of edible and poisonous Fungi.

Niederrheinische Gesellschaft für Natur- und Heilkunde, Bonn.
>Sitzungsberichte, Zweite Hälfte, 1895.
>   "   Erste Hälfte, 1896.

Nova Scotian Institute of Science, Halifax.
>Proceedings, Vol. IX., Part II., 1896.

Oberhessische Gesellschaft für Natur- und Heilkunde, Giessen.
>31. Bericht, 1896.

Observatorio Astronomico Nacional, Tacubaya.
>Boletin Tomo I. No. 25.
>Anuario, 1897.

H. Nehrling. Ornithologischer Verein zu Stettin.
>Zeitschrift für Ornithology und praktische Geflügelzucht, No. 1-8.

Geo. W. Peckham, Milwaukee, Wis.

    Reprint from the report of the Horn Expedition to Central Australia, Part II., Zoölogy.

Physikalischer Verein zu Frankfurt a M.

    Das Klima a von Frankfurt a M., 1896.

    Jahresbericht, 1894-1895.

Physikalisch-Oekonomische Gesellschaft zu Königsberg.

    Schriften, 36. Jahrg., 1895.

      "   37. "   1896.

Physikalisch-Medicinische Societät, Erlangen.

    Sitzungsberichte, 28. Heft, 1896.

"Pollichia" Naturwissenschaftlicher Verein der Rheinpfalz, Dürkheim.

    Mittheilungen, Jahrg. LIII., No. 9 and 10.

      "   Jahr. LIV., No. 11.

Portland Society of Natural History, Portland, Maine.

    Proceedings, Vol. II., Part 4.

Primera Exposicion Centroamericana Guatemala, San José, Costa Rica.

    Flora de Costa Rica, No. 6, 1897.

    Fauna de Cocta Rica, No. 8, 1897.

Royal Irish Academy, Dublin.

    Proceedings, Third Series, Vol. IV., No. 1-3.

Royal Society of Queensland.

    The Geological Structure of Extra Australian Artesian Basins, 1896.

    The Submarine Leakage of Artesian Water.

Schlesische Gesellschaft für vaterländische Cultur, Breslau.

    73. Jahresbericht.

    Litteratur der Landes- und Völkerkunde der Provinz Schlesien, Heft IV.

Smithsonian Institution, Washington, D. C.

    Annual Reports for 1893-1894.

    Special Bulletin No. 1 and 2, 1892-1895.

    International Exchange List of the Smithsonian Institution.

Societé Entomologique de France, Paris.

    Bulletins 19, 20, 21, 1896.

      "   1-12, 1897.

Societé Imperiale des Naturalistes de Moscow.

    Bulletin, Année 1895, Tomo IX.

      "   Année 1896, No. 1, 2.

Society of Friends of Philadelphia.

> An Appeal to Professing Christians, respecting the attitude of the church in regard to war.

Societé De Physique Et D'Histoire Naturelle De Genéve.

> Compte Rendu Des Siances, XIII., 1896.

Stavanger Museum, Stavanger.

> Aarsberetning for 1895.

Thurgauische Naturforschende Gesellschaft, Frauenfeld.

> Mittheilungen, Heft 12.

F. J. Toussaint, Milwaukee, Wis.

> Diarium Sanctorum Seu Meditationes, etc., 1752.
>
> P. Ovidii Nasonis Fastorum, 1586.
>
> 2 Other old Books.

U. S. Bureau of Education, Washington, D. C.

> Report of the Commissioner, 1893-1894.
>   "   "   1894-1895.

U. S. Bureau of Ethnology, Washington.

> 14th Annual Report, 1892-1893, Part 1 and 2.
>
> 15th Annual Report, 1893-1894.

U. S. Coast and Geodetic Survey, Washington.

> Report for 1895, Parts 1 and 2.

U. S. Department of Agriculture, Washington.

> Farmers' Bulletin, No. 54.

U. S. Department of the Interior, Washington, D. C.

> Report on Insurance Business in the U. S. at the Eleventh Census, 1890, Part II., Life Insurance.
>
> Report on Crime, Pauperism and Benevolence in the U. S. at the Eleventh Census, 1890, Part I., Analysis.
>
> Abstract of the Eleventh Census, 1890.
>
> Report on Farms and Homes from the Eleventh Census, 1890.
>
> Report on the Vital Statistics from the Eleventh Census, 1890.
>
> Report on the Insane, Feeble-Minded, etc., from the Eleventh Census, 1890.

U. S. Commission of Fish and Fisheries, Washington, D. C.

> Remarks on the Movements and Breeding Grounds of the Fur Seal.
>
> Stejneger, L. The Russian Fur Seal Islands.

U. S. Geological Survey, Washington, D. C.

> 16th Annual Report, 1894-1895, Part I.
>
> Bulletins, Nos. 124-148.
>
> Monographs, Vols. XXV.-XXVIII.

U. S. National Museum, Washington, D. C.
Bulletin No. 39, Part K, Part I, Part H.
"   No. 47, 48.
Proceedings, Vol. XVII., 1894, Vol. XVIII., 1895.
Report upon the Condition and Progress of the U. S. Nat.
Museum, 1893.
Oceanic Ichthyology, Plates and Text, 1895.
U. S. War Department, Washington.
The War of the Rebellion, Ser. I., Vol. XLVIII., Part II.
Report of the Board of Publication of the Official Records of
the Union and Confederate Armies.
The War of the Rebellion, Ser. I., Vol. XLIX., Part I., II.
"   Ser. I., Vol. L., Part 1, 2.
U. S. Director of the Mint, Washington.
24th Annual Report, 1896.
University of California, Berkeley.
Bulletin of the Department of Geology, Vol. II., Nos. 2 and 3.
Vassar Bros. Institute, Poughkeepsie, N. Y.
Transactions.
Verein zur Verbreitung naturwissenschaftlicher Kenntnisse, Wien.
Schriften, 36. Bd., 1895-1896.
Verein für Erdkunde zu Darmstadt.
Notizblatt, IV. Folge, 17. Heft.
Verein für Erdkunde zu Leipzig.
Mittheilungen, 1895.
Baumann, Oscar. Die Insel Sansibar.
Verein für Geschichte und Naturgeschichte der Baar, etc.
Schriften, Heft IX., 1896.
Verein für Naturkunde zu Kassel.
Abhandlungen und Bericht, 1895-1896.
Videnscabs Selskabet I Christiania.
Forhandlinger, 1895.
Skrifter, 1895.
Vorarlberger Museum Verein, Bregrenz.
.34. Jahresbericht, 1895.
Wiener Entomologischer Verein, Wien.
VI. Jahresbericht, 1895.
VII.   "   1896.
Zoölogische Sammlung zu Berlin.
Bericht für 1896-1897.

ACQUIRED BY PURCHASE.

Heyne, Alexander. Die exotischen Käfer in Wort und Bild.
6. Liefg.

Kappel and Kirby. British and European Butterflies and
Moths.

Browne, Mont. Artistic and Scientific Taxidermy and
Modelling.

Cassino, Samuel E. The Naturalists' Directory, 1895.

Patitz, R. Entwickelung und Bedeutung der Zahl und des
Masses.

Nehrling, H. Die Nordamerikanische Vogelwelt.

Nehrling, H. North American Birds. 2 Vols.

Edwards, W. H. The Butterflies of North America. IV.
Series. Part XVII.

Lydekker, Rich. The Royal Natural History, Vol. I. to VII.

Engler, A. and Prantl, K., Die natürlichen Pflanzenfamilien,
Lief. 106-168.

Kerner von Marilaun, Anton. Pflanzenleben. Bd. 1. II.

Gibson, W. Hamilton. Our edible Toadstools and Mushrooms and how to distinguish them.

Britton and Brown. An illustrated Flora of the Northern
U. S., etc., Vol. II.

The "American Naturalist," Vol. XXIX., 1895.

The "American Naturalist," Vol. XXXI., Nos. 361-368.

Die "Natur," Nos. 1-32.

The "Auk," Vol. XIV., Nos. 1-3.

The "Osprey," Vol. I., Nos. 1-12.

The "Antiquarian," Vol. I., Part 1-8.

"Science," Vol. VI., Nos. 131-137.

v. Heuglin, M. Th. Ornithologie Nord ost Afrika's. I. und
II. Bd.

Sievers, W. Dr. Prof. Australien und Oceanien.

Jordan, David Starr. A Manual of the Vertebrate Animals
of the Northern United States. 7th Edition.

Papers, presented to the World's Congress on Ornithology,
Chicago.

Geological Survey of Illinois, 6 Vols., 1866-1875.

Second Geological Survey of Pennsylvania, 10 Vols., 1874-
1877.

Annual Reports of the University of the State of New York,
18, 20, 21, 27.

Contributions from the U. S. National Herbarium, Vol. III., Nos. 3 to 6, 1895.

The Journal of Mycology, Vol. V., Nos. 1 to 4, 1889.

26th Annual Report of the N. Y. State Museum of Natural History, 1874.

14th Annual Report of Indiana Geology and National History, 1884.

U. S. Geological Survey of the Territories, Vol. IX., Invertebrate Palæontology, 1876.

First and Second Annual Reports of the Geological Survey of Missouri, 1855.

Report on the Geology of the Henry Mountains, 1877.

U. S. Mexican Boundary Survey, 1859.

Memoirs of the National Academy of Science, Vol. III., Part II., 1886.

Memoir on the Fossils of the older Deposits in the Rhenish Provinces, 1842.

D. Schmid's Petrefacten.

Seventh Annual Report of the Geolog. Survey of Indiana, 1875.

Lecture Notes on Geology and Outline of the Geology of Canada, 1880.

Exploration of the Red River of Louisiana, 1852.

Final Report of the U. S. Geolog. Survey of Nebraska, 1872.

Miller, S. A. North Am. Mesozoic and Caenozoic Geology and Palæontology, 1881.

First Report of a Geolog. Reconnoissance of the Northern Counties of Arkansas, 1858.

Reports on the Agriculture and Geology of Mississippi, 1854, 1860.

The American Palaeozoic Fossils, 1877.

Geological Survey of Alabama, 1875, 1886.

23d Annual Report of the University of New York, 1873.

24th Annual Report of the N. Y. State Mus. of Nat. Hist., 1872.

Overman, Fred. Practical Mineralogy, etc., 1875.

Report on Forestry, 1878.

Revision of the Palæocrinoidea, Part I. II., 1879, 1881.

Second Preliminary Report on the Mineralogy of Pennsylvania, 1876.

On the Laurentian Limestones of North America, 1871.

16th Annual Report of the University of the State of N. Y., 1863.

On the Geological History of the Gulf of Mexico.

The Utica Slate and Related Formations, 1879.

Catalogue of the Casts and Fossils, 1866.

Der heutige Standpunkt der Geologie und ihre Bedeutung, 1882.

Useful Minerals of the U. S., 1888.

Hall, James. Contributions to Palæontology, 1858-1859.

Haeckel, Ernst. Ziele und Wege der heutigen Entwickelungsgeschichte, 1875.

15th and 19th Annual Report of the University of New York, 1862, 1866.

Suess, Ed. The Future of Silver, 1893.

Report of a Geological Reconnoissance in 1835 to the Corteau de Prairie.

Catalogue of the College Series of Casts of Fossils, 1870.

Hefe und Gährung nach dem heutigen Standpunkte der Wissenschaft, 1877.

Laws of Wisconsin Concerning the Public Museum.

(330, A.)   (Published April 13, 1882.)

CHAPTER 329.

AN ACT relating to the Natural History Society of the City of Milwaukee.

The People of the State of Wisconsin, represented in Senate and Assembly, do enact as follows:

Section 1. The board of directors of the Natural History Society of the City of Milwaukee is hereby authorized and empowered, in the name of said association or society, to assign, transfer and convey to the City of Milwaukee, all and singular, the natural historical collections of every kind constituting the Museum belonging to said Natural History Society, in trust, to be kept, supported and maintained by said city, as a free Museum for the benefit and use of all citizens of said city; provided, the said city shall accept the trust and assume the care and maintenance of such Museum.

Sec. 2. This act shall take effect and be in force from and after its passage and publication.

Approved March 31, 1882.

(No. 329, A.)   (Published April 14, 1882.)

CHAPTER 328.

AN ACT to authorize the City of Milwaukee to establish and maintain a Public Museum in said city.

The People of the State of Wisconsin, represented in Senate and Assembly, do enact as follows:

Section 1. The City of Milwaukee is hereby authorized to receive and accept from "The Natural History Society of Wisconsin"—a corporation located in the said City of Milwaukee— a donation of its collection of objects in Natural History and Ethnology, or of the greater part thereof, upon such conditions as may be agreed upon by and between said city and said society, subject, however, to the provisions of this act.

Sec. 2. In case of such donation and acceptance, said City of Milwaukee is hereby authorized and empowered to establish and maintain in said city a free Public Museum, exhibitions of objects in Natural History and Ethnology, and for that purpose to receive, hold and manage the collection so donated, and any devise, bequest or donation that may be made to said city for the increase and maintenance of such Museum under such regulations and conditions as are herein contained, or may be agreed upon by and between the donors and said city, or as may be hereafter provided in this act.

Sec. 3. The Museum established and maintained under this act shall be under the general management, control and supervision of a board of nine trustees, who shall be styled "The Board of Trustees of the Public Museum of the City of Milwaukee." Said Board of Trustees shall consist of the president of the School Board and the Superintendent of Schools of said city, *ex-officio*, of three members of the Common Council of said city, designated and appointed by the Mayor thereof, and of four residents and tax-payers of said city, to be appointed by the Mayor as herein provided. The first appointments of trustees by the Mayor under this act shall be made within ten days after the formal acceptance by the Common Council of said city of a donation by said Natural History Society, as authorized in the first section of this act. Of the first three trustees appointed from the members of the Common Council of said city, one shall be appointed from the three-year class, one from the two-year class, and one from the one-year class of aldermen, and they shall serve as such trustees during their respective terms as such aldermen. And annually on the third Tuesday of April thereafter, at the expiration of the term of any such trustee, the Mayor shall appoint his successor for three years, from the aldermen then having three years to serve. In case any such trustee shall vacate the office of alderman before the expiration of his term, he shall at the same time cease to be a trustee under this act, and the Mayor shall appoint some other member of the Common Council of his class in his place for the balance of his term. In the appointment of the four remaining trustees and their successors, the Mayor shall prefer such persons as may be recommended for such appointment by said Natural History Society. Such four trustees first appointed shall, at the first meeting of the Board after their appointment, determine by lot their term of service, so that one of their number shall serve for one year, one for two years, one for three years, and one for four years from the third Tuesday of May next after the organization of such Board. And all vacancies shall be filled by like appointment of the Mayor for the remainder of the term, and annually on the third Tuesday of April a trustee shall be appointed by said Mayor in like manner for the term of four years, in place of the trustee whose term shall expire the following May. None of said trustees shall receive any compensation from the city treasury, or otherwise, for their services as such trustees. And no member of said Board of Trustees shall become, or cause himself to become interested, directly or indirectly, in any contract or job for the purchase of any matter pertaining to the Museum, or of fuel, furniture, stationery or things necessary for the increase and maintenance of the Museum. Said trustees shall take the official oath, and be subject to the restrictions, disabilities, liabilities, punishments and limitations prescribed by laws as to aldermen in the said City of Milwaukee.

Sec. 4. The first meeting of said Board of Trustees for the purpose of organizing, shall be held on the third Tuesday of the month next following their appointment, and the City Clerk shall give at least one week's previous notice of the time and place of such meeting to each member of such Board in writing. At such first meeting said Board shall organize by the choice of one of their number as president to serve until the third Tuesday of May next following, and until his successor shall be chosen. The annual meeting of said Board shall be held on the third Tuesday of May in each year, and at such meeting a president shall be chosen from their number to serve for one year and until his successor shall be chosen.

Sec. 5. The Board of Trustees shall have general care, control and supervision of the Public Museum, its appurtenances, fixtures and furniture, and of the selection, arrangement and disposition of the specimens and objects appertaining to said Museum, and also of the disbursements of all the moneys appropriated for and belonging to the Museum fund, in the manner hereinafter provided. And the said Board shall adopt, and at their discretion modify, amend or repeal by-laws, rules and regulations for the management, care and use of the Public Museum, and fix and enforce penalties for their violation, and generally shall adopt such measures as shall promote the public utility of the Museum; provided, that such by-laws, rules and regulations shall not conflict with the provisions of this act.

Sec. 6. The Board of Trustees shall, at their first meeting, or thereafter as soon as practicable, and every five years thereafter, at an annual meeting, elect by ballot a person of suitable scientific attainments, ability and experience for custodian, who shall so act and be *ex-officio* secretary of said Board of Trustees. The custodian first appointed shall hold his office for five years from the time of the first annual meeting, unless previously removed, and thereafter the term of appointment shall be for the term of five years, and the compensation of the custodian shall be fixed by said Board of Trustees. Said Board of Trustees shall also appoint such assistants and employes for said Museum as they may deem necessary and expedient, and shall fix their compensation. All vacancies in the office of custodian, assistants and other employes, shall be filled by said Board of Trustees, and the person so elected or appointed shall hold for the unexpired term.

Sec. 7. The custodian elected under this act may be removed from office for misdemeanor, incompetency or inattention to the duties of his office, by a vote of two-thirds of the 'Board of Trustees; the assistants and other employes may be removed by the Board for incompetency, or for any other cause.

Sec. 8. It shall be the duty of the Board of Trustees, within ten days after the appointment of the custodian and other salaried employes, to report and file with the City Comptroller a duly certified list of the persons so appointed, with the salary allowed to each, and the time or times fixed for the payment thereof, and they shall also furnish such comptroller with a list of all accounts and bills which may be allowed by said Board of Trustees, stating the character of the materials or service for which the same were rendered, immediately after the meeting of said Board at which such allowance shall be made. And said Board of Trustees shall also, on or before the first day of October in each year, make to the Common Council a report, made up to and including the 31st day of August of the said year, containing a statement of the condition of the Museum and of the additions thereto during the year, together with such information and suggestions as they may deem important, and such report shall also contain an account of the moneys credited to the Museum fund, and expended on account of the same during the year.

Sec. 9. From and after the organization of the Board of Trustees under this act, the Common Council of said city shall levy and collect annually upon all the taxable property of the said city, at the same time and in the same manner as other city taxes are levied and collected by law, a special tax not exceeding one-tenth of a mill upon each dollar of the assessed value of said taxable property, the amount of which shall be determined by said Board of Trustees, and certified to the Common Council at the time of making their annual report to said Council, and the entire amount of said special tax shall be paid into, and held in, the city treasury, as a separate and distinct fund, to be known as the Museum fund, and shall not be used or appropriated, directly or indirectly, in any other purpose than for the maintenance and for the increase of the Public Museum, the payment of the salaries of the custodian, assistant and other employes of the Museum, the purchase of furniture, fixtures, supplies and fuel, and the incidental expenses of the Museum.

Sec. 10. The Board of Trustees shall erect, purchase, hire or lease buildings, lots, rooms and furniture, for the use and accommodation of said Public Museum, and shall improve, enlarge and repair such buildings, rooms and furniture; but no lot or building shall be purchased, erected or enlarged for the purpose herein mentioned, without an ordinance or resolution of the Common Council of said city, and deeds of conveyance and leases shall run to the City of Milwaukee.

Sec. 11. All moneys received by or raised in the City of Milwaukee for Museum purposes shall be paid over to the City Treasurer, to be disbursed by him on the orders of the president and secretary of the said Board of Trustees, countersigned by the City Comptroller. Such orders shall be made payable to the order of the persons in whose favor they shall have been issued, and shall be the only voucher of the City Treasurer for the payments from the Museum fund. The said Board of Trustees shall provide for the purchase of specimens, supplies, fuel and other matters necessary or useful for the maintenance of the Museum; provided, however, that it shall not be lawful for said Board of Trustees to expend or contract a liability for any sum in excess of the amount levied in any one year for the Museum fund, on account of such fund.

Sec. 12. All moneys, books, specimens and other property received by the City of Milwaukee by device, bequest or gift, from any person or corporation, for Public Museum purposes, shall, unless otherwise directed by the donors, be under the management and control of said Board of Trustees; and all moneys derived from fines and penalties for violations of the rules of the Museum, or from any other source in the course of the administration of the Museum, including all moneys which may be paid to the city upon any policy or policies of insurance, or other obligation or liability, or on account of loss or damage to any property pertaining to the Museum, shall belong to the Museum fund in the city treasury, to be disbursed on the orders of the said Board of Trustees, countersigned by the City Comptroller, for Museum purposes in addition to the amount levied and raised by taxation for such fund.

Sec. 13. This act shall take effect and be in force from and after its passage and publication.

Approved March 31, 1882.

(No. 895, A.)   (Published April 15, 1887.)

CHAPTER 521.

AN ACT to amend Chapter 328 of the Laws of 1882, authorizing the City of Milwaukee to establish and maintain a Public Museum, and Chapter 7 of the Laws of 1878, to establish a Public Library in the City of Milwaukee.

The People of the State of Wisconsin, represented in Senate and Assembly, do enact as follows:

*   *   *   *   *   *

Section 2. Hereafter all appointments of members from the Common Council for the Board of Trustees of the Public Museum of the City of Milwaukee, made by the Mayor of said city on the third Tuesday in April, shall be made from aldermen having two years to serve, and in case any person so appointed shall vacate his office of alderman before the expiration of his term, he shall thereupon cease to be a member of said Board of Trustees, and the Mayor shall appoint some other alderman of his class in his place to be such trustee for the remainder of his term. Each alderman appointed shall serve as such trustee during his term as alderman. It shall be the duty of the Mayor on the third Tuesday in April in each year to appoint a sufficient number of aldermen having two years to serve to be members of such Board of Trustees of the Public Museum, to keep the number of members of such Board from the Common Council always three.

All provisions of Chapter 328, of the Laws of 1882, which in any way conflict with the provisions of this section, are hereby amended accordingly.

Sec. 3. This act shall take effect and be in force from and after its passage and publication.

Approved April 14, 1887.

(No. 614, A.)   (Published April 20, 1887.)

CHAPTER 433.

AN ACT to amend Chapter 328, of the Laws of 1882, entitled "An act to authorize the City of Milwaukee to establish and maintain a Public Museum in said city."

The People of the State of Wisconsin, represented in Senate and Assembly, do enact as follows:

Section 1. The Board of Trustees of the Milwaukee Public Museum are hereby authorized to appoint an acting custodian whenever the proper service of the Museum shall require it, and for such time and on such terms as they may deem proper. Such acting custodian shall be *ex-officio* the acting secretary of said Board of Trustees, and his acts as such shall receive full credit. Said Board of Trustees are also authorized to appoint from time to time honorary curators, who shall perform such duties and have such special privileges as may be provided in the by-laws of the Museum, but shall receive no pecuniary compensation. Such appointments shall be made of persons who have manifested a special interest in the Museum or some particular department thereof.

Sec. 2. This act shall be in force from and after its passage and publication.

Approved April 12, 1887.

(No. 403, A.) (Published April 3, 1897.)

CHAPTER 168.

AN ACT to authorize the levy of a tax by the Common Council of cities having a population of one hundred and fifty thousand or more, and authorized by law to establish and maintain a public museum therein.

The People of the State of Wisconsin, represented in Senate and Assembly, do enact as follows:

Section 1. Whenever any city in this state shall have a population of one hundred and fifty thousand or more, and such city is therefore authorized by law to erect and maintain a public museum under the management and control of a Board of Trustees, it shall be competent for the Common Council of such city to annually levy and collect a tax upon all the taxable property of such city at the same time and in the same manner as other city taxes are levied and collected by law, a special tax not exceeding one-seventh of a mill upon each dollar of the assessed valuation of said taxable property, the amount of which said tax shall be determined by said Board of Trustees and certified to the Common Council and to the City Comptroller at the time of making their annual report to said Council; and the entire amount of said special tax shall be paid into and held in the city treasury as a separate and distinct fund to be known as the museum fund, and shall not be appropriated or used directly or indirectly for any other purpose than for the maintenance and for the increase of the Public Museum, the payment of the salaries of the custodian, assistants and other employes of the Museum, the purchase of furniture, fixtures, supplies and fuel and the incidental expenses of said Museum, which said salaries shall not be increased in any manner within two years from and after the passage and publication of this act.

Section 2. All acts or parts of acts contravening the provisions of this act are hereby repealed.

Section 3. This act shall take effect and be in force from and after its passage and publication.

Approved April 2, 1897.

RULES GOVERNING THE MUSEUM.

I. MEETINGS.

Art. 1. The regular meetings of the Board shall be held at the Museum rooms on the third Tuesday of each month at 4:30 P. M.

Art. 2. The annual meeting of the Board shall be held on the third Tuesday of May, at 4 P. M.

Art. 3. Special meetings shall be called by the secretary upon the written request of the president, or any three members of the Board, but the object for which the special meeting is called must be stated in the notice, and no business other than the special business shall be transacted at such meeting, unless all the members of the Board are present, and unanimous consent is obtained.

Art. 4. Five members of the Board shall constitute a quorum.

II. OFFICERS AND EMPLOYES.

Art. 5. At the annual meeting in May the Board shall elect by ballot a president, whose duty it shall be to preside at all meetings of the Board, to sign all warrants drawn on the city treasurer by order of the Board, to appoint the standing committees for the year, and prepare for the consideration and approval of the Board, the annual report of the Board of Trustees, required by Section 8 of the "Public Museum Act."

Art. 6. The duties of the custodian shall be as follows:

To take charge of and exercise control over the Museum and Library, and to see that the regulations relating thereto are properly carried out.

To exercise control over all employes of the Board and the work allotted to them respectively.

To receive all specimens intended for the Museum, and with the advice and assistance of specialists to classify, label, catalogue and arrange them as soon as possible.

To receive all books and other articles intended for the Library, and to label and catalogue them.

To take all precautions necessary for the good preservation of the collections, according to the most approved methods within the means of the institution

To keep running records, containing all necessary particulars, concerning articles received or disposed of.

To purchase specimens, books and other matter under the general direction of the Board,

To inaugurate a system of exchanges with other natural history museums as soon as possible.

To correspond with scientific societies and public authorities for the purpose of obtaining reports and other documents containing information relating to natural history.

To submit from time to time to the Board or to the respective committees, measures for the efficient management and increase of the Museum, and such other matters as he may deem advisable.

To prepare and submit to the Board a monthly report in writing of the work done, stating the number of visitors, and other matters of interest to the Board.

To prepare and submit at the annual meeting in September an annual report of like contents for the preceding year ending August 31st, said report to accompany the annual report of the Board, required by Section 8 of the "Public Museum Act."

To discharge such other duties as usually belong to the office of the custodian and from time to time be prescribed by the Board.

But in the performance of his duties no debt or liability of any kind shall be incurred by him without authority from the Board.

The custodian shall be required to give bonds in the sum of one thousand dollars, with two or more sureties, to be approved by the Board, for the faithful performance of his duties.

Art. 7. It shall be the duty of the custodian as secretary of the Board of Trustees to be present at all meetings of the Board and of the committee, and to keep full and correct records of their proceedings, except when otherwise directed.

To keep exact and detailed accounts of all moneys received from fines and other sources, to report the same monthly to the Board at the regular meetings, and to pay over all moneys so received promptly to the city treasurer as directed by the Board.

To keep books of account in which all the money transactions of the Board shall be set forth accurately in detail, and to make out and sign all warrants drawn on the city treasurer by order of the Board.

To take care of all business papers of the Board and keep the same neatly filed for convenient reference.

To prepare and submit a monthly statement of the finances of the Museum at the regular monthly meetings.

To give notice of all meetings of the Board, and of committees, at least twenty-four hours before the time of meeting.

To receive all documents, letters and other communications addressed to the Board or Museum, and to see to their proper disposal by the proper officer or committee.

To transact all such other business as may be required of him by the Board and its committees in his capacity as secretary thereof.

Art. 8. The janitor shall, under the direction of the custodian, attend to the heating, ventilation and cleaning of the Museum in all its parts, and perform such other work as may be assigned to him at any time by the custodian. The other assistants shall also work under the direction of the custodian and perform such work as the custodian may assign to them.

Art. 9. Engagements of employes or assistants shall be made by the executive committee, subject to approval by the Board.

III. Committees.

Art. 10. The standing committees shall be:

1. The Executive Committee, consisting of the president *ex-officio*, and four other members of the Board.

2. The Finance Committee, consisting of three members of the Board.

3. The Committee on Exchanges, consisting of three members of the Board, to whom, with the custodian, all applications for exchanges shall be referred for recommendation to the Board.

4. The Committee on Furniture, consisting of three members of the Board.

5. The Committee on Purchase, consisting of three members of the Board, to whom, with the custodian, all matters of purchasing specimens shall be referred for recommendation to the Board. The Committee on Purchase shall have authority to expend from month to month in the interest of the Museum a sum not exceeding $50.

Art. 11. The Natural History Society of Wisconsin shall be invited to appoint five scientific persons from among their members to act in an advisory capacity as a joint counsel, in conferences with the Executive Committee; such conferences to take place at such times as the Executive Committee may desire.

Art. 12. The Executive Committee shall have supervision of all matters relating to the purchasing, construction, leasing, repairing and heating of the buildings or rooms occupied by the Museum, and of insurance, the furnishing, order and cleanliness of the rooms and collections; the selection, purchase, preparation, arrangement, exchange, sale or other disposal of catalogues and guides; provided, that in all such matters no action be taken involving an expenditure or liability greater than authorized by the Board. This committee shall assign a suitable room to the Natural History Society of Wisconsin for holding their meetings and receiving their library. It shall be the duty of the committee to see that all persons employed in the service of the Museum are faithful and prompt in the performance of their duties, and that the regulations of the Museum are enforced.

Art. 13. The Finance Committee shall have the supervision of all matters pertaining to the accounts and account books of the Board. It shall be their duty to prepare the annual budget of the Board, to direct the manner of keeping and to examine all the account books; to examine the monthly and other financial statements of the secretary and custodian and certify the correctness of the same to the Board; to examine and audit all vouchers and accounts against the Museum; to report to the Board upon the correctness of the same, and to make such suggestions from time to time concerning the finances of the Museum as they may deem advisable. Said committee shall also, at the regular meeting in September each year, submit an estimate of the amount that will be needed for maintaining the Museum during the following year, and the action of the Board upon such estimates shall be forthwith certified by the secretary to the comptroller of the city of Milwaukee.

Art. 14. A majority of any committee shall constitute a quorum.

Art. 15. The standing committees shall prepare and submit to the Board at the annual meeting in May a report of all matters, subject to their supervision.

Art. 16. The reports of all standing committees shall be in writing.

IV. MUSEUM AND LIBRARY.

Art. 17. The Museum shall be conducted according to the intention of the "Public Museum Act" and the conditions made by the Natural History Society of Wisconsin in donating the "Engelmann Museum," with the following aims in view:

The exhibition of natural history and ethnology, so as to provide material and help for scientific investigation and public instruction.

The collections therein contained are to represent and illustrate as far as possible the natural history and the natural resources of the city and county of Milwaukee and state of Wisconsin in the first order, and then of the United States and remainder of our planet for purposes of comparison and generalization.

The Museum shall be placed in a building reasonably fire-proof, and kept insured for at least five-sixths of its value.

No objects in the collection can be loaned, and the removal of specimens from the rooms can not be permitted, except if sold or for the purpose of exchange or identification, and under proper authority from the Executive Committee. All matters relating to the arrangement, preservation and use of the collection are under the immediate direction of the custodian, subject to the supervision of the Executive Committee, who will give more detailed instructions if needed.

Art. 18. The library is to be considered a reference and working library. Its contents can not be loaned, but may be used for study or reference in the rooms during Museum hours under necessary restrictions.

V. Miscellaneous.

Art. 19. It shall be the duty of every member of the Board to frequently visit the Museum, and of the members of the Executive Committee to do so at least once every week, for the purpose of general superintendence and direction.

Art. 20. The term of service of all the employes of the Museum except the custodian shall be during good behavior. They shall only be removed for cause, of which the Board shall be the exclusive judge.

Art. 21. The records of the proceedings of the Board of Trustees and its committees and the books of account shall be kept in the secretary's office, and shall be open at all times to inspection and examination by any member of the Board.

Art. 22. The order of business of the Board of Trustees, except at special meetings, shall be as follows:

1. Calling the Roll.
2. Reading Minutes of Previous Meeting.
3. Report of Custodian and Secretary.
4. Report of Standing Committees.
5. Report of Special Committees.
6. Reading of Communications.
7. Unfinished Business.
8. Election of Officers.
9. New Business.

Art. 23. All resolutions and amendments before the Board or any committee shall be presented in writing.

Art. 24. All persons employed at the Museum must be promptly at their posts, as directed, and must remain there during the hours of their regular duty. They will remember that their time, while in the Museum, should constantly be occupied in its service, and it is the duty of the custodian and Executive Committee to enforce this rule.

Art. 25. No amendments to the rules of the Board, or the regulations of the Museum shall be acted upon until the next regular meeting after the same shall have been proposed.

REGULATIONS.

The Museum will be open—
> On Sundays, from 1:30 to 5 P. M.
> Saturdays, from 9 to 12 A. M. and 1 to 5:30 P. M.
> On all other days, from 1 to 5:30 P. M.

Visitors are admitted on condition that they observe the following regulations:

Section 1. Any person of good deportment can be admitted during the above named hours. Children less than fourteen years of age will be admitted only if accompanied by parents, teachers or other responsible adults. Dogs or other live animals will not be admitted.

Sec. 2. Admission is free. Employes of the Museum are forbidden, under penalty of discharge, to receive fees from visitors.

Sec. 3. The removal of books, specimens or any other objects belonging to the Museum from any of its rooms, is strictly prohibited.

Sec. 4. The use of tobacco, and all other conduct not consistent with the quiet and orderly use of the Museum, are prohibited.

Sec. 5. Visitors are not allowed to touch any object.

Sec. 6. Visitors will be held responsible for any mutilation or other injury to specimens, books, furniture or other property of the Museum caused by them.

Sec. 7. The time for closing will be announced by three bell signals ten minutes previous to the appointed hour.

OFFICE HOURS OF EMPLOYES.

Custodian, from 9 to 12 A. M. and 1 to 4 P. M.

Assistant Custodian, from 8:30 to 11:30 A. M. and 1 to 5 P. M.

Taxidermist, from 8 to 12 A. M. and 1 to 5 P. M.

First Assistant, from 8:30 to 11:30 A. M. and 1 to 5 P. M.

Janitor, from 7 to 11:30 A. M. and 1 to 5:30 P. M.

In Memoriam.

WILLIAM HOLLE.

Died November 25th, 1896.

Again one of our honorary curators and warm friends of the Public Museum has passed away. Mr. William Holle, of Sheboygan, Wis., died at the home of his daughter, Mrs. W. H. Houghton, in this city, Nov. 25, 1896, and his interment took place at Wildwood Cemetery, Sheboygan.

Though an enthusiastic lover of all that is beautiful in nature, he was especially interested in lepidoptera. His collection of American and exotic butterflies was one of the finest and most complete in the state. Since he retired from business in 1868, much of his time was spent among his collections and in corresponding with scientists and collectors. His life-long correspondent and adviser was Cantor Pfluemer of his native city, Hameln, Germany, a friend of his boyhood, a man of high educational abilities and an ardent collector of North American butterflies. A large number of the butterflies of his collection were raised by himself from cocoons which he obtained while rambling through the woods and fields around Sheboygan. In determining and preserving his specimens Mr. Holle was exceedingly careful. A specimen without the correct scientific name and without the exact data had for him little value.

He also had a small but very fine collection of tropical birds. In his fine garden he was especially fond of observing the birds. He protected them wherever he could and encouraged them to take up their abode in his grounds. In shady garden corners he grew the exquisite Cypripedium spectabile, C. pubescens, the bloodroot and the claytonia, the Polemonium cæruleum, etc. Nowhere have I seen such fine clumps of primulas and auriculas (Primula vulgaris and P. auricula), plants which are exceedingly difficult to grow successfully in this country. They always reminded him of his beautiful native home.

Mr. Holle was born in Hanover, Germany, Sept. 17, 1821. In his early childhood his parents moved to Hameln, a very old and most beautiful and romantic town on the river Weser. Here he received an excellent education and developed a taste for the study of natural history, especially of insect life, which has been one of his characteristics through all his life-time. Accompanied by his teacher and other pupils on Saturday afternoons, he would range the woods and fields, chasing the butterflies, hunting for herbarium specimens and listening to the songs of the birds. At that time the love of nature was created in his heart and directed by his teachers into the right channels. This love for nature proved to him a life-long joy and solace.

After he had graduated from school he became a merchant. In 1847 he came with his young wife to this country. He settled in Sheboygan, where he has resided ever since. He directly embarked in merchandise. His business proved a great success, as many hundreds of his countrymen had settled in and around Sheboygan.

Mr. Holle was a very kind and entertaining gentleman, and a conscientious and painstaking correspondent. He understood also in a pleasant way to stimulate an interest for the beautiful in nature in all those with whom he came more closely in contact.

In the summer of 1895 Mr. Holle donated his collection of butterflies to the Public Museum of this city. The collection represents a value of about $1,000. Nov. 19, 1895, he was unanimously appointed Honorary Curator of Entomology to the Museum by the Board of Trustees of the Public Museum.